# MAKING AND REMAKING THE BALKANS

## NATIONS AND STATES SINCE 1878

# MAKING AND REMAKING THE BALKANS

## NATIONS AND STATES SINCE 1878

ROBERT C. AUSTIN

UNIVERSITY OF TORONTO PRESS
Toronto  Buffalo  London

ISBN 978-1-4875-0469-4

♾ Printed on acid-free, 100% post-consumer recycled paper with
vegetable-based inks.

Munk Series on Global Affairs

_____

Library and Archives Canada Cataloguing in Publication

Title: Making and remaking the Balkans : nations and states since 1878 /
    Robert C. Austin.
Names: Austin, Robert C. (Robert Clegg), 1964–, author.
Series: Munk series on global affairs.
Description: Series statement: Munk series on global affairs | Includes
    bibliographical references and index.
Identifiers: Canadiana 20190053305 | ISBN 9781487504694 (hardcover)
Subjects: LCSH: Balkan Peninsula – History – 1989–. | LCSH: Balkan
    Peninsula – Politics and government – 1989–.
Classification: LCC DR48.6 A97 2019 | DDC 949.605—dc23

_____

University of Toronto Press acknowledges the financial assistance to its
publishing program of the Canada Council for the Arts and the Ontario
Arts Council, an agency of the Government of Ontario.

 **Canada Council** **Conseil des Arts**
**for the Arts** **du Canada**

 ONTARIO ARTS COUNCIL
CONSEIL DES ARTS DE L'ONTARIO
an Ontario government agency
un organisme du gouvernement de l'Ontario

Funded by the   Financé par le    Canadä
Government   gouvernement
of Canada   du Canada

 MIX
Paper from
responsible sources
FSC® C016245

# Contents

# Acknowledgments

I have many people to thank and acknowledge, and it is best to do so chronologically. I will always be indebted to Paskal Milo and Fatos Tarifa. They made my first few visits to Albania possible. Both of them as well as their families were a source of constant support. I am also especially grateful to the Nathanaili family in Tirana for such a wonderful friendship, along with Lindita Bubesi, Spiro and Maria Dede, and Nasho Jorgaqi. The book benefitted from the extraordinary input of many close friends such as Besim Abazi, Shpend Ahmeti, Vlora Basha, Visar Berisha, Srdjan Darmanovic, Thanos Dokos, Jasa Jovicevic, Genc Krasniqi, Ivan Krastev, Ylber Kusari, Remzi Lani, Momchil Metodiev, Veton Surroi, Milka Tadic, Vessela Tcherneva, Ivan Vejvoda, and Arbana Vidishiqi. Thanks to all the local leaders who gave up time to talk to me as well. I enjoyed wonderful access in the Balkans along with the customary hospitality. Outside of the region, the tiny group of Albanian experts kept doing the research so that books like this could be written: thanks to Elez Biberaj, Bernd Fischer, Nicholas Pano, and Louis Zanga for doing all the heavy lifting in Albania studies and for our long friendships. On many trips to the region I was accompanied by my dear friend, Ness Gashi. A better travel companion and friend would be hard to find.

Closer to my home base in Toronto, I am fortunate enough to work at the Munk School of Global Affairs and Public Policy at the University of Toronto. My friends at the Munk School have been extremely helpful, and I am very fortunate to work there. At the Centre for European, Russian, and Eurasian Studies, Director Randall Hansen always encouraged me to pursue my interests wherever they took me. Edward Schatz read some early drafts and actually liked them. Laurie Drake, a PhD candidate in history at the time, did great background research and nice editing too. At the University of Toronto Press, Jennifer DiDomenico saw the value of the book from the start, as did the board of the Munk Series on Global Affairs. Thanks are due to Ron Levi, Anna Porter, Doug Saunders, Janice Stein, and Robert Vipond.

Finally, I have wonderful family and friends. Special thanks to Barbara and Jordan Oelbaum and Jodi and Thomas Ungar. I have two great children, Andrew and Kate, who learned to love adventure, mostly in canoes, but have yet to be in the Balkans. Maybe this book will encourage them to go. My wife, Maureen Hendzel, is the indispensable partner in all journeys anywhere. I dedicate this book to her.

Robert C. Austin
Toronto, October 2018

# Introduction

As an undergraduate at Carleton University in the 1980s, I developed an interest in what was then known as the People's Socialist Republic of Albania – the only country in the communist bloc of states to declare that it had achieved advanced socialism and abolished religion too. Isolated, with a history of subjugation and occupation by Ottomans, Italians, and Germans, Albanians had, as their long-time communist leader, Enver Hoxha, noted, "hacked their way through history." They were, along with the Hungarians, the ultimate survivors in Europe, speaking a language that was unintelligible to their Slavic and Greek neighbors. I started reading everything I could, and there was not much. I then wrote a very mediocre undergraduate thesis on the foreign relations of Albania under the communists who ruled Albania between 1944 and 1991. During this time I was also trying to get there, which was hard, as Albania shunned individual travel. I wrote letters to communist leader Ramiz Alia, Hoxha's successor, in hopes he could intervene and secure me a visa. (I subsequently met Alia years later, and he had no recollection of my pleas for a visa.) The Albanian government, through its mission to the United Nations, which was the only diplomatic outpost it maintained in North America, replied to my letters. They ignored my visa requests but did send me countless books by Hoxha, who ruled from 1944 until he died in 1985. The books were all his classics but totally unreadable, written in that leaden prose that was the hallmark of all of the twentieth century's great communist leaders.

In any case, I finally did get to Albania in the months before the first multiparty elections in 1991. And so began more than twenty-five years in the Balkans. The University of Tirana historian Paskal Milo, who went on to become Albanian foreign minister during some very bad times in the late 1990s and after, invited me to Albania. I remember the letter saying how touched he was that a young person was so interested in Albanian history. Albania then was strange and exotic but also beautiful. No private cars, a nearly unspoiled Adriatic coast, no obesity, extremely hospitable people, and a respectable life expectancy. With very little industry, Albania was pristine in many ways. Only the elite had phones; the sleepy capital Tirana filled every evening with people walking arm in arm, strolling the grand boulevard. It was the only way to get news from your friends. Tirana looked pretty with its tree-lined streets, the fascist-style government buildings built by the Italians in the 1930s mixed in with the Socialist Realist National Museum with its mosaic of Albania's triumphal march to communism, library, and Palace of Culture. There was a feeling that something either really good or really bad was about to happen. It was a tense and even gloomy time. After all, loads of observers, looking elsewhere in communist Europe in 1989, thought Albanian communism just might survive à la North Korea. A *New Yorker* cartoon in November 1989, just when the Berlin Wall fell, showed a peaceful and idyllic village scene, not a soul around, with the caption, "Meanwhile ... in Albania."

Like all foreign visitors, I was put up in the Hotel Tirana on the seventh floor. Built in 1979 with fifteen floors, it was then the tallest building in the country. In 1990 and in the years after, Albania was in very bad shape and on the brink of collapse. Thousands of people flooded the port of Durres on the Adriatic in the hope of getting out. Albania's borders had been shut and militarized since 1948. Some 13,000 people successfully fled between 1948 and 1990. Almost 1,000 were killed trying. In 1990 and 1991, images of young Albanians hanging off rickety ships hoping to make it to Italy or the thousands that stormed Western embassies dominated the headlines. Food was scarce, even in the hotel, where the chain-smoking waiters offered little more than eggs, onions, and acidic Riesling from Korca in the south of the country. The situation was fraught as the county headed to its first free elections since 1924. Albania, almost dissident free due to the depth of communist repression with its vast network of secret police, prison camps, and internal exile, witnessed an explosive growth of new and anti-communist parties that were largely filled with people who had fairly good communist credentials. It was clear from the outset that the Albanian exit would be different and that it would look more like a revolving door. It would not go smoothly. In a testimony to its uniqueness, Albania's communists would easily win the first elections in March 1991, just as they would in Bulgaria and Romania too. In fact, with the exception of Slovenia, the entire region would experience countless disasters during a period that brought war and the inaccurately termed "transition" to market capitalism and democracy.

I was primarily interested in how things would play out in the region over the short and long term. Would Albanians, by far the poorest and most oppressed people in the region, end up with stability, prosperity, and a bright future? On this first visit I had a state-supplied driver, as that was mandatory in a country without private cars and certainly no car-rental agency. Ramadan Muca had always driven for the state, and we plied Albania's few and then-empty roads for two weeks in a nice blue Fiat. The near total absence of a transportation network, some said, was by design. Hoxha wanted to make it as hard as possible for any invaders. The landscape was harsh, even burnt looking. Party propaganda was everywhere. Slogans, such as "Glory to the Party," were placed on buildings and even on the sides of mountains. The itinerary was by no means dictated to us, and we more or less free to go where we wanted but we mostly toured the south, with visits to Berat and Hoxha's birthplace in Gjirokaster. If the communists in power still clung to their vision of a unique path for the country that was different from elsewhere, they were not selling the idea any more. In later trips, we often slept in the car and dubbed it Hotel Fiat. In the early years of the transition many new hotel owners wanted to earn their capital back in a matter of days, making it often far cheaper to sleep in the car.

I also had a series of minders who traveled with me to translate and report back. They were extraordinary people who spoke BBC English even though they had never left Albania. We always ate our meals in the private dining rooms of the shabby Albtourist hotels that were the backbone of Albania's almost nonexistent tourism industry that had catered only to vetted group tours of ideological soulmates. Sitting once on the Albanian side of Lake Ohrid in the town of Pogradec, with Macedonia still part of Yugoslavia on the other side, I was asked what I wanted to eat. We were on a lake. I said, "Fish?" "No fish," was the reply. The official story then was that the unique trout of Lake Ohrid was only for the party elite. My minders periodically asked me questions. I remember one asking me quietly if it was true that in the United States a pet dog could have clothes. Raised on propaganda that emphasized the inequality of capitalism with some really superb cartoons and satire, the dog with clothes went too far for Albanians, especially in a country where pets were forbidden. I told him yes, it was true. He did not want to hear that. He needed to know everything was a lie. And that was long before inequality really took off. Imagine what he would think if he saw an ad for *LunaJets*, the private-jet charter company, that shows a dog occupying a seat in a Learjet. Often when visiting my minders' apartments, I noticed the identical bookshelves, bare lightbulbs, and furniture, and the way they advertised the arrival of the West and their own cosmopolitanism with an empty pack of Marlboros on the shelf or local raki served from a reused bottle of Jack Daniel's.

In subsequent years, I spent more and more time with Ramadan and got to know him and his extended family. I recall meeting his aged mother, who sat perpetually huddled by an indoor kerosene stove dressed in black in one of the horrible flats built by the communists in Tirana. Born in 1910, she was first an Ottoman citizen; she then lived through the proclamation of Albanian independence in 1912, the First World War, the re-emergence of Albania in 1920, its proclamation as a kingdom in 1928, the arrival of the Italians as new rulers in 1939, the Second World War, the triumph of communism in 1944, and now its end. I told her she had seen a lot. She replied that she had seen "only suffering." Mrs Muca captured not just the Albanian experience but also the entire region's, as everyone in the Balkans endured not just wars but countless nation- and state-building campaigns. In 1989, in what was then Czechoslovakia,

Hungary, and Poland, Eastern Europe became Central Europe again, and so began a long and ultimately fruitful march to Europe, which provided prosperity, stability, and mobility. The Central Europeans could claim to be rejoining Europe. In the Balkans the trajectory was less clear – some had to join, not rejoin, Europe. This was certainly true for Albania. It never had a European past and its European future was not secure. The same would prove true for the rest of the Balkans.

In 1989, the end of the Cold War was not necessarily a good thing for Yugoslavia, which was already fragmenting as once subdued and crude nationalisms were back with a vengeance. Slobodan Milosevic, the number two in Serbia's Communist Party in the late 1980s, went to the Albanian-dominated province of Kosovo as an errand boy on behalf of his boss, Ivan Stambolic. The visit transformed him. Taking the mantle of Serb nationalism but claiming he was defending Yugoslavia, he subsequently warned that battles in future could not be ruled out. Anyone who wants to see a man transformed in a moment need only watch the footage of Milosevic in Kosovo in 1988. Charged by Stambolic to quiet the Kosovo Serbs – who were fretting about real and perceived slights by the Albanian majority – and to give the message of "brotherhood and unity" – the mantra of Tito's Yugoslavia – to the quarreling Albanians and Serbs in Kosovo, Milosevic opted for an entirely different message. He quickly turned the Albanians into demons, not socialist brothers, by resurrecting hardly latent Serb antipathy towards the Albanians. The Albanians were the proverbial outsiders in Yugoslavia – the ones your parents warned you about. As the country's small entrepreneurial class, often running sweet shops, the Albanians, rumor had it, would poison the candy. Milosevic, outmaneuvering his boss in a party coup, took over the Serbian branch of the Yugoslav League of Communists and made himself the spokesperson for a new version of Yugoslavia. He started his "Anti-Bureaucratic Revolution," which was a vehicle for establishing Serb dominance in Yugoslavia by replacing the old elite with Milosevic's elite. As Milosevic's first victims, the Albanians of Kosovo unwittingly became the weathervane for the fate of Yugoslavia. Hardly anyone predicted that Yugoslavia would spiral into a series of violent civil wars that ended only in 2001, bringing genocide, war, and massive ethnic cleansing. What happened in Kosovo in 1989 was largely ignored by the outside world.

Bulgaria and Romania had their quasi revolutions too in 1989 but, as we shall see, events there were far less revolutionary than first thought. While long-time communist leaders such as Todor Zhivkov were ousted in palace coups in Bulgaria and even shot, as were Nicolae Ceausescu and his wife, Elena, in Romania, it seemed more like a coup or internal rebellion. Communists did become socialists, but the change was half-hearted as they proceeded to enrich themselves with the fruits of privatization. As Central Europeans largely embraced what was called "shock therapy," which meant aggressive and revolutionary reforms from the beginning, most Balkan peoples could easily claim they got all shock and no therapy. That was true then, and the shocks just keep coming. With the benefit of hindsight, it seems that the Balkans gave us less-than-revolutionary breaks with the past. This was hardly what we saw in the Czechoslovakia in 1990, when dissident and playwright Vaclav Havel declared to citizens their "government had been returned to them." In the Balkans, even today, governments have yet to be returned to them. In short, the democratization and state-building project has largely failed. 1989 in Belgrade, Bucharest, or Sofia, or Tirana in 1991, was not the same as it was in Prague. The question is *why*.

This book attempts to explain why the Balkans are relatively unsuccessful in a number of ways despite a lengthy transition period and enormous amounts of financial aid. According to the cliché, in the Balkans there is too much history in too small a space. Dreams of stable and multiethnic societies are unfulfilled. Some speak of the need for a whole new map, creating homogenous states. Despite the small number of people there and the relatively weak economies, the Balkans have punched above their weight when it comes to creating problems in Europe. Sometimes the problems were not always of their making, but just as often they were. The Balkan states, which now include Albania, Bosnia, Bulgaria, Greece, Kosovo, Macedonia, Montenegro, Romania, and Serbia, are all products of the once-powerful Ottoman Empire. With the onset of a series of wars and failed transitions in the 1990s and after, the term *Balkan* became a pejorative of sorts, with some preferring the more sterile but politically safer term *Southeastern Europe*. Croatia and Slovenia were the first to shed the Balkan adage, especially as their past placed them in the Habsburg Empire, ruled by Vienna, not Istanbul. Greece is sometimes Balkan, sometimes not, although the ongoing economic and political crisis there seemed to be sending the country back to the Balkans.

This book is primarily interested in those states that find themselves outside the European Union (EU), although I have included sections on Bulgaria, Croatia, Romania, and Slovenia as EU members for the sake of comparison. Even as members of the EU, these states exhibit some of the shortcomings that bedevil the non-EU Balkans. The principal focus is thus Albania, Bosnia, Kosovo, Macedonia, Montenegro, and Serbia, which came to be known as the Western Balkans to separate the region from EU members Bulgaria and Romania (or, as some locals note, the "Restern Balkans"); essentially, the former Yugoslavia, minus Croatia and Slovenia, plus Albania. These states in all found themselves on a path that seemed to promise membership in the EU, increased prosperity, and long-sought political stability. Readers may note the emphasis on the Albanians in the Balkans. This is for two reasons. First, I know the Albanians best. Second, given the legacy of isolation, the Albanian story is less well known, even though their fate, especially in Kosovo, was emblematic of some wider trends in the region. Moreover, Albanians find themselves living in large numbers not just in Albania and Kosovo but also in Greece, Macedonia, and Montenegro.

The EU hoped that the lure of membership would be enough to drive reform, as it had done successfully with the countries of Central Europe and the Baltic states. While EU membership was at least the rhetorical goal of every state, the arrival time was highly contested, and despite the relatively small population of the countries combined, the Europeanization process proved to be far more challenging than expected by the decision makers in Brussels and the people living there. As time passed, and the date for membership seemed more and more remote, some spoke of making 2014 the year when the past would really become the past. After all, it marked one hundred years since an assassination in Sarajevo changed the fate of the world, put the Balkans on the map, and gave the region an entirely new map of nation states looking suspiciously at one another. 2014 did not happen. Now policymakers speak of 2025. Now, more than a generation has passed, and the dreams of quick integration have failed. Huge numbers of people simply gave up and moved, leaving the region with among the highest rates of out-migration, youth unemployment, and governments staffed with woefully underqualified people. Hopelessness, particularly among youth, is pervasive. While no longer the powder keg of the early twentieth century, the Balkans, including Greece, in the twenty-first century is a zone of crisis. Weak states dissolving into fiefdoms or those governed by authoritarians in cahoots with oligarchs or ordinary criminals is the norm. Alternative models to liberal democracy, whether from China, Hungary, or Turkey, muddy the waters even more.

This book starts with an examination of the nation- and state-building process in the region in the nineteenth and twentieth centuries, the emergence of rival-national projects, the creation of myths, wars, and communism before turning to the principal questions that emerged after 1989. I started in 1878, as that is when things really get moving. Indeed, Greece was already independent by 1830, but the main changes took place after the 1878 Congress of Berlin, with the creation of the modern Balkan state structure. The Great Powers (what we now call the international community) played a key role in shaping things then and now: deciding boundaries, rewarding some peoples and punishing others.

Chapter 2 assesses the 1989 moment and what followed: the roots of communist collapse, which was categorically different in the Balkans than elsewhere in Europe; the triumph of the nationalist pattern of political change in 1989 in Yugoslavia along with the illiberal pattern of change that took place in Albania, Bulgaria, and Romania. Essentially, while 1989 proved to be a turning point for Central Europe, it was not for the Balkans, with various forms of nationalist authoritarianism surviving well into the 1990s and after. Central Europeans were able to build modern states. Modern state structures still elude the whole Balkans, including Greece. In many instances, the state is a criminal enterprise. The main focus is on the re-emergence of violence and the nationalism that came with it, the road to multiple wars in Bosnia, Croatia, and Slovenia, with particular emphasis on Serbia and the role of Yugoslav/Serb leader Slobodan Milosevic. I say re-emergence, as too many specialists on the region sought to portray the wars in Yugoslavia as somehow unprecedented, as though coming from nowhere. Chapter 2 examines the main features of the ultimately historically rooted political systems that emerged; the independence referenda in Bosnia, Croatia, Macedonia, and Slovenia; and the role of civil society, media, and the international community in setting the stage for conflict. It also seeks to explain why the end of the Cold War meant something totally different in the Balkans. For Albania, the chapter explains its extremely challenging position, given the legacy of almost North Korea-like isolation.

Chapter 3 is devoted entirely to the wars in Yugoslavia. Wars that were largely designed in Serbia came to the Balkans in 1992. However, the leadership in both Bosnia and Croatia contributed to the emerging catastrophe. This chapter assesses the impact of the wars in Bosnia, Croatia, and Slovenia; international intervention; and the legacy of the Dayton Peace Accord of 1995. This chapter is not an account of what happened on the ground but rather an assessment of why it is taking so long for the region to achieve reconciliation. It examines the impact of local and international actors on the peace-making process. It primarily examines the Dayton Peace Accord of 1995 and its role in making a European Bosnia possible or impossible.

Chapter 4 returns to Kosovo and the role Albania played there unwittingly and unexpectedly. As noted, Yugoslavia's disintegration started in Kosovo in the late 1980s, and it ended there with Kosovo's independence in 2008. This chapter examines the road to war in Kosovo between 1988 and 1999. In 1988, the Albanians opted for passive resistance to Serbia, Gandhi-style. This worked only until 1995, when the Dayton Peace for Bosnia failed to even mention Kosovo. The collapse of the pyramid schemes and the Albanian state in 1997 brought weapons, violence, and the Kosovo Liberation Army (KLA) in its wake. This chapter covers the war, NATO intervention, the United Nations protectorate, and Kosovo's compromised independence in 2008 with the high-minded but ultimately flawed Ahtisaari Peace Plan of 2007 and the arrival of the European Rule of Law Mission (EULEX) in 2008.

Chapter 5 examines Macedonia. In the early part of the twentieth century, the struggle for control of Macedonia brought horrible conflicts. Solved partly by Tito's Yugoslavia, the Macedonian question came back with the disintegration of Yugoslavia. A space that is hard to define, with neighboring Bulgaria, Greece, and Serbia often contesting its very existence, Macedonia remains in an existential crisis made worse by a minority population of restive Albanians. Since the fundamentals of Macedonia's contested statehood and very identity were established in chapter 1, this chapter offers a discussion of Macedonian state formation, the drift towards intolerance towards the Albanians, the Macedonian civil war between Albanian and Macedonians in 2001, the peace treaty (the Ohrid Framework Agreement), and the struggle with Greece over just who owns the name *Macedonia*. It takes the reader, in an accessible way, through the now more than twenty-five-year-old name dispute between Greece and Macedonia and the gradual drift of Macedonia from European norms and values to a new form of authoritarianism based on a more aggressive form of Macedonian nationalism embodied in the Skopje 2014 project and the "antiquization" campaign that started aggressively after 2008.

Chapter 6 examines the experiences of the four Balkan states that did enter the European Union: Slovenia in 2004, Bulgaria and Romania in 2007, and Croatia in 2013. Emphasis is on the Slovenian exception and the subsequent hasty, albeit justified, entry of Bulgaria and Romania. While they were made members, they are diminished ones for failures to really deliver on the crucial rule-of-law issues and are saddled with unprecedented post-membership burdens. Croatia, in its post–Franjo Tudjman years after 2000, when it shed its overtly nationalist agenda and its indicted war criminals were sent to The Hague, somehow managed a complete turnaround that could serve as example for the rest of the region.

The epilogue looks at the region today: a mixture of undemocratic, weak, failing, or failed states, mired in corruption, nepotism, state capture (the wholesale plunder of state resources to benefit politically connected people), failed transitional justice, and reconciliation projects and low institutional trust from a population that would prefer to leave. In essence, unmodern states prevail in the region. Things are worsened by an increasingly preoccupied and even disinterested EU that was forced to deal with a financial crisis in Greece, a refugee crisis, Brexit, and the challenge of nationalist and often authoritarian populism as an alternative model, especially in Hungary, Poland, Slovakia, and Turkey. It also assesses the legacy of the main peace treaties in the region – the Dayton Peace Accord for Bosnia (1995), the Ohrid Framework Agreement for Macedonia (2001), and Ahtisaari Plan for Kosovo (2007) – and how they have hindered (or facilitated) the European integration process. As will become clear, policy makers in Brussels and Washington opted for stability over democracy. But it is worth noting that the people of the region opted for that as well.

This book is largely a political history that is not written for an academic audience. It has no citations. It has three distinct audiences in mind. The first is the generalist interested in a big-picture survey of a sometimes-complicated region. The second is the traveler headed to the Balkans who seeks something more than an ordinary tourist does and wants to understand why there is a huge Catholic Cathedral in downtown Prishtina in a majority Muslim country or the presence of Alexander the Great in Skopje. The third is undergraduate students studying the region. While there are solid histories of the region and first-rate journalism, especially the seminal work covering the wars in the former Yugoslavia, this book combines history, journalism, and travelogue. As someone who has taught Balkan history, I can say that this was the book I was looking for to give to my undergraduate classes. As to the periodic anecdotes that appear, often based on conversions with local leaders and people, these are how I remember them.

# MAKING AND REMAKING THE BALKANS

## NATIONS AND STATES SINCE 1878

# 1

# Making Nations and States

The Balkan states broke free from the Ottoman Empire in the nineteenth century, or in the Albanian case, in the early part of the twentieth century. Nationalism, or more precisely the modern nationalism that came with the French Revolution in 1789 and later Napoleon, arrived in the Balkans just as it did everywhere else. Its impact there, however, was different than elsewhere in Europe. After all, the Ottoman Empire was not the Habsburg Empire. How different the Balkans would have been had they fallen under the Habsburg Empire. The Habsburgs were infrastructure and administration builders, a largely benevolent force that most of their people actually liked or at least tolerated, building railways, roads, canals, a developed civil service, and a multinational army that had a place for everyone, almost. Any ordinary Serb can now only weep about the horrible fate of history that gave her or him 500 years of Ottoman rule.

The Ottoman Empire, as a theocratic but not necessarily a proselytizing state, conquered the Balkans between the fourteenth and sixteenth centuries. It took the Ottomans more or less one hundred years to gain control of the whole Balkan Peninsula and another two hundred to lose it in a gradual process made possible by wars and Great Power imperialism, which included nation- and state-building projects designed to carve out client states in receding Ottoman territory. The Ottomans destroyed and subjugated all the great medieval Balkan empires; ruler became ruled, and myths emerged, primarily about the disappearance of once-great and expansive kingdoms. The Ottoman administrative system was based on religion. But the Ottoman Empire was surprisingly tolerant. The Ottomans made it twice to Vienna, destroyed the formerly powerful Kingdom of Hungary in 1526, captured Buda in 1541, and almost took Vienna in 1683. The Ottoman Empire's legacy today in the Balkans is often hard to discern, especially since most of the peoples of the region did their best to wipe it out. The Ottomans did leave some majestic mosques, bridges, vocabulary, baths (especially in Budapest), and certainly better food than what they found when they arrived.

So the Balkan peoples, who were small in numbers and mostly Christian peasants, got stuck in a place that eventually defied modernity. A few people converted to Islam, notably the Albanians, Bosnians, Pomaks, and Vlachs, but since the Ottomans did not actually care, most people did nothing, and the Balkans remained overwhelmingly Christian. You could just as easily stay an Orthodox or Catholic peasant as long as your religious leader paid the taxes. The Islamic peasant may have been higher up in the religious order that the Ottoman's imposed, but the differences were marginal – life in Ottoman feudalism was grim and short for everyone.

In an era of pre-nationalism, people clung to religious or local identities. Hatred for the Ottomans (and often now the Turks) is a near-universal theme among the Balkan Christians and a fundamental part of national-identity formation for most Balkan states. The Serbs speak of the Ottoman "yoke"; the poisonous history books that students read tell of unspeakable horrors – eyes poked out, brigandage, slavery, rape, and worse. Being Muslim in the Balkans was often a death sentence when the "horrors" of the Ottoman "yoke" and revenge for five hundred years of oppression would be trotted out again in the 1990s to turn neighbor on neighbor.

The impact of the Renaissance or even the Enlightenment hardly touched parts of the Balkans. Think of what is now Albania – north of Greece and across from Italy. Despite geographic proximity to the birthplaces of so much, it is as though the soil was poisoned – nothing modern took root there. For the Albanians especially, who were the most isolated of all Balkan peoples, it meant that they had to wait until well into the twentieth century for everything, and they are still waiting for most things.

In any case, nationalism came to the Balkans. While the Serbs were the first to say, "We are here and we want out," the Greeks were the first to actually get out, thus earning them the special place in the eyes of the world that they still have. The Greek independence movement, fortunately for Greeks, caught international attention. Famous people such as Lord Byron were there, and muckraking journalists exposed the depravity of the Ottomans, who emerged as nothing more than anti-Christian barbarians in the media of the day. Byron died before the Greeks won, but his enthusiasm for the Greek cause helped carry the day.

What are the most important ingredients in nation building? There is shared language, territory, religion, or culture among other things. But the most important factor is Great Power support. While we may call the Great Powers the international community now, it is the Great Powers that decide who gets their own state and who does not. The Greeks got the West onside, and the Russians onside too, although the West was by far their most important ally. The Greeks were the first to say two things: "We want to be in the West!" and "We want to be something other than Ottoman." While the Russians came to the rescue of fellow Orthodox Christians in peril, many Westerners saw the Greek revolution as a liberal and nationalist revolt. The Greeks were the first to get out of the Ottoman Empire and they have been struggling ever since to overcome the fact that they were stuck there in the first place. The imprint of the Ottoman Empire proved to be extremely durable. Interestingly, when one looks at the later impact of the collapse of the Ottoman Empire, it is obvious and telling that, despite its shortcomings, Greece remains the most successful post-Ottoman state.

The Greek state, which became a kingdom with a royal family imported from Bavaria, is the original myth factory. Their myth, which still prevails, is the link with ancient Greece – the beacon of humanism – and that they are the inheritors of antiquity, democracy, and (the most exclusive and dangerous of all myths) the owners of the past, as though the past was something you could copyright. They said, and everyone listened, that they have continuity with ancient

Greece and called for a new Byzantine Empire and a Greece of the Five Seas with a capital in Constantinople [Istanbul].

The other great myth, which helped to poison the region just as much, was the nineteenth-century "Great Idea" pushed by the Greek elite. It foresaw a new and much bigger Greece, one where all Greeks would live in one state. At root, since the Greek Orthodox Church was at the service of the new state (although it had originally opposed Greek independence in fear a new nation-state would undermine its authority), the Great Idea meant that if you were Orthodox, you were Greek and, by extension, you wanted to live in a new Greece. You did not need to move there – Greece would come to you, mostly by war. And war they tried. Most of the time, the Greeks lost. This was the first of the many "Greater" projects that would later destroy the region in the 1990s. Suffice to say that the Greater Greek, Greater Serb, Greater Bulgarian, and even Greater Albanian projects draw their inspiration from the Greek "Great Idea."

With the Greeks and their new and imported Bavarian king building a new capital in Athens, the rest of the Ottoman Balkans started to fall apart based on the Greek model – a developing national idea, weak Ottomans, Great Power rivalry, and a benefactor. As noted, the Serbs were really the first to say "help." With the Greek gold standard for revolution and independence established – Christians suffering, Moslems raping and burning, humanitarian crisis, media frenzy, international intervention, and Great Power support – the Serbs hoped for the same outcome. Luckily for the Serbs, they are Orthodox Christians, and so are Greeks and Russians.

The Serbs were subjugated by the Ottomans, starting with their heroic defeat in Kosovo in 1389, on 28 June, or St Vitus Day to be precise, the same day in 1914 on which a Serb nationalist would later assassinate the heir to the Habsburg throne and the same day in 1989 on which Milosevic would whip the Kosovo Serbs there into hysteria in the name of Serb national interests. The Serb leader in 1389, Prince Lazar, died in the battle and, according to the myth, choose the heavenly kingdom over the earthly one and refused to capitulate to the Ottomans. This defeat, which is a cornerstone Serbian myth, set the stage for a Serbian revival in the nineteenth and twentieth centuries. Like the Greeks, their new state drew its inspiration from shared language, culture, and religion made available to a willing people through folklore and epic poems. Where the Greeks established continuity with antiquity, the Serbs drew a direct line to their great medieval kingdom and its churches, located largely in Kosovo: a state destroyed by the Ottomans but destined for a triumphant rebirth and unification. Just who "owned" Kosovo and the rebirth of its myth would return later to help set the Albanians and Serbs on a dangerous collision course in the 1980s and 1990s.

## 1878 and the Emergence of the Modern Balkans

By far the biggest moment for Balkan peoples was the Russian-Ottoman War in 1877–8. This is the real starting point for the study of the modern Balkans. It is important for three key reasons: 1) many states became independent; some did not; 2) the Great Powers remained the decision makers – what you got depended on them; and 3) the Great Powers more or less ruined things by making the region a powder keg. In the Russian-Ottoman War, it is enough to say that the Ottomans lost badly, and the Russians tried to redraw the map to their advantage. With such a humiliating defeat, the Russians imposed a new vision of the Balkans in the Treaty of San Stefano of March 1878, which would have made a gigantic Bulgaria, from the Black Sea almost to the Adriatic, at the expense of everyone else living there – Serbs, Greeks, and Albanians. Russia's "new" Bulgaria violated the spirit of negotiation over the fate of the Balkans. Russia, the Great Powers said, could not impose a fait accompli on the region, Bulgaria needed to be smaller.

So the Great Powers said "no," and the nineteenth century's greatest diplomat, Germany's "Iron Chancellor" Otto von Bismarck, called everyone to Berlin in June to settle things more appropriately. Bismarck, who famously quipped that the Balkans "was not worth the bones of a single Pomeranian Grenadier" also feared that the next war in Europe would be the result of some "silly thing" in the Balkans. The 1878 Congress of Berlin gave Europe a whole new Balkans that lasted only until 1912 – thirty-four years of relative stability – a golden era of sorts for nation building for some and resisting nation building for others. The congress also set the Balkan states on collision courses in that newfound independence meant that they also had to struggle for even more land so that all their ethnic brethren could live in one nationally unified state.

The key aspects of the congress were important for the future of the region right up until the assassination of Habsburg Archduke Franz Ferdinand in Sarajevo in June 1914. Montenegro, which had always enjoyed a degree of independence as it was simply too rugged to conquer, was made formally independent and enlarged in territory; Romania and Serbia were made independent. No greater Bulgaria appeared, but the myth did not die. Bulgaria was divided in two and enjoyed a kind of extensive autonomy from Istanbul. These new states were all monarchies of one type or another. The Serbs and Montenegrins had local dynasties. The Serbs had two in fact – Karadjordjevic and Obrenovic. Bulgarians and Romanians, like the Greeks, got stuck with mostly unemployed and somewhat unqualified Germans.

The Habsburg Empire got the right to occupy and essentially run Bosnia-Herzegovina. This was the beginning of what could have been a golden time for the mixed peoples of Bosnia if not for the First World War. The Ottoman Empire was the biggest net loser, as it lost almost all of its European holdings. In fact, it was left with two pieces of the Balkans that would prove highly contentious in the years leading up to the First World War: the territory that would become Albania and Macedonia.

Let us talk about the Albanians first. Since the Treaty of San Stefano cut right through where the Albanians lived, they were forced to more or less appear for the first time in an organized way. They were reacting to a crisis that was not of their making. In the crisis that came with the Russo-Ottoman war, the Ottoman Empire helped them with their nation-building project at first as they were hoping to use the more loyal Albanians to thwart the plans of the decision makers in Berlin, St Petersburg, and Vienna. Bismarck was totally dismissive of them; saying that there is no such thing as an Albanian nation. In Berlin, the Albanians got nothing. As a majority Muslim nation in the Christian Balkans, the Albanians could not count on the same level of enthusiasm for their project. Vienna would at least see in the Albanians the potential to frustrate the Serbs.

Copying their neighbors, the Albanians established a national defense committee in Prizren, in what is now southern Kosovo. Taking a decidedly different approach, they called for autonomy, not independence, in the Ottoman Empire. Mindful of the fact that their nationalism was a long way from complete, the Albanians were pragmatic: they needed some time to catch up. They lacked the things that other nations in the region already had: they did not have religious unity – the majority were Muslim (Sunni and Bektashi), but there were also Catholics in the north and Orthodox Christians in the south under the sway of the Greek Orthodox Church; they lacked linguistic unity; they had huge regional differences too between the north and south; and they were way behind in the myth-making game, given the small size of their elite and low levels of education. In the Balkans, latecomers to the national revival process paid a high price as their neighbors, independent Greece and Serbia, looked covetously on Albanian territory and continued to deny the Albanian nationality.

While the Greeks looked back to antiquity, and the Serbs to their great medieval empire, the Albanians dug deep into the past for heroic moments. They decided that they were Illyrians, making them the first inhabitants of the Balkans – pre-Roman, in fact – but at the same time equating themselves with Hellenic and Roman civilizations. Being the last nation to appear in the nineteenth-century Balkans but then saying that, well, we were actually here first, was clever. Historians still debate the Illyrian origins of the Albanians. Like all myths, it certainly does not matter if it is true. Being "first," especially in a place like Kosovo, would shape the debate in the 1980s and 1990s with catastrophic results.

The Albanians also found a national hero, Gjergj Kastrioti, better known as Skanderbeg. Born in in 1405, he made a name as a Christian conscripted to the Ottoman armies as a youth, converted to Islam, but then returned to Albania in the fifteenth century, became Christian again, and fought the Ottomans. This tells you just how unique the Albanians are – their national hero in a Muslim majority nation is a Christian fighting Muslims. Since the facts do not really matter in nation building, the Albanians not surprisingly put the "national liberation" stamp on Skanderbeg's "cross versus crescent" war. Skanderbeg's heroic twenty-five-year battle against the Ottomans is very much the source of the Albanian identity, and his presence is recognized in every city or town in Kosovo or Albania.

If the Albanians were left out, so too were the peoples that we come to call Macedonians in the often hard-to-define territory of Macedonia, destined to become the most contentious part of the Balkans. Even though Bismarck brushed off the Albanians, the Macedonians were not even mentioned. The territory of Macedonia often defies definition, and a lot depends on who you ask and where you ask, especially now. In the nineteenth century, Macedonia was a mix of people and stuck next to hostile neighbors – Bulgarians, Greeks, and Serbs. In this mix a Slavic Macedonian identity grew that challenged the goals of the neighboring powers.

Local and small-power imperialisms were made worse by the bigger issues that the Congress of Berlin did not solve. Since Austria had Bosnia as of 1878, its relationship with the new Serbian state was potentially fraught. The Serbs had big ambitions, just like the Greeks, and one of them was to grow and to create a state where all Serbs lived in one place. This introduced another "greater" project into the region: the Greater Serbia one, which sought to expand in places where Serbs did live, such as Albania, Bosnia, Kosovo, and Macedonia. Kosovo, as noted, was still part of the Ottoman Empire. It had a mix of Serbs, Albanians, and others. As the "cradle" or "Jerusalem" of the Serb nation, with its huge medieval Serbian Orthodox Church infrastructure, Kosovo simply had to be Serbian. Without it, nationalists argued, the Serb nation was somehow incomplete. The myth of Kosovo as the very heart of Serbia was crucial to the fulfillment of Serb national dream. Kosovo had its own place in the hearts of Albanians too, but the strength of the Albanian argument lay in demographics: in the twentieth century they outnumbered the Serbs.

However, Serbs had opponents to their Greater Serbian dreams. The key factor was the Habsburg Empire. By grabbing Bosnia in 1878, it had more or less said "check" to the Serbs. It also had another card to play – the Albanians. Recall that the Albanians had announced themselves in Berlin in 1878 and were subsequently told to go home and become someone else. The Ottomans, who at first had supported the Albanian national awakening to use it to their advantage, changed course. Recall also that in 1878 the Albanians had asked only for autonomy, not independence. After 1878, the Ottomans sought to squelch the nascent Albanian identity so as to keep them inside. Like the Serbs, the Albanians charted a national awakening that based its success on developing a standard language. The Ottomans shut down the schools, and the Albanians had to go underground. Going underground to survive as a nation is part of Albanian identity. In the 1990s, the Albanians of Kosovo would be forced underground again, this time by the Serbs.

The Habsburg Empire saved the Albanians by taking on part of their national cause. This is one of the great examples of foreign intervention in the nation-building process. The Austrians, often through the small Catholic community of Albanians in and around the northern Albanian town of Shkoder, provided all kinds of things: schools, hospitals, and Albanian language training in Albanian territory and in Austria. While most Albanians believe in the myth that it was US President Woodrow Wilson who really made Albania after the First World War, it was actually Vienna. To limit Serb territorial ambitions, the Austrians helped put the Albanians between them and the Adriatic Sea. And between 1878 and 1912 that is just what they did. Albania did eventually appear, but in a highly charged and contested environment.

## The Balkan Wars and the First World War: 1912–1914

With the Austrians running around what would become Albania saying, "Become Albanian, come to Vienna or Graz and learn Albanian," many other things had to occur to change the Balkan map again. It was the same combination we have already witnessed: the small-power imperialism of the first Balkan states (Bulgaria, Greece, Montenegro, and Serbia) seeking bigger states combined with the Great Power imperialism of the Great Powers over the remaining Ottoman territories (contemporary Albania and Macedonia). This would bring a world war.

Before the Balkans states would go to war, however, some important events happened that changed things dramatically both inside
the region and in relations between the Great Powers. In 1903, the
Slavic Macedonians found a myth in the Ilinden Uprising against
Ottoman rule and the subsequent Krushevo Republic. Although the
republic lasted only two weeks as it was brutally crushed by Ottoman forces, it remained a pivotal foundational myth for Macedonian
identity. As divided as they were between nationalists who wanted
an independent state and those who wanted to join Bulgaria, the
Macedonians were now there too. In 1908 in Istanbul, the Ottomans
finally had a revolution that should have transformed the empire,
bringing in a more liberal government based on a defined constitution. Some of the subject nationalities, such as the Albanians, for
example, welcomed what was called the Young Turk Revolution. It
was supposed to bring decentralization, tolerance, and humanism.
In the end, the Young Turks brought the opposite, and further disintegration was the result.

The Austrians, worried about the potential of reform in the Ottoman Empire on their rule in Bosnia, decided that simply occupying
and administering Bosnia was not enough: they needed to own it.
So they annexed it. Bosnia became officially part of the Habsburg
Empire. Great news for the citizens of Bosnia, but bad news for a
furious Serb leadership in Belgrade. Internationally, the Russians
were equally displeased because, as part of the deal, the Austrians
were supposed to have consulted with them and agreed to some
important changes to the regulation of the straits in the Ottoman
Empire. After this, Bulgaria declared its independence as it was
nominally under the control of the Ottoman Empire. Less remarked
on in books on the region is another event in 1908 – the Congress of
Monastir in what is now Bitola, Macedonia. There, for the first time,
Albanian elites met and agreed on an alphabet for their language.
They chose the Latin script, hoping to link their fate to the West. The
Albanians were catching up, and time was running short to grab
their territory.

There were two brief but extremely bloody wars in the Balkans
in 1912 and 1913. Agreeing beforehand how to divide the territory,
Bulgaria, Greece, Montenegro, and Serbia went to war with the

Ottoman Empire. Far outnumbering the Ottomans, the Balkan allies won easily. However, during the war, confronted with an impossible situation insofar as they were about to disappear, the Albanians declared independence in November 1912 from the port city of Vlore on the Adriatic coast. The Albanian leadership knew that the only way to prevent partition was through independence, with an appeal to the Great Powers. The Austrian investment in Albania was paying off. Whether or not Albania was to be independent was up to the outside world.

The Great Powers met in London in 1913. The main outcome of the First Balkan War was that it was agreed Albania should become an independent state. It was all very simple: "On the demand of Austria-Hungary, to which Russia agreed, the conference recognized the new Albanian state." The Albanian elite were fanatically pro-Habsburg, hoping that they could join Austria as Bosnia had in 1908. Albania's borders needed to be established, but that would come later. Serbia got Kosovo, Macedonia was divided, and the Ottomans were out of Europe. The Albanians got another unemployed German as a prince, Wilhelm of Wied. He arrived in the port city of Durres in March 1914 and hated it from the start. With the start of the First World War, Wied simply left as he was ill-equipped to deal with the intrigues of Albanian political life. Moreover, at least according to his own memoirs, he hated the food too, and the place terrified his wife.

The First Balkan War, which eliminated the Ottoman Empire from the Balkans, led to a Second Balkan War when the Balkan allies turned on one-time ally Bulgaria. Even Romania joined in this time around. Greece was the big winner here, gaining most of Macedonia, especially the vital port city of Thessaloniki. Macedonia was completely partitioned by the Treaty of Bucharest. Most importantly, it made Bulgaria determined to get revenge on its neighbors.

The bigger-picture outcome was equally important. With the establishment of Albania, Austria had won a small victory in its fight with Serbia and expansionist Serb nationalism. Balkan regional relations were horribly poisoned, especially over Macedonia and Kosovo. The latter had a majority Albanian population that simply became part of Serbia. Making Kosovo Serbian launched decades of

Belgrade-imposed misery. Finally, a new standard of violence had been brought to the region. Known later as ethnic cleansing and very much the hallmark of twentieth-century Europe, the wars gave rise to horrible atrocities – executions, rape, expulsions, and wanton destruction of entire villages. What followed was a series of forced migrations. The Carnegie Endowment for International Peace assembled a commission that documented vast violations in pursuit of new nation-states. The Balkans also developed a reputation for violence. Civilians, facing a choice of move or die, would face the same stark choice again in the 1990s and after. People were not simply exterminated, but their heritage was also eliminated so as to remove their presence entirely.

While the Balkan Wars did solve some local issues, at least temporarily, the bigger issues with the Great Powers remained on the table. Austria's collision course with Serbia continued, made worse by the fact that between Serbia and the Adriatic Sea was a new country called Albania. This is not to say that there is a straight line from the Balkan Wars to the assassination of the Archduke Franz Ferdinand. In any case, the heir's assassin, the Bosnian Serb Gavrilo Princip, was unwittingly the most successful terrorist in the history of the world. He unleashed a chain of events that transformed the Balkans and Europe. All his aims were achieved in a single moment in Sarajevo.

The First World War did not start in the Balkans. Much needed to happen in the capitals of the Great Powers and happen it did. It is enough to say that power and prestige, to avoid becoming a mere holiday destination as opposed to a Great Power, meant everyone needed to be in. Greece, divided as to what side to be on, eventually chose the entente of France, Russia, and the United Kingdom; Serbia joined too, as did Romania in 1916 after being assured Transylvania was theirs. Albania, independent for barely a year, simply disappeared from the map. Bulgaria and the Ottoman Empire joined Germany and Austria-Hungary.

The Great Power juggling act over the Balkans collapsed. The solution over Albania was the last time the Europeans were able to find a workable compromise. After two years of war in the Balkans, the region got four more years of conflict. The costs of the war were immense, especially for the Serbs. An already weak modernization project was dealt a further setback. The destruction of the old empires eliminated whatever economic integration had been achieved. At the war's end, the Great Powers headed to Paris to make a new map. With the Balkan states clamoring to get bigger, there was simply too much history in too small a space to satisfy everyone.

## From Chaotic Democracy to Dictatorship

With the conclusion of the Paris Peace Conference in 1920, the fate of the Balkan states was more or less decided. Only war between Greece and Turkey would bring about more changes with the Treaty of Lausanne in 1923, including the emergence of a new Republic of Turkey and the horrifying population transfers that came with it. The other big change was the emergence of the Kingdom of Serbs, Croats, and Slovenes that would later (1929) become known as Yugoslavia; a somewhat durable occasional federation that would exist, in various forms, throughout the twentieth and early twenty-first century before finally disappearing in 2006. The borders agreed on in Paris managed to hold with only minor changes until the wars began in Yugoslavia in the 1990s. All the Balkan states were constitutional monarchies, at least on paper.

With both the Habsburg and Ottoman Empires gone, along with the tiny Kingdom of Montenegro and the nascent Montenegrin identity with it, the region was poised for a new beginning that, at least at the outset, seemed to promise prosperity and stability through liberalism and parliamentary democracy. However, despite the optimism and even revolutionary atmosphere that prevailed in the war's aftermath, the Balkan states were collectively denied breathing space to make a serious start at anything. A perfect storm of calamities confronted every state that sent all of them into various forms of authoritarianism or dictatorship. To be fair, this was certainly not unique to the Balkans, as the entire period between the two world wars for much of Europe was a catastrophe. Democracy simply failed to meet the challenges of the day.

Before taking stock of each state, let's look at some of the similar challenges faced by all of them. At the outset, it is safe to say that the Balkans did not provide any success stories in the period between the wars. Since these were new states, their national programs were exclusive, dangerous, and largely based on some highly idealized version of medieval greatness that cultivated us-versus-them mentalities. Relations with national minorities were almost always a zero-sum game. The Muslims of the region, as the inheritors of the defunct Ottoman Empire, were subject to horrific persecution and expulsion, especially the Albanians of Kosovo. In fact, even though the new League of Nations made the Balkan states sign on to visionary minority-rights treaties, the legacy of minority rights is shameful. As new states, which were inherently nationalizing states, building up great capitals and trumpeting the achievements of the "state-founding peoples," they left those outside the nation feeling threatened.

The most telling examples of these tendencies were Serb policy towards the Albanians in Kosovo, Bulgarian policy towards the Turks, and Romanian policy towards the Hungarians. When there was no real problem, one was simply invented, as in the case of the Greek claim that the Albanian government was persecuting the small Greek minority living in the south of the country. The Albanian government, unstable as it was, was not persecuting Greeks. Albanians were far too busy fighting each other to worry about the Greeks. Outside Albania, minority policies went from forced-assimilation campaigns to violence, to deportation. Where Central Europe had to contend with the Hungarians left outside the reduced Hungary after the war and a rabidly revisionist Hungary, the Balkans largest minority was the Albanians who found themselves in Yugoslavia and Greece. Despite this, Albania was too weak between the wars to cause trouble, and its leadership never pursued territorial changes. Being a minority was, across the entire region, a disaster. While some groups tried nonviolence to obtain more rights, others, such as the Albanians in Kosovo, tried violent resistance. Neither option got anyone anything at all.

Domestic politics was just as exclusive. It was decisively an urban affair, and the majority Balkan peasants were outside the interest of the mainstream political parties. The few peasant leaders that did emerge in Albania, Bulgaria, or Croatia were either assassinated or chose a life of exile after failing to get the peasant agenda on the table. The failure to advance the peasant or more broadly agricultural interests was possibly the biggest single failure of the interwar Balkans. Political parties fought for a narrow space that was generally center-right. In fact, once the leftist peasant leaders were destroyed, mainstream politics was dominated by right-wing authoritarian parties trumpeting nationalist or religious values or both. The political left hardly existed at all in the Balkans, and as a result the Balkans did not get the low-level (and often high-level) civil wars between right and left that dominated much of Western Europe, especially Austria, France, and Germany. Nevertheless, the marginalization of the vast majority of the populace lent support to extremist parties, nationalist-inspired scapegoating, anti-Semitism, and even homegrown fascism in Romania embodied in the Iron Guard movement.

On the bright side, given the revolutionary fervor that accompanied the end of the war, land was redistributed, with the exception of Albania, which remained practically feudal until 1944, when the communists finally destroyed the old order. However, in the absence of other needed reforms, combined with rapid population growth, land redistribution failed to bring prosperity. The Balkan peasant remained extremely unproductive and poor. State administration was largely overstaffed, inefficient, and corruption prone. As in the transition years that followed the collapse of communism, West European norms were imposed on totally different societies. The much-needed modernization projects never materialized. Modernization was left to the postwar communist rulers.

A number of bigger-picture problems confronted the region. The economy and the lack of capital (foreign and domestic) proved to be the biggest obstacle to stability. There was no money to support economic reform. The United States, which was the key source of cash, pursued narrow economic interests in the region, particularly in oil in Albania and Romania, until the Wall Street Crash of 1929. There were no serious security arrangements for the states in the region, and the League of Nations proved incapable of defending the order established in Paris. States were either in favor of the peace treaties or not, which meant stability was a near impossibility. There was no collective security arrangement, nor were there realistic prospects for regional integration projects given the poor relations between states. The triumph of Mussolini in 1922, and then Hitler in 1933, suggested that if you wanted to be on the right side of history, authoritarianism was the future.

More importantly, the Balkan interwar debacle was largely the failure of its inexperienced, corrupt, and shortsighted elites. Long accustomed to blaming external factors for domestic shortcomings, there is a regional tendency to resist accepting blame. A careful examination of the interwar Balkan political elite reveals a grim picture. Aside from Mustafa Kemal Ataturk in Turkey, Eleftherios Venizelos in Greece, and Nikola Pasic in Yugoslavia, there was a weak field of power-hungry mediocrities best exemplified by Ahmet Zog in Albania, who went from tribal chief with an outhouse to self-proclaimed king, complete with a royal food taster. His biggest success was to make Albania look ridiculous. The other Balkan monarchs were never able to impose the required unity and "above it all" leadership needed to inspire cooperation and civility. Instead, they all played on internal political divisions, the weaknesses as opposed to the strengths of their peoples, and ultimately chose the easier way to stay in power: divide and rule.

A state-by-state survey confirms this grim scenario. Greece had already made huge territorial gains as a result of the Balkan Wars, and in the aftermath of the First World War, decided to take advantage of Ottoman weakness and push for the Greater Idea – the Greece of the "Five Seas." Attacking Smyrna (now Izmir in Turkey) in May 1919, Greece's early victories in this war gave rise to extraordinary defeats and the emergence of the modern Republic of Turkey. Greece forfeited its principal territorial gains and endured what became known as the Asia-Minor Catastrophe. In the quest for ethnic homogeneity that seemed to promise stability, Greece and Turkey engaged in massive population transfers: the Turks sent some 1,300,000 Orthodox Christians to Greece, and the Greeks sent 585,000 Muslims to Turkey.

Horrific as these transfers were, they did create stability between Greece and Turkey. Moreover, the interwar experience of minorities elsewhere in the Balkans was dismal, so the various peoples were probably spared a worse fate later. Finally, the idea of population transfers as a path to stability was back on the table during the Second World War and after, and again during the wars of the 1990s.

In the wake of the Asia-Minor Catastrophe, Greece faced some daunting challenges. The legacy of the national schism played out in various negative ways that resulted in a struggle between monarchists and republicans, resulting in the abolition of the monarchy in 1924, only to see its return in 1935 and the imposition of a dictatorship by General Ioannis Metaxas in 1936. Greece's complex democracy survived the longest of any state in the Balkans. Greece's interwar inexperience was similar to the rest of the region – some democracy, more chaos, followed by dictatorship, war, occupation, and civil war. Emerging as a victor from the First World War, Greece's very participation in the war brought about the "national schism" that divided Greek society on every level – divisions that would be reinforced by the coming bitter civil war of the 1940s.

If Greece was the strongest Balkan state, Albania was the weakest. Independent first in 1912, Albania barely escaped disappearing after the First World War. Greece, Italy, and Serbia would have happily done away with it altogether. In fact, the secret Treaty of London (1915), which brought Italy into the war in the first place, foresaw Albania as nothing more than an Italian protectorate, something that it was destined to become in the long run anyway.

As noted, the Albanians wrongly credit US President Woodrow Wilson for Albania's survival at the Paris Peace Conference, and the tiny state, which had almost as many Albanians living inside the country as out, was on the map again, even though its borders were still up in the air. It should have been a revisionist state but it was not. Survival with few gains took precedence over adventurous policy. Albania's only advantage was relative ethnic homogeneity as there was only a small number of Greeks living in the south, contiguous to the Greek border.

The state- and nation-building challenges were simply mind-boggling. An illiterate population, feudal peasants in the south, tribal mountaineers in the north, no standardized language, three religions, no schools (Albania did not get a national university until the 1950s), an Ottomanized elite, no organized political parties, hardly any infrastructure, no money, and surrounded by neighbors who tarred them as "Turks" or subhumans who preferred anarchy to self-government.

In this horrible milieu, Albania too had its brief experiment with chaotic democracy, Balkan style. Elections came and went, parties emerged, but stability remained elusive. Two Albanian leaders fought it out in a battle that was often characterized as east versus west. It was partly true as US-educated Fan S. Noli sought to bring about reform, especially for the peasantry, while Ahmed Zog, the aforementioned tribal chieftain, sought mere power (and stability too.) Zog won out, seizing power in a coup with decisive support from Belgrade and Serb forces in December 1924 that ended Albania's fragile democracy without a peep from the outside world. Noli wandered around Europe a bit then settled in the United States to run the Albanian Orthodox Church in Boston before retiring in Florida.

The end of democracy in Albania by outside forces would later play well for the communists, who built the myth of encirclement and siege. In any case, Zog was no democrat. He established a presidential authoritarian republic in 1925; then, responding to the "will of the people," he made himself king in 1928. In a country with 90 per cent illiteracy, it is not clear how Zog gauged the will of his people. This started the gradual de-Europeanization of Albania. Zog claimed his role model was Ataturk in Turkey, and his wife compared him to Napoleon. His only nod to westernization, which he claimed he was committed to, was to send his three sisters in various white military outfits on tour around the country. In any case, he largely left Albania as he found it.

Lacking cash, Zog turned to Mussolini's Italy to finance his grand lifestyle and some modest infrastructure projects, such as turning tiny Tirana into a European capital with fascist-style government buildings on the main square and a grand boulevard for parades. Zog's legacy is otherwise empty. He never even bothered to tackle Albania's biggest challenges: land reform and education. Although Mussolini is often rightly characterized as a buffoon lacking serious ideological underpinnings, his brand of fascism was extremely dangerous. Zog, however, was truly the real buffoon of the era, with his garish military outfits, tiny castles, food tasters, a court surrounded by acolytes, and his omnipresent mother. His dependence on Italy was a direct path to Albania's invasion in April 1939 and the absorption of the Albanian kingdom into the Italian one. Zog, telling his people he would fight to the last drop of blood, fled two days later with the state treasury. He spent the rest of his life in a rather opulent exile, trying to find a way to get home. He died in Paris in 1961, leaving the hopes of the monarchy's return to his son, Leka, who was two days old when the family fled.

Bulgaria's interwar story is equally disappointing. Having lost important territories, obligated to pay reparations, and coping with a wave of refugees from the lost territories, Bulgaria wanted treaty revision. The quest for a better deal would later send it into an alliance with Germany. Like Stjepan Radic among the Croats, or Fan Noli among the Albanians, the Bulgarians started out with a progressive-minded peasant leader, Alexander Stamboliyski. He actually tried to fix some of Bulgaria's internal and external problems. Sadly, he drew the ire of Macedonian irredentists, who murdered and butchered him in 1923. Bulgaria's experiment with democracy ended there, more or less.

The fight over Macedonia continued with terrorist groups fighting for different visions for the region. Some struggled for the Macedonian independence, others sought its unification with Bulgaria. Serbs were doing their best to make Macedonians Serbs, and the Bulgarians were saying that Macedonians were Bulgarians. In trying to bring peace, Stamboliyski ensured his own murder, as peace was not the terrorists wanted. The terrorism did not end with Stamboliyski's murder, and Bulgarian political life between the wars was perilous – political infighting, murder, and mayhem. Elections ended in 1931, and a military coup, with the king's support, came in 1934. Parliament was dismissed, political parties dissolved, and censorship put in place. The military coup morphed into a royal dictatorship that drifted towards Germany in hopes of territorial rewards and the return of Greater Bulgaria.

Unlike Bulgaria, Romania found itself on the winning side of the war as it more than doubled its size, primarily by taking territory from Hungary but also from Bulgaria. It never turned the windfall of territorial gains into political or economic success. Of all the states in the region, where there was often a race to the bottom, Romania's performance was certainly the worst. Political instability and the dominance of an urban and disconnected elite over a poor peasantry certainly contributed to general discontent. As a result, Romania provided the one true mass-fascist party in the entire Balkans, the Iron Guard, complete with its own messianic leader. As well, Romania emerged as one of the more openly anti-Semitic countries.

Its early political life was dominated by Ion Bratianu's Liberal Party until Bratianu's death in 1927. King Ferdinand died the same year. The old structure gave way to rule by the National Peasant Party of Iuliu Maniu, which on the surface seemed to herald the possibility of real change. But peasant democracy failed utterly. Within this mix was the Romanian monarchy. King Ferdinand's son, Carol, had renounced his right to throne because of a contentious love affair with the "wholly unsuitable" Magda Lupescu and was told get rid of her or exit. He exited, and Carol's son, the one-year-old Michael, came to the throne with a regency.

Since the Maniu government was not up to the challenge and was in the midst of constant instability, the National Peasant Party government collapsed in 1930. One of the biggest changes was that Carol came back, and he brought Ms Lupescu with him. Maniu simply resigned in protest, and so ended the Romanian experiment with constitutional democracy. Carol's divide-and-rule policies yielded him total control of the country, with the customary bad results. During Carol's reign the most problematic issue was the growth of the Iron Guard under the leadership of the charismatic Corneliu Zelea Codreanu. This was true fascism, Romanian-style, fusing nationalism, necrophilia, mystical Christianity, a leadership cult, and virulent anti-Semitism. Its handsome leader succeeded in growing the party's support from a low of just above 1 per cent to almost 20 per cent in the 1930s. Part mass movement, part cult, part social service agency, and part political party, Codreanu and his legionnaires, as they were called, combed the villages and exploited the very fact that the peasants had been betrayed by both mainstream parties: Liberals and Peasants. The charismatic Codreanu would arrive at villages on his trademark white horse to bring a helping hand, digging a ditch or burying a loved one. King Carol willingly used the Iron Guard to advance his own ambition of establishing a personal dictatorship. In 1938 he did just that. Romania's fragile democracy ended there. His erstwhile allies in the Iron Guard were rounded up and jailed. In November 1938, Codreanu and thirteen of his followers were brutally murdered while "attempting to escape" during a prison transfer. The king established a single political party, and the country was firmly in the German camp, just waiting to sign on the dotted line.

Yugoslavia – like the first Czechoslovakia, which also appeared in 1918 – was a pragmatic solution to a complex problem after the war. It was a truly mixed country: a little more than 40 per cent Serbian, 23 per cent Croatian, 9 per cent Slovenian, 6 per cent Bosnian Moslem, 5 per cent Macedonian Slavic, and a mix of Albanians, Germans, Hungarians, and others. Although the Yugoslav concept (the idea that Southern Slavs – Croats, Serbs, and Slovenes – at that time should live in one state) had serious intellectual roots, especially among young people and intellectuals, it had equally strong geopolitical origins. In 1919 bigger was better (the opposite would be true in 1989, when smaller was better), and for Croats and Slovenes, being in something big was better because it protected them from Italy, which had entered the war solely for territory but ended up with almost nothing and still hoped to expand. Sadly for the Croats and the Slovenes, with the end of their Habsburg glory days, they joined the Balkans. For the Serbs, this move put everyone in one state, which had been the Serb dream since the nineteenth century.

If the Serbs built a nation partly around the Kosovo myth of a lost but heroic battle, the First World War is an equally important milestone. Serbs suffered terribly – their losses during the war outstripped those of either Britain or France – and with the Serb army retreating by foot through Montenegro and then Albania to Corfu, it was a period of incredible heroism and sacrifice. Given that the Serbs had paid such a high price, they more or less demanded a role that was more than just first among equals in the new federation. Unlike Croats or Slovenes, the Serbs had a state before the war and were thus better equipped to run one, so they more or less ran the first Yugoslavia. For the most part, the new state was a Serbo-centric one. The Serbian Karadjordjevic dynasty was in power (the Petrovic dynasty in Montenegro was sent off to exile in Italy), and the government was staffed by Serbs and run by Serbs, who obviously served the interests of the Serbs. The key issue of discord, competing visions of the future state between Croats and Serbs, was never solved.

In 1928, testimony to the tensions inside the state, the Croat Peasant Party leader Stjepan Radic was shot, in parliament, along with four other members of his party. The conflict had reached an entirely new level, and in January 1929, King Alexander took some extraordinary steps by ending the constitutional order, abolishing political parties, and dissolving the assembly; and with a new constitution in 1931, he established his personal rule in the form of a centralized unitary kingdom, which ended any attempts at federalism. In a further attempt to solve the national question, he also redrew the state's internal boundaries, with nine provinces that were decidedly mixed so as to enforce a new, top-down form of Yugoslavism that still gave the Serbs the advantage. King Alexander's dictatorship lasted until he was assassinated in Marseilles in 1934 by the joint forces of Croatian and Macedonian nationalists seeking Yugoslavia's destruction. In essence, the first Yugoslavia failed to solve the national question. The federal experiment ended in 1941 with German occupation and the Second World War. A second Yugoslavia, led by Josip Broz Tito, would try to solve the national problems in the war's aftermath.

## From Right-Wing Authoritarianism to Left-Wing Dictatorship

Given the complexity of the internal and external challenges, even the most gifted of interwar politicians would have found the situation almost impossible to fix. As noted, many, although not all, of the problems that confronted the region were beyond the control of the local elite. It was a perfect storm of external and internal calamities, given the global economic crisis, the rise of Mussolini and Hitler, and the fact that Western Europe more or less abandoned the entire region, with the partial exception of Greece. Moreover, the Great Powers had set extremely low expectations for the region. A preference for stability over democracy prevailed, and Hitler's Germany proved the most capable at exploiting the weak, failed, or failing states in the Balkans.

The drift towards various forms of authoritarian rule, and the complete failure of the liberal order, was by 1938 established everywhere in Europe, so the Balkans were no different. The international fate of the region is best told in terms of 1938 – the most decisive year, which marked the beginning of the total destruction of the Europe made by the Paris Peace Conference. Any leader of any small state in either Central Europe or the Balkans understood the events of that year as leading towards one kind of disaster or another. Nobody was safe. In March 1938, the Republic of Austria, after enduring a right-left civil war and its own brand of Austro-fascism, disappeared from the map without a shot fired or a single comment from the Great Powers. After all, Hitler needed only to placate Mussolini to take Austria. Austria's disappearance meant the end of Czechoslovakia. Hitler's seizure of parts of that country, agreed to by the Great Powers in Munich in September 1938, spelled another disaster. In March 1939, what remained of the Czech lands also left the map, just as Austria had. A quasi-independent Slovakia emerged that was pro-German, and the Czech lands became the protectorate of Bohemia and Moravia under Hitler.

In the Balkans, things would not play out much differently. On 7 April, Italy invaded Albania and announced the end of Zog's "kingdom," making Albania a part of Italy. As previously noted, Zog, his wife Geraldine, and their two-day-old son, Leka, fled two days later, preferring exile to a fight the Italians. As we shall see in chapter 4, Leka would attempt to reclaim the throne in 1997. Mussolini's next step was to invade Greece from Albania. When Mussolini asked the dictator Metaxas to surrender territory in October 1940, Metaxas's defiant "No" started the Greek-Italian War, which the Italians lost, prompting Hitler to intervene. "Ochi" or "No" Day in Greece is a national holiday. Despite some initial victories, Greece was later invaded by Germany in the wake of the Yugoslav invasion in April 1941, which led to a horrific occupation that resonates in German-Greek relations to this day.

In Yugoslavia, the situation was not resolved until 1941, when the Germans and Hungarians invaded the country, split it up, and Yugoslavia, like Czechoslovakia and Poland, simply disappeared. The fascist Croatian Ustase was the main beneficiary, grabbing

Bosnia and imposing a violent anti-Semitic, anti-Serb, anti-Roma regime based on violence. The Italians (along with Germans and Hungarians) got the territory they coveted in Slovenia and Croatia. In essence, by 1941 a new and enlarged fascist Croatia emerged that was a puppet of Germany. Albania, Greece, and Serbia were occupied. In a bid to curry favor with the Albanians, the Italians created a Greater Albania by adding Kosovo and parts of northern Greece. Romania, which had lost Bessarabia to Stalin as a result of the August 1939 Nazi-Soviet Pact, was humiliated again by Hitler in 1940 when he gave Transylvania "back" to Hungary in the Second Vienna Award. Romania emerged as a satellite of Germany, with the Romanian army and the Germans running the country. The country's leader, the authoritarian (some say fascist) Marshall Ion Antonescu, allied with Hitler in 1940 and joined, with catastrophic consequences, the invasion of the USSR in 1941. Romania was among the most enthusiastic participants in the Hitler's Final Solution. Antonescu tried to get Romania out of the Nazi camp after the defeat at Stalingrad. Bulgaria, still whining over territory lost in 1913 and in the First World War, was a pragmatic ally of Hitler, until it formally joined an alliance in 1941. The impact of all this is inconceivable, especially when one factors in the horrifying aspects of occupation, especially in Greece. Out of this came resistance struggles and horribly violent civil wars in Albania, Greece, and Yugoslavia, the near destruction of the Balkan Jewish communities by the Final Solution, and the liquidation of others groups in the region.

It is not my intention to provide an assessment of the Second World War in the Balkans. Instead, I will look at the establishment of the socialist/communist order and offer a quick overview of the various types of socialism and communism that prevailed between 1944 and 1989, from the absurd national communisms of Albania and Romania to the more benign system in Yugoslavia. Chapter 2 will then examine the crisis of 1989 and its implications for the subsequent transitions. The region was transformed by two key factors: the successful resistance of the often communist-dominated resistance groups and the presence of the Red Army. For Romania and Bulgaria, which had destroyed the left-wing political forces before the war, the arrival of the Red Army transformed things entirely.

Both countries had tried to switch sides in 1944, but the facts on the ground determined that their fates would be decided in Moscow, not London or Washington. Stalin was determined to build loyal Stalinist-style states in both countries. The wartime conferences of the Allies, particularly the percentages agreement between Churchill and Stalin in October 1944 and Yalta in 1945, consigned the Balkans, except Greece, to the Soviet sphere of influence. With the notable exceptions of Albania and Yugoslavia, where communist-dominated national liberation armies had won fair and square, the Red Army was in control.

## The Communists in Power: Ceausescu, Hoxha, Tito, and Zhivkov

A terrific if depressing entry point into the study of any of the communist states is a reading of some of the publications of the era that came from official state publishing houses that excelled at outlandish claims about the achievements of socialism. Or better still, read Malcolm Bradbury's 1983 *Rates of Exchange*. Bradbury tells the story of a hopeless British council visitor to a fictional country called Slaka, which has the combined absurdity of Albania, Bulgaria, and Romania. Or read the Tintin classic, *King Ottokar's Sceptre*. The bigger question that remains unanswered for the Balkans during the communist period is just how such ordinary, even subordinary men, often dull and largely from the periphery, imposed their will for so long on so many people. Some of the dictators who eventually ran the Balkans and died in office were not even good Marxists.

Shortcomings aside, the Soviets and their communist allies in the region had some important advantages in the war's aftermath. For a start, based on wartime agreements, Greece retained its special status and became the only non-communist state in the Balkans. But it first had to exit a disastrous civil war that in many ways reflected the schism of earlier years. Civil wars elsewhere were won by communists, who proved to be better equipped than the nationalists, who were often tainted by alliance with the German and/or Italian occupation forces. Political consolidation was made easier since the pre-war political elite was completely discredited.

The Balkan kings were especially guilty of incompetence, and the monarchies were swiftly abolished. Given their collective dismal failure and the near-total absence of royal nostalgia, it is surprising that all of them attempted a return to their "thrones" when communism collapsed in 1989 and after. For all the states of the region, there was the hope that the new order would bring modernity, stability, and prosperity – the very basics of life that had eluded the totally discredited interwar elite. The success of communists in the region is not solely because in some places (Bulgaria or Romania) they had the Red Army to back them up, or because they were simply the most unscrupulous in their willingness to use extraordinary violence against their enemies, but also because there were enough real believers who saw the new era as a needed break with the horrible legacy of the war and the years that preceded it. Everything prior to that had failed, so it was perfectly reasonable to try something new.

Rather than examine specific countries, it makes more sense to provide an overview of the main features of the communism that came to the region in 1945. The original systems put in place replicated the Stalinist economic and political model at all levels. Given that the interwar years were marked by the near-total absence of pluralism, the shift to left-wing authoritarianism and then totalitarianism was not the abrupt break it is often construed as. The Stalinist model implied a vertically integrated political system; a single political party; rigid censorship; a centrally planned economy; the collectivization of agriculture in Albania, Bulgaria, and Romania (Yugoslavia kept small plots for private use); the destruction of civil society; and the militarization of the populace. In short, nothing could exist outside the state's control. Significantly, the consolidation of these regimes required extraordinary violence against real and fake enemies. For ordinary citizens, who could see with their own eyes just how predatory these parties were, when even a top leader could perish, the message was abundantly clear – if you are not with us, you are against us. All the Balkan communist states were also nationalist in one way or another, and national communism was very much the hallmark of Balkan communism.

Until 1948, the Stalinist economic and political system prevailed for the entire communist Balkans. However, a deep and profound change to the region came in 1948 that altered the region's fate in a number of important ways. This dramatic realignment revolved around a deep disagreement between Yugoslav leader Josip Broz Tito and Soviet leader Josef Stalin. The source of the break, which sent Yugoslavia on totally different path, was that Tito was seeking too much power in the region. On the one hand, he seemed to have a solution to the perpetual instability of the region – create a Balkan federation with Bulgaria, thus solving the Macedonian question, and at the same time absorb Albania, thus solving the Albanian question in Kosovo.

Until 1948 the Albanian communist leadership was fine with becoming a republic in Tito's new federation. Stalin was not, as geopolitical changes were his to make, not Tito's, and he expelled Tito from the bloc. Local lore has it that Stalin sent five assassins to murder Tito. From his side, Tito allegedly wrote Stalin that he himself would need to dispatch only one if he decided to have Stalin killed. In any case, Albanian communist leader Enver Hoxha quickly switched sides, becoming anti-Tito and latching on to a very willing Stalin. By doing so – and succeeding – Hoxha essentially saved his own life. Had Tito's supporters in Albania prevailed, Hoxha would have been executed, as he had been quick to execute real and perceived supporters of the pro-Tito faction. His number two in the party, Koci Xoxe, was quickly shot. The year 1948 marked the beginning of some of the region's worst internal violence in the name of consolidation of one-party rule. Tito's national communism meant that all the other communist parties of Eastern Europe and the Balkans used the opportunity to clean house. A charge of "Titoism" or being a "Titoite" meant jail or death. While the USSR did mend fences with Tito after Stalin's death in March 1953, Tito's break with Stalin also meant the end of Stalinism in Yugoslavia. The break and the general defiance of the USSR gave Tito an unprecedented degree of legitimacy that other communist leaders could only dream of. As well, Tito established a kind of third-way system, called workers' self-management, that began in the early 1950s and avoided some of the more villainous aspects of Stalinism.

By creating a new federation of six republics (Macedonia, Serbia, Bosnia, Montenegro, Croatia, and Slovenia), Tito would attempt to solve the national question within an increasingly decentralized federation under the rule of a single, multinational party. Citizens of Tito's Yugoslavia would spend much of their lives in a kind of constitutional revolution, as Tito tinkered with the federation endlessly. In 1966, Tito dismissed the feared head of the Secret Service, Aleksandar Rankovic, which opened the way for more decentralization and the hope of more change. Most importantly, he would recognize the Bosnian Muslims (later called Bosniaks) as a nation in the 1960s and would make the majority Albanian Kosovo an autonomous province with rights approaching those of a republic. The same status was bestowed on Vojvodina in northern Serbia, where a smaller Hungarian community resided. The result was that Yugoslavia had eight relatively equal federal units – Bosnia, Croatia, Kosovo, Macedonia, Montenegro, Serbia, Slovenia, and Vojvodina. The main distinction between provinces – Kosovo and Vojvodina – was that they lacked the secession rights that were granted to the other republics. Moreover, the big changes made the republics essentially proto-states. But at the same time, Tito destroyed the emerging liberals who sought even deeper reforms, especially in Croatia.

These decisions, embedded in the 1974 constitution, would later provide fodder for nationalist Serbs claiming Tito's Yugoslavia was by design anti-Serb, given that Kosovo and Vojvodina were historically Serbian territory, especially as there had been talk of making Dalmatia in Croatia a separate province too, but the Croats beat that back. Yes, the Kosovars could claim to be the majority in Kosovo but they were still a minority in Serbia, which had owned Kosovo since the First Balkan War. Tito successfully designed a system that was a success as long as he was alive to arbitrate disputes between nations. A dictatorship, yes; but when compared with its neighbors, Yugoslavia, with its relatively open borders, membership in the Non-Aligned Movement, and workers' self-management, was a stunning achievement – which goes a long way to explaining why it generated so much nostalgia after the whole edifice came crashing down, especially in Bosnia and Macedonia.

Neighboring Albania was indeed Yugoslavia's opposite. It was ruled by a single person, Enver Hoxha, between 1944 and his death in 1985. Hoxha emerged as the region's most oppressive and paranoid leader and the only member of the ruling circle with a university education. Only Romania's Nicolae Ceausescu could rival Hoxha for a stunning combination of cunning, love of violence, and sheer megalomania. As noted, Hoxha communists did "win" their own liberation war. Upon assuming power, they violently dispensed with their enemies, especially the Catholics in the north, who they deemed the most hostile to communism. At first beholden to Tito's communists, who had been instrumental in establishing the Albanian communist party, as luck would have it, Hoxha maneuvered out of the Yugoslav orbit straight into Stalin's in 1948. Taking over a country that King Zog had left more or less as he found it, Albania was faced with the greatest obstacles. It is worth recalling that Albania was still feudal, with a few large landowners owning the limited arable land. Hoxha's main goal, in a country where 80 per cent of the population were illiterate peasants, was to industrialize based on the Stalinist model and make Albania self-sufficient. He also had to electrify the country, build roads, create a national education system and, most importantly, finalize the only partially completed nation-building project by making Albanians into Albanians.

Hoxha's Albania would maintain a commitment to Stalinism long after everyone else did, and he would manage to avoid virtually even the hint of reform that drifted in and out of the region. After Stalin's death in March 1953, there were hopes that Albania would liberalize. Stalin's successor, Nikita Khrushchev, pushed Hoxha to alter course plus mend fences with Tito. While Khrushchev clearly found Hoxha stubborn and annoying, Hoxha outright rejected his vision of Albania as some kind of beacon to the Middle East while supplying fruit to socialist bloc. Hoxha wanted steel mills, not olive groves, and he opted for Stalinism. Fearful of changes that would have endangered his own position, he left the Soviet bloc altogether. He kicked the Soviet advisors out and sent their submarines home but, according to local lore, allegedly kept a nuclear bomb or two. Taking advantage of Albania's general irrelevance and the emerging ideological split between China and the USSR, Hoxha established Albania as a Chinese satellite in the Balkans. When the Soviets tried in the 1960s to pressure the Albanians to get back in line by stopping grain deliveries, Hoxha declared, "We will eat grass rather than give in." While Hoxha and his leadership lived in relative opulence, Albanian-style, in a sealed-off quarter of Tirana called the "block," complete with televisions, refrigerators, loads of food, and drink, the rest of the population was indeed stuck with grass, horrific food rationing, and an insidious secret police as well as informants. The majority of the population was rural and forced to eke out an existence on collective or state farms.

With the Soviet advisors out, in came the Chinese with tractors, terraced agriculture, and cash, but less cash than the Soviets had. Hoxha's Chinese period lasted only as long as the Chinese commitment to Stalinism was maintained. When Mao died in 1976 and new policies came in with Deng Xiaoping, Albania chose Stalinism again. Hoxha decided to go it alone and opted for self-reliance and isolation, which inevitably delivered more hardship. The new 1976 constitution, which established Albania as a People's Socialist Republic, declared that Albanians have "blazed the path of history sword in hand" while struggling with foreign and "domestic enemies." Its Article 28 legalized the state of self-reliance. This period, which lasted until the mid-1980s, ultimately devastated Albania, pushing it further and further behind the rest of the region and making Albania's exit from communism even more challenging.

In addition to Stalinist economic and political policies, Hoxha maintained a very tight grip on Albanian society. Outside of a very powerful secret police, the Sigurimi, party propaganda drilled home the idea that Albania was threatened by all its neighbors. Albanian history was rewritten to tell a story of Albanian exceptionalism and survival against all odds. A couple of features of the Hoxha system deserve further explanation as they serve to highlight its built-in absurdities. In the 1960s, as Hoxha was moving closer to China, he implemented an Albanian version of the Chinese Cultural Revolution. The Albanian variant, which was much less violent, included a new emphasis on nation-building by banning all religions and declaring Albania the world's first atheist state. Religion, Hoxha argued, divided Albanians.

In the wake of the USSR's invasion of Czechoslovakia in August 1968, Hoxha militarized the country even further. Although the USSR never considered invading Albania, that did not matter: invasion could come from Yugoslavia or NATO members Greece or Italy. The made-only-in-Albania TV model, the Illyria, which was available only to those with permission, was modified to prevent tuning in to foreign broadcasts. In 1971, the government approved a bunker-building campaign that covered the country in 175,000 big and little bunkers on mountain tops and borders, ruining Albania's beautiful coasts. The building stopped only in 1983. Vine poles had bayonets on top to greet those who tried to parachute in. The slogan of the time was that with a population of two million, "We are two million soldiers." The party also built a massive complex in the base of Mount Dajti overlooking Tirana. The 110-room super bunker would keep the party elite alive in the event of a chemical or nuclear attack. It is now one of Albania's best museums of the communist past.

Although never at the level of North Korea, so successful was the propaganda that many Albanians, despite the grinding poverty, believed that they had achieved something great, especially since they had no comparisons. Isolated and alone, no televisions, no phones, no private cars, a single light bulb in a tiny apartment built by a youth labor brigade, when they saw what the world outside looked like after communism fell, they could only weep as they realized just how far behind they actually were. In a world of big lies, the Albanians were told the biggest one. Anti-Western propaganda was constantly leading many to believe that the West was awash in class struggle, massive inequality, and on the verge of revolution. Hoping to foment revolution, the Albanian communists funded all kinds of pro-Hoxha Marxist-Leninist parties around the world. Radio Tirana, known throughout the entire Soviet-dominated bloc, broadcast the Albanian alternative in multiple languages.

Things were just as bad in Romania, and it is never exactly clear just which state – Albania or Romania – had the most repressive form of communism. Romania's communism is mostly associated with Nicolae Ceausescu. Unlike Hoxha, who had somewhat serious intellectual credentials, Ceausescu was a small-minded and suspicious peasant who ruled brutally over a cowed and terrified people. Taking over from leader Gheorghe Gheorgiu – Dej in 1965, Ceausescu ruled until he was executed by his own soldiers on Christmas Day 1989, in what amounted to a coup, not a revolution, although it is highly unlikely we will ever know exactly what happened.

The main feature of Romanian's communism was similar to Albania's – a strong emphasis on exclusive nationalism. While he never really left the bloc like Tito and Hoxha did, Ceausescu functioned as a kind of maverick, pursuing his own foreign policy. Despite his appalling domestic policies, he was feted by Western leaders for his independence from the USSR with visits to the United States and France and was even hosted by Queen Elizabeth and praised by US presidents. Rumors suggest that Ceausescu always stole from his hosts. He also flirted with the east too, copying some of Mao's policies and even Kim Il-Sung projects in North Korea. His visit to Pyongyang in 1978, during which he was given the most outrageous display of faux love from adoring North Koreans, is probably the best example of the depth of absurdity that had reached both states by then. He returned home to Bucharest with some very bad ideas for which the population paid dearly.

When not flitting around the globe stealing ashtrays and towels from his hosts, he relied on a combination of Romanian exceptionalism (trumpeting the Dacian roots of the Romanians), anti-Russianism, anti-Hungarianism, and anti-Semitism to maintain power. His personality cult rivaled Hoxha's and Tito's. He called himself the Great Conductor or the Genius of the Carpathians. His regime, like Hoxha's was also ultimately a family dynasty as ugly as anything Carol had. His wife, Elena, also executed alongside her husband, pretended to be a world-renowned chemist with a doctorate, even though she never finished high school. Like Nicolae, she was an uneducated peasant who nearly flunked out of school and ordered her underlings to grant her degrees she did not earn and to publish books she did not write. The Ceausescus' children, especially the heir apparent, the sinister son Nicu, a well-known pervert, were integral to the regime.

In terms of domestic policy, his secret police, the Securitate, complete with an army of informants, ensured that Romanians were likely the region's worst conformists. Forced urbanization, the destruction and rebuilding of Bucharest, the criminalization of abortion, taxing people without children, and, to raise money, selling the country's remaining Germans to West Germany and the Jews to Israel were the hallmarks of his policies. Unlike neighboring

Yugoslavia or Hungary, which maintained social peace partly through a consumerism paid for with foreign loans and crushing debt, Ceausescu's regime was austere, at least for ordinary people. He spent the money saved on grandiose projects, such as his House of the People, which was the world's second-largest administrative building, after the Pentagon. It was built in the 1980s at the height of austerity and food rationing. To make room, forty thousand buildings were destroyed. Ceausescu's own extravagant lifestyle was equally unrestricted by the economic concerns of the day.

The Bulgaria of Todor Zhivkov was not much better, although less destructive than Ceausescu's Romania. Zhivkov, like Ceausescu, was born a poor peasant and raised in the school of hard knocks. He took over in 1954 in the wake of the major changes that came with Stalin's death in 1953. He ruled until the changes of 1989. Unlike the other Balkan leaders, he was unquestionably loyal to the USSR. Despite this, nationalism also became the cornerstone of regime policy, which earned the Bulgarian communists a degree of loyalty from the ordinary population. Like all communist states, they were prone to big lies. One propaganda book produced for foreign consumption claimed that the small and dynamic Bulgaria had achieved an unbelievable feat: abolishing misery forever.

The nationalism of Bulgarian communists found its expression primarily in the attitudes towards the Muslim minorities, particularly the Turks, who made up roughly 10 per cent of Bulgaria's population, but also the Roma. Bulgaria declared these groups to be part of the Bulgarian nation, and by the 1950s had adopted an intense assimilation campaign and the gradual elimination of minority-language schools. In the 1960s, people were encouraged to Bulgarianize their names, and Bulgaria and Turkey struck an agreement that led to large numbers of Turks leaving Bulgaria for Turkey.

By far the most odious aspect of these various attacks on minority rights was the 1980s' "Revival Process." This took things to an entirely different level. The government declared that the Turks were Bulgarians who converted to Islam. The government was just helping them to "rediscover" their roots. Name changes became mandatory, enforced by the secret police and other security organs. In 1989, as the communist world was unraveling, Bulgaria tried something new: it opened its border with Turkey and encouraged the Turks to leave, and almost four hundred thousand did. Local media said they were taking a holiday. To make sure Bulgarians got the point, the 1988 film *Time of Violence* was made to whip up anti-Turkish hysteria by dragging out the old horrors of 500 years of Turkish rule. The film depicts the violent destruction of Bulgarian Christians in a small village.

## Conclusion

As the region headed towards the miraculous year of 1989, none of the Balkan states were ready for what lay ahead. Even non-communist Greece, which should have been the main beneficiary of the collapse of communism in the Balkans, found itself unprepared and squandered an opportunity to be "back in the Balkans" on its own terms. While Greece may have been poor in west European terms, it was the wealthiest and most successful state there and the one best suited to reap the rewards of regime change. On the surface, Yugoslavia, with its third-way socialism, open borders, and thriving tourist business, seemed the best prepared to weather the storm and rejoin Europe. Tito died in 1980, and the national questions were still on the table. While the slogan "After Tito, Tito" may sound silly now, it was just what was needed – but there was no Tito. The country was left in the hands of a collective presidency within a highly decentralized federation, which reduced the likelihood of Yugoslavia making a successful transition, even though on paper, Yugoslavia should have been a frontrunner. Making matters worse, Yugoslavia, like Hungary and Poland, owed huge amounts of money to international financial institutions. Maintaining social peace through consumerism, with stores filled with Western goods, had a high price. Whatever the outcome, harsh austerity was in the cards.

In Albania, the situation was the opposite. Hardly any change had occurred, and in 1985, Hoxha's chosen successor, Ramiz Alia, was not up to any challenges. Hoxha's death had long been expected, and thousands of Albanians, in what was probably the first time they formed an organized line, lined the Boulevard of Martyrs to the Nation to file past Hoxha's coffin to shed real and fake tears. Even though Alia was in charge, it was Hoxha's widow, Nexhmije, a real hardliner, who called the shots. Comparing himself to Deng Xiaoping, Alia would attempt to put a square peg in a round hole and fail by offering some modest economic changes but nothing dramatic on the political front. Owing to such tight internal controls and regular party house cleaning, there were no dissidents inside Albania. Unlike Yugoslavia, Albania was at least solvent.

Romania was destroyed by the Ceausescu dynasty. The Ceausescus' executions confirmed where things would go there. Ceausescu's repressive policies meant that the first real demands for change came from the minority Hungarians in Transylvania. His execution brought to power a group of people who would resist reform but not the promises of state capture that came with power. Zhivkov's Bulgaria was no better. Loyal to the USSR to the end, Zhivkov never saw change coming. His fate, and those of people like him, is best captured by Julian Barnes's novel *The Porcupine* (1992). The nouveau riche, pseudo-Marxist vulgarians who ruled with an iron fist were replaced by the only things the old system could produce: communists turned fair-weather democrats, state security hacks with the right connections, criminals, and bureaucrats lacking vision but with a real knack for political survival.

Although the end of the Cold War in 1989 meant things were different in Czechoslovakia, Poland, and Hungary, it meant something different in the Balkans. Always looking for a fundamental break with the past, aside from the Greek exception, the Balkans never got that break, moving from one kind of intolerant authoritarianism to another. The ordinary people of the region sought a revolutionary break for sure. They were to be disappointed. Albania, Bulgaria, and Romania got permanent transition, brain drain, and kleptocracy. Yugoslavia got the same – plus civil war.

# 2

# Good News, Bad News: Before and After 1989

Even though communism fell last in Albania, it makes some sense to start the story there and return to the issues in Yugoslavia with the ascendancy of Slobodan Milosevic, and then examine events in Bulgaria and Romania. 1989 brought a series of changes that were largely unanticipated by most seasoned observers. While many identify the fall of the Berlin Wall in November 1989 as the moment when the east really unraveled, things in the Soviet bloc had been rotten for a while. Reform communists were tinkering with the system in Hungary already, and events in Poland really got the ball rolling. The regimes everywhere were decrepit, based on a weird compact between ruler and ruled that amounted to a kind of grumbling conformity, lacking any kind of legitimacy. Everyone, ruler and ruled, was simply faking it. With the whiff of decay and environmental degradation everywhere, the moral basis for rule was gone, and when the Soviet leader Mikhail S. Gorbachev made it clear that he would not use force to uphold Soviet dominance, the jig was really up, except where the USSR had no influence: Albania, Romania, and Yugoslavia.

But when the Berlin Wall did fall, and the communist regimes of Central Europe disappeared like a morning fog in the sun, things looked relatively stable in a place like Albania. I even wrote a piece for Toronto's *Globe and Mail* that spoke of Albania as the last Stalinist holdout, and I was certain the communists would survive. The level of Albania's isolation was extraordinary, and the success of the propaganda machine was real. The siege mentality convinced ordinary people who had never traveled or watched foreign television that a new and advanced society had been built. They were to be extremely disappointed when they were forced to see, with their own eyes, just how huge the gap was between them and everyone else. This is not to say there were no gains. Albanians had a small flat, some electric lights, schools, and they were literate. The ruling party lived differently of course: in the bloc, inaccessible to ordinary people, in nice houses with pools, gardens, and multiple refrigerators. When compared with the ostentatious luxuries that the likes of Ceausescu, Tito, and Zhivkov bestowed on themselves, the Albanian leaders were modest, even austere. Not seeing too far into the future, they did not have foreign bank accounts; for that matter, they did not even have domestic ones. Where the Albanians really blew cash was in funding all kinds of fringe Marxist groups around the world and letting their diplomats based in New York fly on the Concorde to ensure that nobody would ever assume the Albanians were poor.

The Albanians had started a controlled opening of sorts in 1990 and sent some trusted emissaries out to spread the word about Albanian exceptionalism. I met two of them during a visit to Toronto. But even by December 1990, the ruling Albanian Party of Labour (Communist Party) gave in to massive street demonstrations and agreed to multiparty elections in 1991. An emerging opposition coalesced around two key figures with good, even great, communist credentials: Sali Berisha, a cardiologist and incorrectly rumored to have been Hoxha's physician, and Gramoz Pashko, an economist, who quickly eclipsed the until-then ascendant student protestors and called for an end to one-party rule by establishing the Democratic Party (DP). By early 1991, the gigantic statue of Enver Hoxha in Tirana's main square was down, and Albania began a very hectic and ultimately failed exit from communism.

Albania's communist boss, Ramiz Alia, had been handpicked by Hoxha to replace him after he had his other heir apparent, Mehmet Shehu, killed in 1981. Shehu's death deserves some further explanation as it sheds light on the nature of the regime in its last decade. Shehu had been number two in the regime since the 1950s and the main beneficiary of the execution of Koci Xoxe after the break with

Yugoslavia in 1948. In a world of "bad cop, bad cop," Shehu was the really bad cop. He was deeply interwoven into the Hoxha family dynasty, but rumor had it that Hoxha's wife, Nexhmije, preferred Alia. What happened to Shehu remains an extremely murky affair. In what the regime termed "a fit of nervous crisis," Shehu killed himself. He was likely murdered, some say even by Hoxha himself. The party announced that the country's long-time prime minister was actually a spy for multiple foreign governments, including the USSR, the United States, and Yugoslavia. Imagine living in a country where you were asked to swallow that? History books had to be rewritten, and everything had to be revised. Citizens were asked to remove references to Shehu in any books they had. Even more telling, I had a friend in the upper echelons of the party in the 1980s, and Shehu had been part of her family's lives. After 1981 she meticulously used her fingernail to remove Shehu's face from family photos. Better to do that than destroy the photos altogether, she said.

As Shehu's replacement, Alia was an extraordinary mediocrity, typical of the people that Hoxha had elevated in his forty-one years in power: largely uneducated toadies unwilling to question the absurd policies Hoxha pursued. The cult of personality that Hoxha established ensured that he needed people of very dubious credentials around him. Since his life and achievements were essentially fabricated, he had eliminated anyone who knew the truth. I recall, in later interviews with Alia, his lack of depth and even pedestrian understanding of things. Later lamenting that his successors embraced "shock therapy" for the transition, he likened what they were doing to throwing a baby into cold water. Prior to my interviews with him, my Albanian friends always warned me to be careful for he was clever and they thought he could spin me. He was not clever, not in the least. For people who lived under his rule, it made sense to at least believe the leadership was smart. There was no other way to accept what was happening in a society where you were completely unable to act as an individual. It served to partially justify a life of utter despair.

Alia did embrace reform at first and he largely succeeded in preventing the type of violence that would come to Romania. His main goal was to preserve his mentor's principal goals while allowing a modest reassessment of economic policy designed to alleviate Albania's isolation and incredible poverty. He was still essentially an "Enverist," best understood by his book *Our Enver*, in which he extolled the never-ending virtues and God-like features of his mentor. His reassessment included a partial opening up to the West. But Alia only offered controlled change. He failed miserably as events got ahead of him and he was not up to the job. It is to his credit that there was so little violence as he could have acted differently. Violence would come but it would be in 1997 during a period of pseudo-democracy. It would not be long before Alia's opponents would put him in jail for a variety of crimes that were certainly not the ones he deserved to be in jail for. A telling anecdote was a conversation he related to me about his time in jail. He said that one of his guards was ironically someone who spent time in jail under the communist regime. Alia enquired, "What did you do?" The guard replied, "I tried to flee the country." Alia responded, "But you broke the law and you knew that." What remained astonishing about Albania's communists was how they simply refused to reflect on the past: there were no mistakes.

Once, in a quest for Alia to say something new, I did ask him if he had made mistakes. Surprisingly, he said, "Yes." He asked me if I was staying in Tirana. I said, "Yes." He asked me if the call to prayer from the mosque had awakened me. "Yes," again. He said that was his fault. As culture minister in the late 1960s, Alia had presided over Albania's abolition of religion in 1967 and its declaration as the world's first atheist country. As discussed, the war on religion was part of a wider battle against competing centers of loyalty to the communists that included regional identities, different dialects of spoken and written Albanian, and the centuries-old Kanun of Leke Dukagjini. Dating back to the 1500s, this code was passed down orally until it was first published in the 1930s. The Kanun served as a code of behavior, and a guide to life and blood feuds for many of Albania's northern tribesmen. As for religion, Alia later suggested to me that the resurgence of religion after communism's collapse was the result of the ban. He argued that had religion not been forcibly banned, it would have simply disappeared. This was true as the war on religion in Albania did in fact place the seeds for radicalization of

Islam in Albania and for Albanians later joining Islamic State. Burying the Kanun of Leke Dukagjini did not work either, because the blood feud was back as old and new scores needed to be settled.

As noted in chapter 1, the communists had already destroyed Catholicism in Albania's north after the war. The 1967 ban dealt mostly with Albania's Orthodox population and the Muslims. By the time communism came to end, there were no clerics for any religion, which meant that the rebuilders of religious life had to come from abroad. The Vatican helped the Catholics, the Greek Orthodox Church helped the Albanian Orthodox community, and the Saudis were active in Albanian Islam. Albania's leaders embraced the Saudis at first, hoping for cash, but instead all they got were hastily built mosques that looked rather temporary, situated in the weirdest locations. The mosques were strategic, in fact, often near Albania's few main roads, never in a village, added as a kind of roadside advertisement to say, "This is Muslim territory."

Under Alia's leadership, Albania headed to the polls in March 1991. With only a few months to prepare, the opposition to the communists had too little time to mount effective campaigns. In the end, without even bothering to change the party name, the Albanian exception prevailed, and the communists were still in power in what were partially free elections. Partially free because the communists really held all the cards, particularly by controlling the message given on state television. Moreover, the nascent DP of Berisha and Pashko remained mostly an urban and student phenomenon. Albania was then roughly 65 per cent rural, and the peasants were out of the DP's reach. In addition, they were instinctively conservative. Recall that when the communists took over in 1944, Albania was feudal. The peasantry working the land feared the massive privatization offered by the DP. For some, it meant the return of the old landowners and more misery. Overwhelmingly they stuck with the communists. However, the DP won most of the urban centers and, in an electoral tradition that started then and never really ended, the opposition contested the results, took to the streets, and provoked a never-ending crisis in what were extremely perilous times. The international community had to intervene even to provide food aid. In the meantime, the communists tried to become mainstream, got rid of the aging men in Hoxha's politburo, and became the Socialist Party of Albania with a much younger leadership. A technocratic government took over, and new elections were set for March 1992, which the DP won in a landslide. It appeared that Albania had made a decisive break with its past.

In the carnival-like atmosphere of 1992, Albanians thought they had reached a turning point. They had not. The DP remained in power until 1997, using methods that were primarily authoritarian in nature. A turning point could have come in 1992, but given the nature of the Albanian exit from communism, Albania failed to embrace a democratic system and drifted towards disintegration and conflict. As we shall see later, even ethnically homogenous Albania ended up in conflict. Berisha's rule was characterized by the very features that would shape the entire region: a strong presidency, weak institutions, state capture, fraudulent elections, control of media, and an illegal war on opposition parties. Since the West set a very low bar for Albania, democratic shortcomings were ignored, more or less. As well, the Albanian fanatical devotion to the United States ensured that very little criticism came from Washington. Berisha, in what was then a very controversial move, brought Albania into the Organization of Islamic Conference (OIC), which angered many Albanians who were undeniably proud of their religious diversity and tolerance and did not see themselves as part of an Islamic alliance. Berisha saw only cash in the OIC, and besides, the Americans told him to do it so they could have an ally there, even though the Albanians hardly attended any meetings. The United States was especially eager to trumpet its success with a majority Muslim state. As the country's new president, Berisha's main preoccupation was the destruction of the opposition Socialists, and to accomplish that he initiated a series of trials that were highly politicized and even unnecessary. Berisha's initial decisions meant Albania would head down the path of permanent polarization, which continues to shape political life.

In neighboring Yugoslavia, which by the low Albanian standards was like Switzerland, analysts who saw in Yugoslav exceptionalism an easy transition to democracy and free markets were horribly wrong. Most Western academics were too enamored of the Yugo-sphere and Yugoslavia to see any problems, and few of them knew just what was happening in Kosovo, where ethnic hatreds were alive and well. Besides, they liked the hospitality there too – the slivovica, the cevapcici – and generally asked the wrong questions of their interlocutors and talked to the wrong people. They drifted between Belgrade, Zagreb, and the coastal resorts in Croatia and Montenegro. Even more disturbing, many academics were apologists for Milosevic. I can recall one scholar even comparing Kosovo and Quebec as though they were somehow similar. Serbian diplomats, as we shall see, hoped that Canada would not recognize Kosovo's independence, precisely because of Quebec again assuming the situations were similar when they were not.

In any case, the belief in Yugoslav exceptionalism became an echo chamber. In what was still a dictatorship, if more benevolent than some but not all of the Soviet satellites (the goulash communism of Hungary was similar), Yugoslavia had many admirers, as it did have a degree of legitimacy. It had broken from the USSR, maintained a nonaligned foreign policy, had a relatively freer economic system, and was known to many as it was a major tourist destination. Unlike most other communist bloc states, Yugoslavs had passports, which meant that they could travel; and more importantly for the economy, work abroad as remittances, then and now, was a cornerstone of a very weak economy. However, in the wake of Tito's death in 1980, the federation faced numerous challenges that would put communists-turned-nationalists into power. More challenging was that with the end of the Cold War, Yugoslavia simply lost its geopolitical significance, and its leaders were told so.

Even before Milosevic made his first fateful visit to Kosovo in 1987, the federation was under extraordinary strain. The legacy of Tito meant that the omnipresent nationality question was solved by a complex federal arrangement that was supposed to solve the national question by providing a single party with branches that represented the nations and nationalities. It was an extremely decentralized state, which was an important factor in its undoing in the 1990s as the center was too weak to combat the power of the republics, especially when they were taken over by nationalists. This structure had eight units with almost equal rights and a rotating presidency. Nations and nationalities deserve some clarification.

What it meant was that republics were nations: Bosniaks (Bosnian Moslems were recognized as the sixth nation in Yugoslavia in 1968), Croatians, Macedonians, Montenegrins, Slovenians, and Serbians. Nationalities who already had their own nation-states included the Albanians of Kosovo (and elsewhere) and the Hungarians living in Vojvodina, Serbia's north.

The Albanians of Kosovo, who became part of Serbia in 1912 in the First Balkan War, later experienced successive horrors until Serbian rule. Although exact population numbers are highly contested, with Serbian historians arguing that the Kosovo was historically majority Serb, it is fair to say that in the twentieth century the Albanians were the majority. Until the substantial changes to their status in the late 1960s, which were made concrete with the 1974 constitution, Belgrade's policy towards them was essentially a mix of genocide, expulsion, colonization, and assimilation. Nothing worked to change the fact that the demography plus the League of Prizren in 1878 were the foundations of their claim. For the Serbs, Kosovo was not just the epicenter of the Serbian Orthodox Church legacy but also the cradle of the Serbian medieval empire – the very heart of Serbia, as the cliché went. Nonetheless, the Albanians saw their rights grow under Tito's rule and later became an autonomous province with federal status.

The key difference between a republic and province was that the 1974 constitution did not offer secession rights to the provinces. This was to become extremely contentious when Yugoslavia began to disintegrate. What this meant for the Albanians of Kosovo was that they enjoyed a tremendous degree of self-government, control over policy, and generally were in a better position to start getting back at the Serbs. They got better representation in the governing party and more fairness in what the Yugoslavs called socially owned enterprises. There were other unavoidable but unintended consequences as the changes led to a state-sanctioned growth in Albanian identity, particularly with the opening of a university in Prishtina, the province's capital. Thousands of young Albanians flocked there to study all things Albanian, which served to make them aware of their identity but hardly provided the basis for a future career. This ensured that Kosovo had 50 per cent youth unemployment, a figure that continued to define its economy well after it achieved independence in 2008. Finally, the Belgrade-sanctioned Albanianization of Kosovo hurt the minority Serbs as they felt more and more excluded. ·

An explosive growth in new and young nationalists – who were aware of their relative poverty when compared to the rest of Yugoslavia and somehow smitten with the official line from Tirana that a paradise had been constructed – was accompanied by an equally fast growth in Albanian population numbers, making Albanians the fastest-growing population in Europe. The Albanian numerical advantage was made even stronger by the out-migration of Serbs, who felt increasingly isolated in what was quickly becoming Albanian space. An important side note is that while the Albanians in Kosovo were empowered, the substantial Albanian community in Macedonia got nothing. They would have to wait until 2001 before they had the chance to make their grievances known. Emerging Albanian awareness, along with calls for closer ties with neighboring communist Albania, were becoming greater. There were also growing calls for Kosovo to be made a republic alongside the six existing republics, giving Kosovo full federal equality. This became particularly acute with massive student demonstrations in 1981 and a violent response from Belgrade. While Kosovo retained its autonomy until Milosevic arrived on the scene, the events of 1981 meant that Kosovo was kept under the watchful eye of Belgrade, along with an outsized presence of troops from the Yugoslav National Army in the event things got out of hand.

If the Albanians were becoming the key political dilemma, things on the economic front were even more potentially catastrophic. Like Hungary and Poland, social peace was bought with loans from international financial institutions. Yugoslavia was living under its own form of goulash communism, paid for with money they did not have, which was a testament to Yugoslavia's outsized importance in the Cold War. By 1988, Yugoslavia's economy was in grave condition, and international creditors were sounding alarm bells that the massive debt could no longer be serviced. The International Monetary Fund called for painful restructuring. The crisis hit hardest the country's poorest places: the province of Kosovo and the republic of Montenegro.

Facing dire economic and political problems, Milosevic offered a new vision under the guise of the aforementioned "anti-bureaucratic revolution." He heeded calls from emergent nationalist opinion, particularly in academia, that bemoaned the weakening of Serb national interests. Some extremists even spoke, inaccurately, of an Albanian genocide against the Serbs. Milosevic was prepared to alter the constitutional structure of 1974, which, he argued, was contrary to Serb national interests. His triumph in Belgrade allowed him to place his people in power in Kosovo, Montenegro, and Vojvodina, thus ensuring that he now had four federal votes. To rally an already insecure population, not long after his first visit to Kosovo, Milosevic seized the state media to demonize the Albanians and develop his own hero cult. Lurid but fabricated tales of Albanian depravity, violations of women (and men), and desecration of Serb graves were the norm, along with the usual tropes about the legacy of Turkish occupation, which worked well because the Albanians of Kosovo were neither Christians nor Slavs but primarily Sunni Muslims and ethnically distinct. Left untouched with their growing population, Milosevic argued, the Albanians would completely destroy not just the Serbs but also the Serb legacy in Kosovo.

Negative myths were back with a vengeance. Nowhere was this more obvious than when Milosevic – and a million other Serbs – descended on Kosovo Polje (Fushe Kosove in Albanian) on 28 June 1989 to celebrate the sixth-hundredth anniversary of the Battle of Kosovo. Prior to the anniversary, the bones of the dead Prince Lazar toured the country in a scene totally befitting the arrival of bad news. At the speech, displaying his now-trademark pose, which was a bit Mussolini – chin stuck out, filled with bitterness and threats – Milosevic warned that while armed battles had not started, they could not be ruled out in the future. The Milosevic-controlled media reminded the audience that Kosovo was the essence of Serb unity, had been wrongly taken from Serbia, and without action the Albanians would seize it. The June 1989 display was a stark warning, a disgrace, and testimony to the capacity of vulgar nationalism to mobilize. For Albanians, the speech was a warning and sent waves of fear throughout the province. While violence would come later, Milosevic put huge psychological pressure on the Albanians. The Albanians had no choice but to submit and head underground. In the ensuing instability, Milosevic effectively destroyed Kosovo's (and Vojvodina's) autonomy and the emerging semi-democratic projects there, and he reversed all the major constitutional gains the Albanians had made. As will become clear later, the simple fact that Belgrade effectively eliminated Kosovo's autonomy made it subsequently impossible for the Albanians to accept autonomy again when the Belgrade government offered it in 2007 as an attempt to prevent Kosovo's imminent independence. If autonomy could so easily be swiped away by a rigged parliamentary vote, why accept it ever again?

What happened in Kosovo sent Yugoslavia into a series of unending crises, and there is no doubt that Kosovo caused Yugoslavia's disintegration. This is not because the other republican leaders fretted about the fate of the Albanians – after all, only Slovenia reacted with solidarity with Kosovo – but because they understood Milosevic's vision and saw in his actions a simple constitutional coup d'état. One of the great tragedies is that the non-Serb nations in Yugoslavia never formed a coalition to stop Milosevic. In 1989, Serbia approved Milosevic's changes to the constitution, and a rigged Kosovo Assembly followed suit. Serbia was united again, and Kosovo more or less disappeared. As a provocation, in the heart of Prishtina, beside the university, is a gigantic yet abandoned Christ the Savior Serb Orthodox Church. To the uninitiated, it tells the story of the Albanian attack on historic Serb religious infrastructure because it looks like a relic. It is not: its construction started in 1995 as a simple act of aggression by Milosevic. Milosevic's message was clear to the Albanians: you were a majority in Kosovo but now you are minority in Serbia.

With the Kosovo branch of the Yugoslav communist party simply taken out of the picture, new political forces emerged that sought, at first, to respond to Serb actions with non-violent resistance. As the Albanians were excluded from state structures, they were forced to go underground. They developed a unique "parallel society" to respond to marginalization, which meant activities once paid for by the state now ran in peoples' homes. The Albanians were quasi-stateless, so they created their own state. What began was a period that Albanians rightly refer to as Serb occupation and that lasted until 1999. The period of the parallel society had a lasting impact on Kosovo society in that the parallel society could not really deliver on the education and medical needs of Kosovo and left the population barely prepared for what came after Serb rule ended.

Belgrade's policy was racist, and that needs to be acknowledged in open terms. What always astonished me about mainstream Serb attitudes towards Albanians was how easily even some of my cosmopolitan interlocutors slipped so easily into ethnic slurs. They always demonized the Albanians. While Belgrade propaganda ironically deemed them as ungovernable anarchists bent on unification with Albania and the destruction of the Kosovo Serbs, they, according to Belgrade, were capable of organizing a fertility campaign. Living on the margins created a remarkably cohesive society that benefitted immensely from the financial support from Albanians living around the world. The Kosovo para-state was also corrupt in that conditions imposed on them forced them to seek alternatives and to avoid, as one friend noted, "simply dying a noble death." If the Serb leadership in Belgrade later complained about the criminalization of Kosovo, they failed to acknowledge their role in creating it.

Among Albanians, power largely went to the successor to the Kosovo League of Communists, the Democratic League of Kosovo (LDK in Albanian) and its leader, Ibrahim Rugova, a Sorbonne-educated literary scholar. The soft-spoken and chain-smoking Rugova, with something verging on an extremely compelling anti-charisma, was an unlikely leader. His survival, given that not only Serbs wanted him dead but his opponents in Kosovo also wanted him out of the way, suggests that he had a number of hidden talents that were not always apparent, since he managed to be the most important figure in Kosovo until his death in January 2006. Sadly, he did not live long enough to see its independence in 2008 but he did more to align Kosovo with European values than all his successors combined. His fundamental premise was passive resistance. Violence, he argued, would only bring an even more violent response from the Milosevic regime, which would invite a catastrophe. He also worked tirelessly to generate international interest in the fate of the Albanians, who, after all, were the first victims of Milosevic's new order. He was not without his critics: some argued Rugova made too many concessions to Belgrade and thus held Kosovo back. The international community liked him for that very reason. Rugova's passive resistance would fail because of events beyond his control, but a lot had to happen before Albanians realized that Mao was a better role model than Gandhi. For. some, Rugova's passive resistance was too passive to even be called resistance. Nevertheless, Rugova's most lasting legacy would be the foundation of a distinctly Kosovo identity as Kosovars, separate from neighboring Albania.

A brief comparison with the fate of the Hungarians in Vojvodina also sheds some light on Rugova's policy, as the Hungarians had a lasting impact on Kosovo. Hungarians never had the numerical superiority that Albanians had, as they generally made up 25 per cent of Vojvodina's total population. Moreover, they were far better integrated into Yugoslavia, having never faced the oppression or demonization that was the hallmark of policy in Kosovo. With Milosevic's restructuring, the Hungarians simply reoriented themselves towards Budapest, where they have focused ever since. Rugova could not do the same with Tirana. Albania was behind Kosovo, not ahead, and Rugova had no wish to see Albania and Kosovo unified. (He even developed Kosovo-specific national symbols, which were later shelved after Kosovo became independent in 2008.) Rugova also worried about how the fact that the Albanians were majority Islam would impact their struggle. To that end, his notion of identity was largely secular, although he was closest to Catholicism: he gave Christmas greetings sometimes to the citizens, and by far the most prominent photos in his office were those of him with Pope John Paul II. Those photos were the backdrop that Rugova chose to project to the outside world. For Rugova, the "eastern" identity was extremely dangerous if he was to get Western attention and support. Kosovo, especially in media footage in the 1980s and 1990s, was always stereotyped – the mosque as background with men wearing white caps, traditional clothes, and looking very Ottoman. One of Rugova's most lasting legacies was creating the foundation for a massive Catholic cathedral in downtown Prishtina named after the ethnically Albanian Mother Teresa. Inside the building, in addition to dramatic stained glass images of Skanderbeg and the pope, there is a mural that includes the saint-like Rugova, surrounded by religious figures, lifting a shovel at the ground-breaking ceremony.

After giving up on a demand to become a republic, elections took place, and Kosovo had its own clandestine independence referendum in 1991, with 89 per cent in favor. Kosovo then declared an independence, which was recognized only by Albania. Kosovars consistently refused to participate in any elections organized in Belgrade, which many argued helped keep Milosevic in power. The Kosovars have often been criticized for the boycott, in that their numbers could have undermined Milosevic's rule if they had voted. This makes little sense, given the total absence of free and fair elections. The refusal of Belgrade to negotiate with Rugova, who was truly a moderate, was an epic blunder that later would cost the Serbs dearly.

It felt like 1878 all over again, with the Albanians pleading for international support. Sadly, no one listened. The Europeans and Americans had their eyes on Central Europe, especially the two Germanys. When examining the European response to the collapse of communism and the imminent disintegration of Yugoslavia, one can only acknowledge just how much policy makers in the West longed for simpler times and the status quo. Research has shown that the West's response was tepid at best to the monumental changes taking place. And, after all, the Albanians of Kosovo were largely Muslims, and no one seemed keen on establishing a Muslim state in the Balkans.

Elsewhere in Yugoslavia, the remaining four republics gradually drifted towards independence, and some ended up in a war. In Bosnia, Croatia, Macedonia, and Slovenia, what was happening in Belgrade and elsewhere meant that independence was the only option. Only tiny Montenegro, with its mixed population of Montenegrins, Serbs, Albanians, and others, stayed within the Serbian sphere of influence, due to Milosevic's machinations, which ensured they toed a pro-Belgrade line, at least until the late 1990s. What happened in the other republics mirrored to an extent what was transpiring in Belgrade, where communists quickly became nationalists and, goaded by a vitriolic state media, neighbors turned on neighbors.

The big difference was that the Serbs had an overwhelming presence in Yugoslavia's federal institutions, particularly the army, which allowed Belgrade to exercise predominant influence in the ensuing struggles. The presence of Serbs in almost every other republic, as

Serbs numbered between 35 and 40 per cent of the entire country, also worked for Belgrade when it needed local paramilitaries to do the dirty work. What happened to a degree was the re-emergence of the interwar conflict between the Croats and the Serbs. In the middle was Bosnia, which would suffer in the years to come. Despite some laudable calls for a new confederation, Yugoslavia's republics went their own ways. By the late 1980s, most Yugoslav republics were already nation-states looking out for their own interests, teaching their own highly glorified but hardly inclusive versions of the past, and they were often reluctant to keep footing the bill for places like Kosovo. Only two republics, Bosnia and Macedonia, with their heavily mixed populations, needed Yugoslavia to survive, which goes a long way towards explaining the nostalgia you can find there for the good old days of ethnic harmony under Tito. You can find Tito cafés in Sarajevo and Skopje but nowhere else.

Outside of Serbia (which then included Kosovo and Vojvodina) and Montenegro, multiparty elections took place throughout 1990, and various referenda followed in 1991 and 1992. The response by the international community was to allow for independence based on the 1974 constitution's republican borders, as long as a viable referendum took place. Slovenia had the easiest escape. It was the further west, most advanced of all the republics, and generally homogenous. With only 10 per cent of Yugoslavia's population, it produced one-fifth of its GDP and one-third of all exports. In April 1990 a coalition of democratically minded political parties (DEMOS) won Slovenia's first free elections since before the Second World War, with 55 per cent of the vote, and the country's new president, Milan Kucan, had no interest in staying in Yugoslavia. Given the relative homogeneity of the country, Slovenia's elections were not as controversial and divisive as they were to become in Bosnia or Croatia. In December 1990 the Slovenes held a referendum in which 88 per cent voted for independence. On 25 June 1991 Slovenia declared independence. However, in the wake of this event, the Yugoslav National Army, from barracks in Croatia and Slovenia, intervened on 27 June 1991, thus beginning the Yugoslav wars. The Slovenes put up fierce resistance, and fortunately for Slovenia, the war lasted only ten days, at a cost of eighty-three lives. The European Community (the

EU's institutional predecessor) and others intervened, met in Tito's former summer home on the Croatian island of Brioni, and with the Brioni Declaration of July 1991, Milosevic agreed to withdraw the Yugoslav army. Slovenia agreed to freeze its independence plans for three months. For Milosevic, Slovenia was not worth the trouble. The Slovenes did the quintessential disappearing act: they left the Balkans, joined Central Europe, and never looked back. Slovenia's independence was largely recognized in 1992.

Croatia and Bosnia would be different, proving that the Balkans really were Hotel California – you can check out but never leave. While Slovenes elected moderate, pro-European politicians, the course of events in Croatia and Bosnia would put people in power who replicated, to a degree, Milosevic's strategies: fiery use of state media to generate fear and insecurity; a strong presidency; weak civil society; destruction of opponents as anti-national; and use of negative myths to maintain power. Croatia had its first free elections just two weeks after Slovenia's. The republic was mixed, with Serbs making up 12 per cent of the population. Croatia's main opposition to the renamed communists, the Croatian Democratic Union (CDU), was decidedly nationalistic, authoritarian, and paid for largely by Croatians living in Canada and the United States, who were later given the right to vote – which often proved decisive for CDU elec-toral victories. The CDU's leader, Franjo Tudjman, a former Second World War partisan and general turned nationalist dissident, began a fraught ten-year rule of Croatia that would leave the country out-side the integration process with the European Union. Croatia fol-lowed up with its own independence referendum in May 1991, in which 93 per cent voted in favor of an independent Croatia. The minority Serbs boycotted the poll. Like Slovenia, Croatia was for-mally independent in June 1991. In terms of power, the Tudjman presidency resembled Berisha's in Albania until 1997. He built an authoritarian state based on a twisted form of historical legitimacy, controlled state institutions, interfered in civil society, allowed only limited media freedom, and plundered the economy.

The international community did not get involved in the early disintegration process. It is doubtful there was much it could have done, as the elections and subsequent referenda, which proved to very blunt instruments, decided the day, even though they effectively marginalized hundreds of thousands of people. Whether or not 50 per cent support was enough of a mandate to break up a county is another question altogether. The problem in Croatia was that the process alienated the Serbs, and Milosevic was determined to protect their interests. Three things are important to keep in mind. First, while Croatia was a nationalizing state, even a more inclusive approach to the Serbs there would have failed, given Milosevic's obvious agenda. Second, the Serbs were not about to give up the status they had in Yugoslavia in exchange for becoming a minority in Croatia. Third, Croatia was in a frenzy of nation building and saw minority rights for the Serbs as a zero-sum game. It could only lead to partition.

The nationalist tone of the elections and the referendum spelled trouble for the Serb minority. For the Serbs, Croatian fascist symbols from the Second World War Ustase regime brought only legitimate fear, and Belgrade media reinforced those fears. Moreover, as the Croatian leadership could hardly be deemed visionary, there was no attempt to reach out to the Serbs. If Milosevic could be blamed for trying to build a Greater Serbia under the ruse of defending Yugoslavia, in Croatia one could just as easily say Tudjman had his sights on a Greater Croatia that harked back to the events of the Second World War. If Milosevic and even his successors made clear in Kosovo that they wanted the territory, just not the Albanians, Tudjman's message to the Serbs was just as obvious. The Serb response was not that dissimilar from what occurred in Kosovo: most rejected the Croatian state and established their own para-state, supported by Milosevic, within the new Croatia. Even before independence, with an ethnic-inspired killing here and there, it was clear that Croatia was on the road to a war that would last until 1995.

If Croatia was on a knife edge with Serbia, Bosnia had to contend with Croatia and Serbia to ensure its very survival. Bosnia was worse off, with three Yugoslav nations inside the republic's borders. The Bosniaks made up more than 40 per cent, the Serbs 33 per cent, Croats 17 per cent, and a mix made up the remainder. Bosnia had always been a bone of contention among the Great Powers in the nineteenth century and between Belgrade and Zagreb in the two Yugoslavias (interwar and communist). For some Croats, the Bosniaks – as Sunni Muslims who had converted during the Ottoman era – were Croats who had converted. For Serbs, they were Serbs who had converted. In any case, they all spoke the same language.

As elsewhere, Bosnia's first multiparty elections in 1990 brought nationalists to power among all three groups. The results split Bosnia along national lines, with the Muslims voting primarily for the Party of Democratic Action (PDA), the Serbs for the Serbian Democratic Party (SDP), and the Croats for the CDU. For the Muslims, the key person to emerge was Alija Izetbegovic, who became Bosnia's president. A controversial figure, with a past that allowed him to be labelled an Islamist due to some writings earlier in his career, Izetbegovic was not surprisingly painted by the Serbs as someone determined to establish an Islamic republic in Bosnia. His writings on Islam landed him in jail for five years in the 1980s. Hardly a strategic thinker, he would do things that would play right into the hands of his opponents, such as visiting Turkey in 1991 and suggesting that Bosnia join the OIC. As an indication of his consistency of thought, on his deathbed in 2003, he asked the Turkish leader Recep Tayyip Erdogan to be Bosnia's guardian. Izetbegovic was set to become the ultimate loser in the years ahead.

For the Serbs, their leader was the infamous Radovan Karadzic. A psychiatrist and failed poet from the margins of Bosnia, he would go on to cause incredible hardship for all of Bosnia due to his single-minded pursuit of Serb national interests. Karadzic spewed even more poison than Milosevic when it came to reviving negative myths about Islam in the Balkans. Revenge for the Turkish occupation of the Balkans was due, he argued. From the start, there was absolutely no common ground as Bosnia headed for its own referendum. For a real glimpse into the heart of Karadzic's and Bosnian Serb provincialism, watch Pawel Pawlikowski's *Serbian Epics* (1992) as Karadzic and company descend into madness through peasant folklore, myth, and hard liquor. As noted, Bosnia's position was certainly the most precarious of the republics, and therefore Bosnia was the most vocal supporter of preserving some form of Yugoslavia. When it became clear that preservation was no longer an option,

Bosnia too went for independence and hoped that the international community would quickly recognize and even protect it from its predatory neighbors. Bosnia's choices in the early 1990s were either bad, very bad, or catastrophic. Given what Milosevic was up to in Croatia, cohabitation was impossible.

Bosnia's referendum in 1992 was the beginning of the end. For Izetbegovic, there was no choice. For Karadzic, there was no way the Serbs would live in a unitary state called Bosnia. The results not surprisingly reflected ethnic divisions. In the February 1992 vote, voter turnout was 64 per cent, and there was 93 per cent support for independence. The vote was boycotted by the Serbs, who rejected the new state and, with support from Milosevic, began to prepare for war by establishing their own state along ethnic lines. As we shall see, Croatia would later play the same game in hopes of gaining land. Bosnia declared independence on 1 March 1992, which remains a Bosniak holiday. Tellingly, the Serbs celebrate a different day – 9 January 1992 – when they declared their unwillingness to leave Yugoslavia. Holidays aside, the stage was set not for a classic war but one that was based entirely on ethnic cleansing. Karadzic and his entourage loved violence and the rhetoric of revenge and division. Before the war started, Karadzic warned of an imminent bloodbath, that the capital Sarajevo would be made "a black cauldron," and that the Muslims would be wiped out. He was correct on the first two assertions.

Montenegro, as noted, avoided war on its territory until NATO, eager to destroy equipment belonging to the Yugoslav National Army, bombed it during the Kosovo War in 1999. Having succeeded in grabbing control of the Montenegrin leadership, Milosevic had two allies in the coming conflict, Momir Bulatovic and Milo Djukanovic, school buddies who ran the place like a fiefdom together from January 1989 until 1997. The former was the perfect stooge for Milosevic – you need only watch him in part one of *The Death of Yugoslavia*. So excited to be part of history-making moments as the new president of Montenegro when he attended his first party congress, he said his parents "were proud of their clever boy." Bulatovic, it turned out, was not so clever after all, but his one-time ally Djukanovic was. Djukanovic would end up as the region's greatest survivor, going from pro-Milosevic stooge to smuggler, to darling of the West, to Russophile, to independence in 2006, to Russophobe, to NATO membership in 2017 and all the while staying alive and in power. Montenegro was the real Balkan exception. Even if you include Greece, it enjoyed suspiciously high levels of political stability.

Identity was very fluid in Montenegro, as indicated by the changing numbers of people claiming to be Montenegrin or Serb. Moreover, you could have in one single family a pro-Montenegrin-independence advocate and a Serb nationalist. In Tito's Yugoslavia the Montenegrins played the same role that Austrians did in Nazi structures: overrepresented in communist-party upper echelons, given the small size of the republic's population. In 1990 the majority of the population overwhelmingly declared Montenegrin as their nationality, but as Yugoslavia fractured and Montenegro drifted towards independence, the number of people declaring themselves Serbs increased dramatically. In 1990 Montenegro also had its first multiparty elections, and the communists won easily. In 1991 the party changed its name to the Democratic Party of Socialists (DPS) and governed with Bulatovic as president and the then twenty-nine-year-old Djukanovic as prime minister, at that time the youngest prime minister in the world. In 1992 Montenegro had its own flawed referendum and decided to remain in Yugoslavia. Montenegro was hit harder by Yugoslavia's economic crisis than other republics, mired in unemployment and poverty, especially in the north. At the outset, this kept it under Milosevic's thumb, and it bought into his defense-of-Yugoslavia thesis. The subservience and depravity of the Montenegrin leadership would be laid bare in September 1991 when Montenegro began an attack on Dubrovnik in neighboring Croatia. As the Montenegrin army shelled the city, the "clever" Bulatovic also announced that Montenegro was declaring itself an ecological state "committed to the purity of nature," among other lofty goals. It would be a long time before Montenegro would apologize, and even longer for Croatia to forgive them.

The last Yugoslav republic to examine is Macedonia. As noted earlier, the Macedonian identity was by far the most contested. Macedonians have experienced a constant existential crisis, with neighboring Bulgaria and Greece contesting everything about them.

The ethnic mix in Macedonia suggested a possible scenario along the lines of Bosnia, but war avoided Macedonia until 2001, ten years after was started in Slovenia. Macedonia's population is contested, and talk is always divisive and often filled with the same racism that permeates the Serb view on Kosovo. In the 1990s, Macedonia was roughly 65 per cent ethnic Macedonian, 23 per cent Albanian, with smaller communities of Roma, Turks, and Serbs making up the rest of the population. After its first-ever multiparty elections in 1990, power largely, although not exclusively, went to a nationalist party, the Internal Macedonian Revolutionary Organization–Democratic Party of Macedonian Unity (VMRO-DPMNE). The party's main platform was independence and to a degree, Macedonia for the Macedonians, which left the Albanians and others isolated. In its referendum of September 1991, more than 90 per cent voted in favor, but the Albanians boycotted, fearing their rights would not be protected.

Macedonia's entry onto the world stage was fraught from the start, which threw it into permanent crisis. As will be discussed in chapter 5, the very use of the name *Macedonia* was rejected by Greece. But external problems aside, the internal issues were just as daunting. Macedonia, like Croatia and Serbia, was a nationalizing state. This was evident from the first constitution of November 1991, which, while giving a slight nod to non-Macedonians there, was essentially an ethnic constitution that created first- and second-class citizens. As the largest minority, the Albanians were not granted full equality but appeared only as an afterthought. That this did not result in a war until ten years later deserves some further explanation. As noted, although the Kosovars had been nationalized by the changes to their role in the federation in the late 1960s and 1970s, no corresponding changes took place among Albanians in Macedonia. If they wanted Albanian-language university training, they had to go to Kosovo, and indeed the Albanian elite in Macedonia was largely educated at the University of Prishtina. Not surprisingly, of all the Albanian communities in the Balkans, the Albanians in Macedonia were the least educated and most committed to Islam. In some ways, they needed to be nationalized. Finally, even though ethnic Albanian parties did participate in multiple coalitions after Macedonian independence, they were engaged primarily in shared state capture and corruption. When Albanians did finally take up arms against the Macedonian government in 2001, one could argue that it was not just the Macedonians who had let them down but their own political elite too.

Bulgaria and Romania, which in some ways were Balkan success stories, given the poor performance of Yugoslavia and Albania, also offered fake revolutions in 1989. There were other striking similarities. Both returned mostly communists to office in the first free and fair elections. Both had absolutely ruinous economic situations in 1989. Both had kings in waiting – Simeon for Bulgaria and Michael for Romania. Nonetheless, there were important differences. Bulgaria was the most loyal of Soviet satellite states. Romania was somehow independent, and for a while Ceausescu was treated as a normal statesman because of his maverick foreign policy. The two would not be in the first round of EU enlargement in 2004 when the Central European states plus Slovenia joined, but politics would play in their favor, and they would get a kind of second-tier membership in 2007.

In a 1959 book produced by Bulgaria's state publishing house, the authorities noted that the "small and energetic nation" had banished "misery forever." However, by 1989, misery had certainly returned as Bulgaria also began a fraught and flawed transition. In 1989 Bulgaria was bankrupt. Looking for an out, as noted in the preceding chapter, Zhivkov again whipped up anti-Turkish fever and announced that the Turkish minority would have to be expelled. But the Turks had already been systematically repressed for long enough and they stood their ground. Even Zhivkov's allies in the party started to desert him, and Gorbachev chastised him for the stupidity of the move against the Turks. In what was probably a totally unexpected move, in November the seventy-eight-year-old Zhivkov, in power for more than thirty years, was "retired" by his own people. A simple palace coup. He was replaced by Petar Mladenov as president. Mladenov would do his best to hold on to the communist monopoly on power and would even be caught on tape mulling over whether or not to use tanks to crush demonstrations and defer democratization as long as possible. Mladenov was ousted in July 1990 as things in Sofia started to get out of hand with the torching of the communist party headquarters. His replacement, Bulgaria's first non-communist president, Zhelyu Zhelev, would hang on until 1996 after winning a direct presidential vote in 1992. He was a former communist until he was expelled from the party in the 1960s. Zhelev was a dissident too, with serious credentials. He was much maligned for his refusal to wage a real war on the former communists. By August, street politics forced the former communists to form a coalition government with the Union of Democratic Forces (UDF).

Domestic instability aside, it is extremely important to note that Bulgaria could have easily descended into ethnic war just like Yugoslavia had. The communist demonizing and scapegoating of the Turks as the last breath of the regime could have easily continued. Thankfully, Bulgarians had somehow taken different lessons from being on the losing side of wars in the twentieth century: it always ended badly. That said, as one friend noted, Bulgaria's protection of its Jewish community during the Second World War (Bulgaria did, however, facilitate the deportation of Jews in territory they occupied in northern Greece) and its avoidance of a full-out war with the Turks in the late 1980s and early 1990s stand out as Bulgaria's only two real successes. That somewhat "liberal" and open Yugoslavia ended up in war and Bulgaria did not is due to a number of factors. First, although there were nasty nationalist parties clamoring for a Bulgaria for Bulgarians, these were marginal and never got enough support to make a difference. The mainstream parties opposed any form of discrimination, and Bulgarians in general displayed considerable tolerance for the Turks. The same could not be said for the Roma. Most importantly, by avoiding the word *autonomy*, the Turks largely got what they wanted without violence or war.

The Bulgarian communists became socialists and tried to emulate Gorbachev in the USSR – implement modest economic reform but keep the party in charge. They had their opponents too, mostly in the cities, who saw what was happening in Central Europe and wanted the same. They won the first multiparty elections in 1990. The key feature of Bulgaria is that the former communists more or less controlled the country at the national and local level. They rejected the shock therapy applied in Poland and elsewhere and stuck to a version of the old pre-1989 ideals. Delay prevailed, while the former elite and security services colluded to steal everything they could in the name of social democracy. Only Bulgaria's financial collapse in 1996–7 would herald the beginning of a real transition.

Two final factors are worth noting for Bulgaria. First, as noted, some fairly hopeless royalty was waiting in the wings for all the Balkan states. Only Bulgaria had someone who could be taken seriously. The exiled Tsar Simeon would return to Bulgaria in 1996, start a serious political party, and go on to rule Bulgaria as prime minister between 2001 and 2005. Unlike other unemployed monarchs of the Balkans, Simeon was prepared to work hard. The second factor was the then more than a million strong Turkish minority. They established their own political party, the Movement for Rights and Freedoms, which was the sole voice for Turkish concerns in Bulgaria.

In Romania, Ceausescu's austerity policies had sent most people into darkness, and when they were not lining up for food, the only news they got on state TV was bad. Grumbling conformity was the norm there, but the tight grip of the Securitate kept Romania mostly Stalinist and stable. However, in April 1989, there was some good news – Romania had paid all its foreign debt – Romania was free, and paradise was around the corner. To get there, Romania sold everything, rationed the few things they retained, and living standards were horrible as people sat in the cold and dark. Worse still, by the summer of 1989, the changes underway in Central Europe made Romania geopolitically irrelevant. Ceausescu was no longer the bloc maverick, and invitations abroad were no longer coming. As people froze in their beds, the Ceausescus built the People's Palace in a spot that forced them destroy the center of Bucharest so as to put in place what they claimed would be the biggest building in the world. The Genius of the Carpathians destroyed much of Bucharest to realize his dream.

If Zhivkov went against the Turks, Ceausescu had the Hungarians to demonize. Hungarians made up roughly 6 per cent of Romania, living largely in Transylvania. And trouble started there when a local priest in Timisoara started to ask the wrong questions. Laszlo Tokes had been in trouble with the authorities before, including jail and random beatings from the dreaded Securitate. As unrest grew in the region, Ceausescu, goaded by his villainous wife Elena, simply called for more repression and violence in early December. His left his minions to do the dirty work and went on an official visit to Iran, one of the few places willing to host him. When he returned, things were about to become different.

On 21 December, Ceausescu called for a massive rally in downtown Bucharest, which was designed to show the world that Romania was different. His speech to the crowd would be his last and it is a must see on YouTube. In a single moment, Ceausescu and his wife are exposed as frauds. He goes from tyrant to frightened child, with his bellicose wife calling on the hostile crowd to be quiet as though she was a teacher in an elementary school. Ceausescu tried to buy them with some promises in pensions but he was finished in an instant. He fled the next day in a helicopter to Snagov, where they had a summer home. Nobody was sure what would happen next. The young revolutionaries thought a new era had begun à la Budapest or Prague. They were wrong, as the elite would again conspire to steal their future.

The events of 1989 in Romania are still not entirely clear. We do know that power fell to the National Salvation Front headed by Ion Iliescu, a former aide to Ceausescu, and other diehard communists who had also been part of the inner circle. When not in power, Iliescu would make a living as a laughable speaker on democracy and democratization in places like authoritarian Azerbaijan, always as a guest of the people in power. Iliescu and a group of second-tier communists consolidated power and arrested the Ceausescus, who had been first flying and then driving around Romania looking for a safe haven. They never found one. In the end, they had a very short trial. That too can be viewed on YouTube. Elena Ceausescu comes across as the most brazen and brave, asking for a lawyer and telling a soldier she was like a mother to him. They were convicted, shot multiple times on Christmas Day in a courtyard, and buried in unmarked graves. Romania, which had been beset by violent demonstrations until then, ended the Ceausescu era with executions, the only bloc country to do so. Revolution or coup? Nobody knows for sure.

The National Salvation Front, which morphed into the Party for Social Democracy (PSD), easily won Romania's first multiparty elections in May 1990. In June 1990, as a harbinger of their type of democracy, they did their best to destroy the emerging opposition parties. In June 1990 they even brought ten thousand angry miners to Bucharest to beat up opponents, including students and intellectuals. In their attempt to destroy the opposition, the miners were joined by former members of the security services. The miners, eager to defend the PSD, would come again in September 1991 and topple a government. Nobody was ever charged. Iliescu would go on to win the presidency again in 1992. His strength lay in his popularity in villages and the countryside, where a fear of change prevailed. As an open nationalist, he exploited the Hungarian minority issue whenever he had to. As elsewhere in the region, the media, especially television, remained a tool of the governing party. Red-carpet journalism prevailed – endless and lavish coverage of government activities. Like Bulgaria, the Romanian transition would not start in a serious way until 1997.

## Conclusion

Unlike in much of Central Europe, events before and after 1989 in the Balkans did not provide the fundamental break with the past that was required for the region to chart a new course. In fact, there was a degree of systemic continuity. This is partly because specifically domestic causes of the "revolutions" were hardly there. In Albania, for certain, the events of 1990 and 1991 happened only because they were happening somewhere else – there were hardly any domestic sources of revolution. In short, the Balkans did not get a 1989 moment like Budapest or Prague. No Balkan state, except newly independent Slovenia in 1991, established anything resembling a democracy. What emerged were authoritarian, corrupt, sometimes nationalist but always predatory states that barely managed to disguise the narrow self-interest of their leaders. Hiding behind the tired "defense of the nation" thesis were low-level felons plundering the state. Publicly, they argued for the slow path to reform as a means to protect the people from the hostile and debilitating shocks of quick reform, but their real concern was capturing the state for their own ends.

Already by 1989, the Balkan states displayed some very obvious shortcomings that hindered positive developments. In all states, prior to 1989, there were very weak dissident cultures. This was most obvious in Albania and Romania, but even in the less repressive Yugoslavia many previous dissidents had been co-opted by the new nationalist regimes, such as the Serbian academics who led the attack on the changes embodied in the 1974 constitution. Croatia had to contend with in emergent nationalist diaspora that was intent on reviving the myths of the Second World War and bent on revenge. As we shall see, nationalist Croats from North America played an ultimately negative role in the new Croatian state. They came to settle some old scores. Bosnia and Croatia emerged as the main battlefields in the 1990s.

Every Balkan state went from one kind of authoritarianism to another – the interwar authoritarian state, through war, occupation, to varying forms of communism to opportunistic authoritarianism made legitimate by exclusive nationalism. There was no transition at all in fact. Some went on to develop highly centralized presidential systems with strongmen presidents in very weak institutional settings. The new presidents had at their disposal a state-controlled media that became the most effective weapon among populations that were facing political, economic, and sometimes even existential crises. Those states that opted for strong prime ministers did not fare much better. Regardless of regime type, strongmen dominated the scene. As well, the army and the organs of state security worked for them. Lastly, a cross section of the elites that came to power between 1987 and 1990 tells a dismal story. These were not Vaclav Havel–like thinkers offering humanism and a way out, but largely hacks who chose the laziest path to power: the politics of fear, negative myths, and the promise of living in an imagined past. As we shall see in the next chapter, the fact that Yugoslavia ended up in a series of wars should not have been such a surprise.

# 3

# Hero-Free Wars and Ethnic Purity

As we saw in the preceding chapter, four of Yugoslavia's eight federal units had a referendum that led to independence and subsequent
international recognition. Croatia and Slovenia were the first to go,
soon recognized by Germany in December 1991, which the government in Belgrade claimed was tantamount to restoration of German
hegemony in the region, with the obvious allusions to the Second
World War. Recognition followed for Bosnia and Macedonia. Kosovo
was stuck in the quasi-apartheid of the Milosevic regime, living in
a para-state. Montenegro, for the time being, was prepared to toe
Milosevic's line, and in the March 1992 plebiscite, it voted to stay
in Yugoslavia. A series of wars began that did not really end until
2001, with the conclusion of the Albanian-Macedonian conflict.
However, this chapter focusses on the events in Bosnia and Croatia
between 1992 and 1995. Subsequent chapters deal with the unfortu-
nate events in Kosovo and Macedonia and the peace treaties that followed those conflicts. There is an extraordinary amount of academic
literature, plus some excellent journalism, on the wars. The works of
Misha Glenny, Allan Little, and Laura Silber are must reads. There
are also any number of excellent documentaries. It is not my intention to detail the day-to-day conflict but rather highlight the main
features of these horrible years and then provide some analysis of
what happened when war did finally end. Many of the issues discussed below remain highly contested and politicized, as Bosnia in

particular (and Croatia too) is a very long way from developing an agreed-upon narrative for the period between 1992 and 1995.

For those interested in a local description of the war in Bosnia that tells a bigger story, Joe Sacco's *Safe Area Gorazde: The War in Eastern Bosnia 1992–95* is incredibly insightful as he deftly illustrates the plight of Bosniaks in one of six "safe" areas set up by the UN during the war. Or stare at the infamous picture of the Serb warlord Arkan (real name: Željko Ražnatović) and his masked paramilitary fighters posing for the camera. Arkan, a member of the secret services with a criminal past, holds a baby tiger aloft that later died because he failed to look after it. Doing violent service for Belgrade, he was one of the most notorious warlords responsible for any number of brutal crimes in Bosnia, Croatia, and Kosovo. Charged with war crimes and then later gunned down in a Belgrade hotel in January 2000 by people who feared he was about to spill the beans to the International Criminal Tribunal for the Former Yugoslavia (ICTY) to maybe save his own skin, Arkan's methods defined the war – drunkenness, rape, executions, ethnic cleansing, and looting. His paramilitaries were the most feared during the war. Along with his wife, the turbo folk star Ceca, they were the height of the Belgrade elite and very much role models and symbols of just what was possible in Milosevic's criminalized Yugoslavia.

There is now a degree of consensus emerging on the origins of the wars and the subsequent war aims of the parties involved. Since Slobodan Milosevic ended up in The Hague in 2001, charged with war crimes in Bosnia, Croatia, and Kosovo by the ICTY, there is an extraordinary amount of material available that documents his actions in Bosnia, Croatia, and Kosovo. In any case, as things unraveled it was clear that the West was caught completely off guard. The then European Community (EC) was busy taking the next steps in intensified integration that would lead to the creation of the European Union, and the George H.W. Bush administration in the United States had its hands full with events in the USSR, Central Europe, and the Gulf War. In an attempt to limit violence, the UN established an arms embargo on the whole of Yugoslavia in 1991 that would end up doing extraordinary harm to the Bosniaks and the region more generally because it made a lot of bad people very rich and created the basis for a mafia-based economy that has been difficult to undo. Turkey would do its best to get arms to the Bosniaks, although, interestingly, they would not later do the same for the Albanians in Kosovo.

Bush's secretary of state, James Baker, famously quipped that the US "had no dog in that fight," referring to Yugoslavia's disintegration. Alternatively, the Europeans claimed it was "their hour," but somehow forgot to act. In late summer 1991 the EC established an arbitration commission, headed by Robert Badinter of the French Constitutional Council and four other European legal scholars, that was supposed to apply the rule of law to the end of Yugoslavia. The EC initially hoped to keep the federal Yugoslav state together. In the end, pushed particularly by Germany, the commission concluded that Yugoslavia "was in the process of dissolution" and that an orderly dissolution was possible based on the existing republic boundaries and the fact that the 1974 constitution permitted secession. Among other things, it meant Kosovo's case was lost. EC policy eventually gravitated towards recognition of the independence of Croatia and Slovenia, even though the Badinter Commission concluded that Croatia (and Bosnia) needed to do more for the Serb minority in order to qualify for recognition. In the end, Bosnia and Macedonia applied to the commission for recognition, and thus the commission essentially oversaw the dissolution of Yugoslavia based on the borders established by Tito's communists after the Second World War. It was, of course, unable to prevent the violence that accompanied it, leading some to conclude that Tito's republican borders should not have been taken as inviolable. But that does not matter now.

Policy failures aside, one cannot situate the entire blame for the war on the EC, the United States or the UN. Some saw in the eventual wars the return of what were called "ancient ethnic hatreds" in so far as the peoples of the region were destined for bloodshed and that conflict was ultimately ethnic in nature. While this idea has been partly debunked and is unsatisfactory as single explanation, one still needs to acknowledge that elites in Bosnia, Croatia, and Serbia were able to build on something that was already there. The hatreds may not have been ancient, but many people were still looking for revenge, and revenge is always in the air in the Balkans. Plus, there was a lot of intolerance. All too often in the Balkans things are personal, shaped by the notion that the apple does not fall too far from the tree. Sure, so-and-so might be a nice person, but his dad was a communist or a fascist, and that settles that.

It would be hard to deny that most Serbs held negative views of the Albanians of Kosovo. In fact, poll data always suggested Serbs did not trust Albanians. Anti-Albanian sentiments were rife in Macedonia too. Only the Serbs in the North American diaspora hated the Albanians more. The grandparents and parents of second- and third-generation Serbs in Canada and the United States had filled their heads with the dangers posed by the never-ending fornication, terrorism, and criminality of the Albanians. What we saw happening in the extreme in Kosovo was replicated elsewhere to great effect, especially with Muslims of Bosnia, who, like the Albanians of Kosovo, had increased their power (and population) at the expense of the Serbs during Tito's Yugoslavia. In Bosnia especially, the Bosniaks were far more urbanized than the largely rural Serbs, which created resentment. Serbs in Croatia needed only the reminder of Serb propaganda, which revived the horrors of Croatia's wartime fascist regime and its murderous policies. Armed with the success of the Kosovo media model, Serb state media, along with some very willing academics and dozens of journalists, revived the Croat crimes against Serbs with endless serials and documentaries. This created the conditions for mass indifference to the fate of one's neighbors and later war crimes and even genocide.

As we saw in chapter 2, violence started in Slovenia but ended quickly. Croatia was almost immediately partitioned by forces of the Yugoslav National Army and local paramilitaries seeking to create the basis for the Serb-dominated part of Croatia to become part of Milosevic's "Greater Serbia" project. After a series of skirmishes, with dead on both sides, and ethnic drum beating by the media, Tudjman opted for war in September 1991, counting on US help. According to the last US ambassador to Yugoslavia, Warren Zimmerman, he urged Tudjman to offer autonomy to the Serbs. Tudjman said no, with good reason. On the one hand, it was a totally naïve suggestion. Plus, the Serbs would have never accepted it, especially if they bothered to look at the fate of Kosovo. *Autonomy* by then was a poisoned word. Autonomy, according to Tudjman, led only to one place: separation.

The local Serbs rebelled against rule from Zagreb and established their own territorial space, the Republic of Serb Krajina (RSK), administered from its capital, Knin, which also sought recognition from the Badinter Commission. By the end of 1991, the Croatian Serbs would grab just over 26 per cent of Croatian territory with a cease-fire, which was signed in January 1992. The war in Croatia brought the meaningless destruction of the heavily mixed city of Vukovar. As noted earlier, a similar fate came to Dubrovnik, a UNESCO World Heritage site, which did not have either defenses or a Serb population. It was a public-relations fiasco for the Serbs and, as noted earlier, the Montenegrins too. The UN attempted to implement a peace plan for the region that, while accepted by Zagreb, was rejected by Knin, which planned to unite with the Serbs in neighboring Bosnia anyway. Things would change dramatically in 1995 to the disadvantage of the Serbs when the Croats, with help from the United States, would retake the territory and ethnically cleanse the Serbs by sending them to Serbia, where Milosevic would attempt to resettle them in Kosovo in hopes of altering as much as possible the Albanian numerical superiority.

In Bosnia, things were destined to be even more deadly. As would be proved later by evidence presented at The Hague (telephone intercepts between Milosevic and the Bosnian Serb leader Radovan Karadzic), Milosevic's original plan was the include all the Serbs in one state, which explained the withdrawal from Slovenia and the creation of a para-state in Croatia (RSK). That said, his new state would include all of Bosnia and part of Croatia. As we shall see, Milosevic did not count on such fierce resistance from the Bosniaks and thus was forced to alter his plans considerably, in that he sought to gain as much territory as possible for the Serbs.

The first year of the war saw some astonishing victories by the Bosnian Serb forces as their forces grabbed 60 per cent of Bosnia in just six weeks. It was hardly a fair fight: they got decisive help from alcohol-fueled paramilitaries, forces of the Yugoslav National Army, plus the embargo on Bosnia. As a result, by the end of 1992 the Serbs controlled roughly 70 per cent of the country. Already confronted by atrocities committed by the Bosnian Serbs, including gruesome images of emaciated men in concentration camps on television in August 1992, the international community convened its first major conference in London at the same time, which was supposed to galvanize international action to stop the war in Bosnia. The group established a formal team, the International Conference on the Former Yugoslavia, led by Lord David Owen, former United Kingdom foreign secretary, and Cyrus Vance, former US secretary of state. The group intended to examine all aspects of the Yugoslav crisis. It would set down three possible peace plans, all of which would remain unimplemented due to failure to gain support among the warring parties in Bosnia. In addition to various peace plans, in July 1992 a UN sanctions regime was put in place. While the UN Security Council supported sanctions, most Balkan states opposed them, and the sanctions had disastrous implications for the region's economic outlook in terms of destroying regional trade and shifting economic activity to the black market.

The first comprehensive peace plan for Bosnia was presented in early 1993 by Owen and Vance. The Vance-Owen plan gave Bosnia a new constitutional framework and created ten ethnically based provinces with massive decentralization of powers. The plan had the support of Europeans, Croatia, and Serbia but it was rejected by the Bosniaks, the Bosnian Serbs, and even the United States. While the Bosniaks and Americans eventually came on side, the Bosnian Serbs could not be persuaded, and the plan died. The Owen-Stoltenberg Plan of 1993 offered a three-way partition, more or less, and was rejected by the Bosniak leadership. Everything the international community offered had a common thread: weak central government, the end of Bosnia as a unitary state, partition of a sorts – hard or soft – but partition nonetheless. It raises the question, why not partition in the first place? After all, Tito made the borders and he was dead. When peace did come – in Dayton, Ohio, in the winter of 1995 – it was just another partition that largely rewarded the Bosnian Serbs.

Having failed to bring peace, the EU was at least forced to acknowledge that the active participation of the United States and Russia was required. To that end, the Contact Group was established in April 1994, which brought the Europeans, Americans, and Russians together with their own peace plans, which were largely rejected by the Bosnian Serbs. However, facilitated mostly by US prodding, a joint Muslim-Croat federation was established in 1994 that ended the on-again/off-again fighting between Bosniaks and Croats and thus dealt a heavy blow to the Serbs. It must be noted that – and this is based on documentation by the ICTY and others – until then Croatia had played a key role in the plans to destroy Bosnia. The most telling example of this is the fate of ethnically mixed Mostar, where among other crimes, the Croat forces shelled and destroyed the sixteenth-century Ottoman bridge. The Contact Group focused on obtaining a cease-fire but held to the previously agreed plan that any peace would mean that the Serbs were to receive 49 per cent (far more than they deserved) and the Bosniak-Croat Federation 51 per cent. The Serbs rejected the plan for the simple reason that it meant that Bosnia would survive as a state and they were stuck in it.

The year 1995 proved to be a watershed for Bosnia and Croatia. In July, in what was called Operation Storm, the Croats, with logistical help and encouragement from the United States, retook the Serb-occupied territories in only two days. For President Clinton, it was about time the Serbs suffered some losses, something he correctly assessed would help get them to the negotiating table for Bosnia. Although Croatian military leaders would face subsequent war-crimes indictments for what happened in the RSK, Croatia was unified, and the Serbs were more or less gone because three hundred thousand fled to Serbia and another forty thousand went to the Republika Srbska (RS) in Bosnia. The Croat victory, which later led to war-crimes indictments from the ICTY, was followed by looting, and several hundred Serbs were murdered. Holding the moral high ground was not on the table. The Bosnian Serbs responded by expelling the Bosnian Croats from territory they controlled. This time around, there was nothing Milosevic could do. The Croats gained a new national holiday: 5 August, the day Knin fell, became the Day of Homeland Thanksgiving. There is little doubt that President Tudjman was pleased with the departure of the Serbs, and for that he was widely vilified outside Croatia. It is worth acknowledging that the Serbs had to bear some of the blame for what happened, given the local leadership's behavior. Moreover, Tudjman did believe that Croatia's ethnic purity was the endgame anyway. Ethnic cleansing in Europe had been the endgame since 1914. The defeat of the Serbs changed the lie of the land in Bosnia too as Bosniak-Croat forces gained the upper hand and soon controlled almost 50 per cent of Bosnia. Peace was in the air.

But in Bosnia, in the last year of the war, things got a lot worse, which indicated just how certain the Serb leadership was of imminent victory, since they were prepared to ramp up what was already a genocidal campaign against Muslims. To protect civilians, who were the primary victims of the war, in 1993 the UN established a number of safe areas in Bosnia where citizens were protected from armed attack. There were six in total: Bihac, Gorazde, Sarajevo, Srebrenica, Tuzla, and Zepa. The safe-area policy was a dismal failure that reflected poorly on the international community. The safe areas also put on display for the world just what the Bosnian Serb policy was towards Bosniaks who had fled their homes due to ethnic-cleansing campaigns. All the safe areas were subjected to harassment by the Bosnian Serb forces. Sarajevo suffered a three-year siege that sought to destroy the very multiethnicity the city was famous for. Deliberate shelling from the mountains above targeted hospitals, state institutions, and market places, including the Markale market, which was attacked in February 1994 and August 1995. The former attack killed sixty-eight people. The latter killed thirty-seven people and intensified NATO's resolve to use force to get the Bosnian Serbs to the negotiating table.

But it is the story of Srebrenica that stands out as the worst moment of the war and that gave Europe its first genocide since the Second World War. The Srebrenica massacre also led to war-crimes indictments for the Bosnian Serb Army leader Ratko Mladic and Bosnian Serb leader Radovan Karadzic. For what transpired in and around Srebrenica in early July 1995, both would be charged with genocide, crimes against humanity, and violation of laws or customs of war. What happened is still contested by some and remains a serious issue for both Bosniaks and Serbs in Bosnia and Serbia proper in terms of the long road towards reconciliation. There is no agreed-on narrative.

Srebrenica was a safe area and under the control of Dutch UN peacekeepers, but Mladic and his army nevertheless began shelling Srebrenica and attacked UN observation posts. On 12 July, according to the ICTY indictment, Mladic and his ever-present TV crew arrived at the UN compound. He told the Bosniaks that they would not be harmed but simply transported out of Srebrenica. It later became clear that when buses arrived to transport the Bosniaks, Mladic and his men oversaw the separation of men from women and children. Between 12 and 13 July the Bosnian Serbs executed more than eight thousand people and buried them in mass graves. Satellite photos of the massacre were shown to US president Bill Clinton in early August. Enough was enough, according to Clinton and UK prime minister Tony Blair.

As it turned out, it was the American hour, because the United States stepped up air attacks in Bosnia and forced the parties to the negotiating table. Intensification of the air attacks began in the spring of 1995. The Bosnian Serb Army responded by using UN soldiers as human shields to protect their heavy weapons and munitions. By July NATO was authorized to use air strikes without joint approval from the UN. Three important things happened in August. First, Richard Holbrooke of the US State Department was put in charge of negotiations alongside a stellar team of Balkan specialists. Second, Slobodan Milosevic basically took over as the representative of Bosnian Serb interests. Despite his past brutality, he was considered essential to peace and he was desperate to end the sanctions imposed on Yugoslavia. Finally, on 30 August, NATO's Operation Deliberate Force was launched, NATO's biggest military action ever. While military force did bring about peace talks, it did not fundamentally alter the lie of the land on the ground since there was no attempt to roll back Serb territorial gains. This permitted the Serbs to maintain more territory than their numbers warranted. What this meant was that there would be no reversal of three years of ethnic cleansing. Always remember that Srebrenica is in the Serbian-controlled entity that emerged with the Dayton Peace Plan.

By 8 September the contours of peace for Bosnia were in place. Bosnia would remain a country but divided into two entities: the Republika Srbska (RS) and the Bosniak-Croat Federation. Forty-nine per cent of the territory went to the RS, and the remaining 51 per cent to the federation. The big challenge was to determine just what type of central government Bosnia would have. Even before arriving for the final talks, the three sides had agreed on a parliament, a constitutional court, and a three-person presidency. In short, the bad decisions – especially the 51/49 division – came before peace talks began. There was no way to get the three sides to find any kind of consensus on just what type of state should emerge. The Bosnian Serb premise was basic: they would not become a minority in a Muslim state, and their rights had to be territorialized. But progress was made. In October, a cease-fire began, and on 1 November peace talks started at the austere Wright-Patterson Air Force Base near Dayton, Ohio. Hoping to avoid endless talks and a replication of the failed peace talks that came before, the United States took the lead and in the end found a peace after three weeks of exhausting and intense negotiations. The Europeans were kept updated but not much more.

As noted, while there was a Bosnian Serb presence, it was relatively junior, and Milosevic was in charge. Mladic and Karadzic were left behind due to war-crimes charges, although no one was actually looking for them, even though everyone knew where they were. After three weeks of intense and by all accounts exhausting talks, by 21 November a deal was initialed, and everyone went home. The formal agreement was signed in Paris in December. Milosevic and Tudjman were hailed as statesmen by people back home. Serb soldiers returning from the Bosnian or Croatian fronts were hailed as heroes. The writer and curator Bojana Pejic noted that the soldiers said the best things about the war were "shooting and fucking." Milosevic exported war, but the wars had yet to come to Serbia, only sanctions that impoverished the majority and enriched Milosevic and his cronies. It is important to keep in mind that Milosevic craved international acceptance and he was accepted by the United States as the only person who could get the Bosnian Serbs on side. He did just that and, for the time being, despite massive, ongoing, and even escalating human rights violations in Kosovo, Milosevic was a peacemaker. For the Bosniak leader Alija Izetbegovic, Bosnia survived but it was a weak state and a far cry even from his minimum goals.

Thousands of articles have been written on the Dayton Accords and its obvious shortcomings – and these articles have had astonishingly little impact on how Bosnia is governed. There is really nothing to do other than outline the agreement's main features and discuss its flaws. It is an extremely easy agreement to criticize, especially more than twenty years later. The most obvious problem is that it was prepared in haste and failed to anticipate what was ahead. While everyone later argued that Dayton really ruined Bosnia forever, that was not apparent at the time. Dayton's defenders argued that it served its primary purpose: it ended a three-and-a-half-year war. The biggest losers were the Bosniaks, who suffered disproportionally. For them, a unitary state would have been better, not a hyper-decentralized one that basically rewarded the war's victors. Bosnia was largely segregated with the possible exception of Brcko, Mostar, and Sarajevo. Bosnia, for the West, had to avoid partition to prevent the emergence of a weak Muslim statelet in the Balkans, surrounded by hostile neighbors and under the patronage of another Muslim state. The agreement was basically a form of ethnic segregation that combined massive decentralization with strong international oversight in the form of the presence of sixty thousand NATO troops and the Office of the High Representative (OHR), who was there to ensure that all sides adhered to the agreement. In the end, the agreement was based on the simple idea that power was to be pushed down as much as possible to the local level, which meant that, at least in the short and medium term, ethnic reconciliation was simply off the table.

In terms of the big picture, its goals were sound. It sought (but ultimately failed) to establish stable multiethnicity and it laid the basis for elections that mostly entrenched the war's ethnic divide. Multiethnicity was always considered a long-term goal that would go hand in hand with the Euro-Atlantic integration process. Bosnia's internal boundaries would become irrelevant. It established the basis for an end to ethnically inspired violence and it was capable of preventing its return. It tried (but also failed) to lay the foundation for integration into the EU. It tried to promote refugee return, maintained a vibrant international presence, transformed the dreaded police services, hoped that war criminals would be arrested, and gave Bosnia the makings of a new constitution embedded in Article 4 of the agreement.

The Dayton-made Bosnian constitution deserves some additional description. First, it was designed to be temporary in that it was imposed from above, hoping that further down the road the Bosnian people would design and approve a homemade constitution. They have yet to do that. Power is held by the entities, essentially, and it is up to them to deliver the promises of Dayton. It is worth noting that the structure only includes three ethnic groups. If you are not one of these or somehow a combination, you are therefore excluded – and this is blatant discrimination that has been challenged in the European Court of Human Rights. All Bosnia's institutions are based on ethnicity. For example, there were three presidents and multiple ministers based on two-thirds for the federation and one-third for the RS. The same two-thirds/one-third model applied to the House of Peoples and the House of Representatives. The constitutional court was the same. Consensus decision-making was a stated goal, but ethnic presidents had the right to block decisions deemed harmful to their entity's interests. There were even three power companies delivering electricity to each group. More regrettably, Dayton impacted the political-party structure in a decidedly negative way in that parties in Bosnia defend purely ethnic interests, making Bosnia-wide consensus impossible.

The central government has few powers, largely limited to foreign affairs and other international obligations. Most importantly, the Dayton constitution requires consensus among the three ethnic groups. For example, the House of Peoples has fifteen members – five from each ethnicity. Quorum is nine, as long as there are three each for each ethnicity – a great idea to prevent all kinds of miserable outcomes but also a recipe for deadlock. Only two years later, in 1997, the international community decided to override this by giving more power to the OHR. These so-called Bonn powers made the OHR the ultimate ruler of Bosnia, allowing the High Representative (always a man; no woman has ever held the office) to intervene at will in domestic politics. The OHR can issue or veto legislation and can fire elected officials too. A strengthened OHR has not solved Bosnia's problems, and despite on-again/off-again talk of its imminent closure since 2006, it is still there. At the time, there were few alternatives to Dayton, but it doubtful that anyone intended it to still be the law of the land almost twenty-five years later. As we shall see in subsequent chapters, Dayton not only created enormous domestic challenges for Bosnia, it also had a negative impact on the region as a whole. The passive-resistance policy of Ibrahim Rugova in Kosovo no longer seemed relevant, and Milosevic emerged as a peacemaker. In gloomy Prishtina, it was Groundhog Day.

A final word about the fate of Mladic and Karadzic, two of the principal, but not the only, war criminals of the Bosnian war. Both would end up doing incredible harm to the region long after the war ended. Mladic's behavior was particularly vile, and as a professional soldier, he displayed extraordinary cowardice, especially in Srebrenica. The fact that both he and Karadzic were often lauded as heroes by Serbs in the RS and Serbia too shows the depth of the sickness that engulfed large parts of the Serbian nation. Mladic and Karadzic were war criminals to Bosniaks and most outside observers, but most Serbs were fed on the myth that they were the "defenders of the Serb nation." The NATO force in Bosnia (IFOR or Implementation Force) was not concerned with capturing ICTY indictees: major and minor war criminals wandered around in plain sight. There were the big fish, like Karadzic and Mladic, but countless others too. In any case, Karadzic maintained that he cut a deal with Richard Holbrooke that would allow him to avoid jail as long as he avoided politics. Holbrooke denied such a deal existed, but the consensus is that a deal was indeed made. Things started to change in 1997, and the hunt became real. Both Karadzic and Mladic went into hiding, consistently protected by Serb authorities in Bosnia and Serbia. Karadzic was arrested in Belgrade in 2008, where he was found living the quiet life as a mystic healer. Mladic was arrested in 2011, also hiding in Serbia. Both men went sent to the ICTY for trial. The decision of both men to head for the hills instead of facing the charges did enormous harm to Serbia's Europeanization agenda because the EU tied any talks to their arrest. In real terms, that meant that these men cost Serbia more than fifteen years. If you had been a fifteen-year-old Serb youth in Belgrade dreaming of a European future, you were thirty-one when you got to return to that dream. The

ICTY subsequently convicted Karadzic in 2016 and sentenced him to forty years. In November 2017 Mladic received a life sentence for the Srebrenica genocide along with other crimes against humanity. He promised to appeal the verdict. In 2018, in his hometown of Kalinovik in Bosnia, a mural went up.

## Conclusion

The statistics of the war in Bosnia are telling. More than one hundred thousand Bosnians were killed, almost half of them were civilians, and the majority of those civilians were Bosniaks (66 per cent of the total killed). The killings were largely perpetrated by the Yugoslav National Army and the Bosnian Defense Forces, along with paramilitaries often under Belgrade's authority, according to the ICTY indictments. Srebrenica, as the war's biggest single massacre, was the most emblematic example of Bosnian Serb war aims. The Bosniaks were subjected to a terror that sought not just their destruction, as Karadzic promised, but the end of Muslim life in Bosnia. That meant the siege of Sarajevo and the bombing of cultural heritage sites, hospitals, and other state infrastructure. Since the war was largely fought for ethnic purity, two million people were moved from their homes. The borders of the new entities were established by war crimes.

In the now twenty-plus years since the war ended, Croatia managed an abrupt turn when Franjo Tudjman died in December 1999. Croatia began a meaningful reform and Europeanization process that led to its entry into the EU in 2013. Bosnia has not experienced the same transformation and remains mired in the made-in-Dayton peace package that has not permitted it to chart a path towards stability and prosperity. Dayton's defenders remind everyone that Dayton's primary job was to end the war and start a process. The main thrust of the literature is that Bosnia can move ahead only with either dramatic constitutional reforms or partition. The latter option is unpalatable for the international community because so much cash has already been spent. Moreover, as we shall see later, partition does not solve all problems.

Two anecdotes are worth telling that serve to illustrate at least part of the problem. If you visit Sarajevo now, especially in the parts where the Bosniaks dominate, not only can you feel the nostalgia for Tito, especially in the crowds in front of the memorial to Yugoslav liberation after the Second World War but also in just how far the sides are from serious reconciliation. In June 2014, Bosnia prepared to mark the anniversary of the start of the First World War. Gavrilo Princip means different things to different people: to some Serbs he is a hero who fulfilled great goals. To others, he is simply a terrorist. He ended Bosnia's Habsburg dreams. Annexed in 1908, Bosnia had a bright future in the central European Empire. It could have left the Balkans behind. Instead, Princip's success ended the dream. Even now, school children in Bosnia learn different versions of that fateful day. In the RS, film director Emir Kusturica, with cash from tennis star Novak Djokovic, opened Andricgrad, but not just to celebrate the Nobel-prize-winning Yugoslav author Ivo Andric. A mosaic shows Princip and the other assassins sent to Sarajevo that day, with Vienna's Belvedere Castle in the background and an alleged quote from the wall of Princip's prison cell, on which he wrote, "Our shadows will be walking through Vienna, strolling through the court, frightening the lords." So complicated was the anniversary that there was no real way for Bosnia to mark the day without conflict. It was a low-key affair, too messy for everyone. The Serbs had their celebration, which included an unveiling of a statue of the hero Princip in Serb-dominated East Sarajevo, while the Bosniaks and Croats did something else. There was an open-air concert for everyone in Sarajevo by the Vienna Philharmonic, in front of the restored National Library – which had been torched by Serb forces in 1992 – that actually ended up being for VIPs only. Sarajevo's citizens were herded into a dusty parking lot across the river to watch the concert on a screen.

Just as telling are the plaques that one can find in and around Muslim-dominated Sarajevo. Sarajevo, as noted, suffered the longest siege in the twentieth century, and much of the city's cultural patrimony was destroyed by Serb shelling. Memorialization of these events is of critical importance but must be done properly. Plaques note the destruction by "Serbian criminals" in the 1990s, which could be deemed provocative. In 2014, I asked a Sarajevo-based analyst why the reconciliation process seemed to be taking so long in Bosnia and alluded to Franco-German rapprochement after the Second World War, which happened much faster. He said that the Franco-German conflict was state-to-state. In Bosnia, after years of relative ethnic harmony, it was not a person from another state attacking your home but could have very well been your neighbor or even a former friend. His answer made sense.

Moreover, among political elites in the region there is no political will at all to deal with events of the past in a meaningful way. Nation building in the Balkans still requires a lot of denial, and schools teach different things to different ethnicities. As well, the highly complicated and lengthy trials in The Hague did little to promote closure, reconciliation, or understanding. Milosevic died in The Hague in 2006. With the ICTY's closure at the end of 2017, the process of bringing everyone to justice is far from complete. In addition, the ICTY's legacy in terms of promoting reconciliation is mixed. It was a necessary step, as huge cases like those against Serbia's Milosevic, Croatia's Ante Gotovina, Bosnia's Radovan Karadzic, and others could not have been managed by local courts. With the ICTY shutting down, it now falls to local courts to continue to prosecute the hundreds of cases still outstanding.

If you live in a weak state like Bosnia, you may be without a future, which explains the out-migration of mostly young people, as well as a general malaise. The political parties pander almost exclusively to narrow ethnic interests. "All Bosnia" parties do not stand a chance. Reconciliation is by far one of the biggest remaining challenges. Despite really incredible bottom-up efforts by activists, the political elite drives things the other way. School curricula is one thing, but visualization in the form of monuments is equally worrying. Take, for example, the debate over whether Srebrenica was a genocide. In July 2015, Russia's then ambassador to the UN, Vitaly Churkin, who also represented Russia in Bosnian peace talks in the 1990s, vetoed a Security Council resolution condemning the Srebrenica massacre as a genocide. To honor Churkin, who died in 2017, a Serb-run group in Srebrenica planned to erect a statue to thank him for his decisive "NO."

While officially Belgrade recognizes Srebrenica as a "grave crime," it does not call it a genocide. Milorad Dodik says Srebrenica is the "the greatest deception of the twentieth century." Not even after a video was aired in 2005 that showed Serbian paramilitaries executing Bosniaks did Belgrade acknowledge that a genocide had occurred. In fact, given the nature of Serb crimes in Bosnia, Croatia, and Kosovo, the failure to really confront the past head-on stands out. To understand the Srebrenica genocide, it is best to take the advice of one of the best observers of the Yugoslav disaster, the Croatian writer Slavenka Drakulic. In a series of posters that documented life in Srebrenica twenty years after the genocide, she wrote that "the best way to remember Srebrenica is for each of us to remember at least one face from the photos of or documentaries about Srebrenica, one sentence spoken by an eye-witness or war refugee, or at least one victim's name."

The international community, particularly the UN, failed Bosnia. To best capture the absurdity on the ground of the countless UN missions to Bosnia, a good starting point is Bosnian filmmaker Danis Tanovic's classic 2001 *No Man's Land*. Sarajevo 1914 gave us the clash of Great Power interests in the Balkans, which turned them into the famous tinderbox. In 1995 it was the opposite: there were no Great Power interests, but only narrow national interests that precluded decisive action. The international community did try to avoid intervention. Only later would President Bill Clinton understand that what was happening in Bosnia also undermined US credibility, and the United States did finally lead a decisive intervention that ended the war. The biggest failure was the EU's though. The European non-response, during Europe's so-called "hour," proved that the European integration project was limited to the success stories in Central Europe and the Baltic states. European policy certainly aided and abetted the "elite" who took over the newly created Balkan states. However, the fiasco in Bosnia, picked apart by thousands of scholars, did provide some lessons for the conflicts that came later: Kosovo in 1999 and Macedonia in 2001. While the international community would again impose peace treaties that often ignored local input, they would not replicate Dayton. That does not, however, mean they would get it right.

# 4

# Albania Implodes, Kosovo Arms

It is difficult to decide just where to begin the Kosovo story. As we saw in the preceding chapter, under the passive-resistance policy of Ibrahim Rugova and the Democratic League of Kosovo, the Albanians worked to internationalize their predicament and prevent a Serb attack on them. In the late 1980s, when Milosevic stripped the Albanians of their power, they went underground and tried to survive – and survive they did, thanks to the inclusiveness of society in Kosovo and help from their brethren abroad. Two events occurred in the 1990s that changed things, which meant violent resistance to Belgrade's occupation triumphed over Rugova's plan. The fate of Kosovo, and indeed the entire Rugova strategy, was tied to what happened in Dayton, Ohio, in 1995 and Tirana in 1997. Without these two events, Kosovo's trajectory would have been completely different. For the first time in the twentieth century, Kosovo simply got lucky.

But to Dayton first. When the Americans brokered the peace for Bosnia, Kosovo was not on the negotiating table, even though President Rugova said it would be. In hindsight, it was a mistake to leave Kosovo out of the discussion because Kosovo had started the whole disintegration of Yugoslavia, and in late 1995, things there had hardy improved. In fact, every informed observer knew just how bad things were there, given the ongoing human rights violations and discrimination against the majority Albanians. Kosovo endured a heavy police and military presence, and rural communities especially were subject to late-night searches by police looking for weapons. As to the elections in what was left of Yugoslavia, the Albanians simply boycotted them. Even the warlord Arkan won a parliamentary seat in Kosovo.

Rugova had visited every capital that mattered and made clear just what was happening. Although he was technically president of Kosovo, elections in Kosovo in the 1990s were never recognized. As such, he was never received as a head of state but more as a well-meaning missionary of sorts, with his trademark scarf and his ever-present bag of geological marvels from Kosovo to present as gifts to his interlocutors. No doubt he reminded everyone that passive resistance could not hold as long as the Albanian fate in Kosovo remained the same. As noted, Rugova was the ideal interlocutor for the West since he eschewed violence. And things needed to get a lot worse in Kosovo before the West would react. It is regrettable that the West did not take what was going on in Kosovo more seriously or recognize just how much the fate of Kosovo would determine the fate of the rest of Yugoslavia.

None of that matters now. Kosovo, as a province and not a republic, was sidelined for the sake of a deal on Bosnia, which made sense at the time. Plus, the negotiators needed Milosevic on side, and there was no way he would have allowed Kosovo on the agenda. He easily abandoned the Croatian Serbs and later sold out the Bosnian Serbs, who had started to annoy him, but Kosovo was too much to lose, and he would not abandon the Kosovo Serbs. Finally, the United States had set very tight deadlines for the Dayton talks, knowing that if left open ended, Izetbegovic, Milosevic, and Tudjman would deliver endless history lessons. Negotiations on Kosovo in the aftermath of Dayton focused on getting the Albanians back into the system, and nothing more, in what were largely fake deals with Milosevic that skirted the main issues and focused on human rights issues such as access to schooling and health care. Rugova's ability to hold back the extremists took a blow, and new forces emerged that had different ideas. It was time to try violence, but guns needed to be found.

If Dayton really undermined Rugova, events in neighboring Albania would change things even more. Albania in 1995 was hardly a functioning democracy. The governing Democratic Party (DP) of President Sali Berisha focused mostly on destroying the opposition

Socialists, currying favor with the United States, and not much else. The international community largely turned a blind eye to what was an emerging authoritarian state. Albania, to observers, was stable, and Berisha was a faithful ally, and despite some nationalist rumblings at the start of his career, he avoided stirring the nationalist pot. Berisha had already tried to introduce a new constitution in 1994 that would have made Albania a strong presidential republic and cemented his rule. However, when put to a nationwide vote, the constitution was rejected in a fall 1994 referendum. This was a major setback for Berisha and had been totally unexpected.

When Albania went to national elections in 1996, the failed referendum loomed heavily as the DP could not afford to lose again. In the end, it won easily, for mostly the wrong reasons. In the months prior to the election, the DP passed a number of laws that effectively made it impossible for the opposition to function. Under the broad heading of seeking redress for the communist past, the DP used the new laws to get rid of not only communists who had served the old regime but also ordinary opponents. Armed with new electoral laws and tons of cash from emerging pyramid schemes, the DP won 122 out of 140 seats in the assembly. The Socialists, with their leader, Fatos Nano, in jail since 1994 on spurious charges, were effectively destroyed. But the election was flawed, rigged, and filled with irregularities. Unable to stop the stolen election, the opposition walked away because the DP had stuffed the ballot boxes and frustrated the counting process. As the DP walked towards the creation of a one-party state, Albania's economic situation headed down the tubes.

If you visited Tirana in 1995 or 1996, you would have been surprised by just how much money seemed to be floating around the capital. Albania experienced truly impressive economic growth in the 1990s, the highest of any transition country, which was primarily owed to US$700 million in remittances per year from an estimated four hundred thousand Albanians working in Greece and elsewhere. Cafés and restaurants were full, and the mood was exuberant. But there was no real basis for the wealth. Albania had received very little foreign investment, and the economy was largely dependent on remittances from Albanians working abroad, sometimes more than 10 per cent of the GDP, especially in Greece. What

Albania had in the mid-1990s was a huge number of small kiosks that grew like mushrooms throughout the entire country. Kiosks grew to cafés, which grew to restaurants and then small hotels.

But the weakest link was the banking system, and it was there that trouble would start. In some ways, even twenty years later, Albania is still associated with the catastrophic collapse of the pyramid schemes and the civil unrest that followed in 1997. The basic facts are essential to understand just what happened and how it impacted Kosovo. Banks were not getting deposits and they were not lending much money either. The loans they had were largely bad. Businesses were turning to an informal credit market to raise cash. Some of the companies borrowing cash at high interest rates were ones that would become pyramid schemes. Some of them grew out of busting the sanctions imposed on Yugoslavia during the wars because Albania was a main artery for gas and oil. Others grew out of criminal activities. Even now, you can see the remnants of dozens of gas stations built near the border with Montenegro. When sanctions ended with the Dayton accord, cash had to be found. Some of the pyramid companies made high-profile investments in the tourism sector. The point was to show people they owned something. The life and death of pyramid schemes is easy to conceptualize. People are attracted to high rates of return, and doubts are assuaged as money keeps flowing in and payments continue. People hope they can exit before a crash. The scheme collapses when new investment is no longer enough to pay old investors.

Albania followed this path to a tee. Owing to shortcomings in the formal banking sector, which was hardly functional, much of the domestic savings, which were under people's mattresses in cash, flowed into what were irresistible pyramid schemes. Although schemes like the Albanian variant showed up elsewhere in the post-communist Europe, particularly in Romania, the level of enthusiasm (and investment) from the Albanians was totally unprecedented. The net liabilities of the schemes at their peak was half of Albania's GDP. What started as one or two companies grew as new players entered the field and the money flowed. The more players, the higher the interest rates, as the competition among the schemes was vicious. It is extremely hard to find in Albania a single person that did not invest, because the schemes were simply irresistible at the beginning – one company alone boasted a million investors in a country with a population of three million. People sold their houses to get the money there. Farmers sold all their livestock. It was mass hysteria. Educated, uneducated, rural, urban – everybody. I asked a friend if he fell for it. He said, "Yes, my wife made me. She said look at the neighbors with all their money and look at us." Lucky for him, he lost only $1,000. Talk to any Albanian – they all have a story to tell about 1997.

Interest rates just went up and up – 4 per cent a month, 8 per cent a month, 10 per cent a month. One company offered to triple your investment in just three months. You had to line up to deposit the cash. Warnings came from the IMF and the World Bank, but the government, for the most part, said nothing – because the people were happy and some of the companies had pumped money into the DP election campaign. As everyone knows, such schemes work as long as money comes in – but the money stopped. By November 1996 the first scheme collapsed, and the rest soon followed, and when people realized they were not getting their money back, they took matters into their own hands. The collapse of the schemes brought down the government of Sali Berisha, led to widespread civil unrest, anarchy, the deaths of two thousand people, and the total breakdown of the state in Albania. Reminiscent of 1991 when the Albanians attacked the communist state infrastructure and destroyed it, they did it again in 1997 as government institutions were destroyed and libraries burned. Taking part in the melee were not just ordinary criminals freed from prisons, but MPs too. Albania's descent into chaos said quite a bit about Albania's transition. For one, it proved just how little of a modern state had been built, because the state's institutions simply evaporated. Even the defense minister, Safet Zhulali, fled the country in a government-owned helicopter. Few were willing to defend any institutions. It was also extraordinary how many until-then mainstream politicians were willing to join the violence. Finally, it made clear that conflict in the Balkans did not have to be ethnic, as what happened in Albania was Albanian-on-Albanian violence.

Armed and masked gangs loyal to the Socialists controlled the south, and gangs loyal to Berisha controlled the north. The country was awash in weapons that had been stockpiled since the communist days. The hitherto bruised opposition parties used the chaos to advance their own agendas. The prisons were emptied; the army and police deserted. Foreigners were evacuated by their home countries. The US sent a ship, helicopters, and heavily armed forces to get their people. The Italians were called in to rescue others by boat from the port of Durres. The huge numbers of stockpiled weapons from the communist era ended up on the streets and then made it to training camps in Albania for the emerging violent resistance to Serb rule in Kosovo, embodied by the nascent Kosovo Liberation Army (KLA), which made its first appearance in November 1994. Its emergence was greeted as a sign that things did not always have to be the same. But, without the 1997 collapse, Kosovo would have endured a much more protracted guerrilla war.

An interesting aside to the whole story is the return of the Albanian "king," Leka I, Zog's only child. Recall that Leka was born on 5 April 1939. The Italians invaded two days later; Zog pledged to fight and then took off. The young Leka began a life of exile that would not end until much later, after two failed attempts to get back the throne. Leka made his first attempt to return home in 1993, when he arrived at Tirana's then Rinas Airport on a plane lent to him by the king of Jordan. The Albanians had been expecting him but were not sure how or when he would come or even what he looked like. They knew only that he was tall like his father. Louis Zanga, an Albanian by birth and then the key analyst of all things Albanian at Radio Free Europe/Radio Liberty in Munich, arrived at the airport in fall 1993 and was asked by a border officer if he was the "king." When Leka actually did arrive, he was kept at the airport by the Albanian authorities on a technicality: he was carrying a passport issued by the Royal Court of Albania that listed his occupation as "king" in Albanian. The Albanians were happy to admit him in so much as he was an Albanian citizen but they said no to that passport – come in as citizen, not the king. He returned to his home in South Africa and sat it out for a better moment.

Later, taking advantage of the chaos of 1997, he returned, hoping that this was his moment. His return was a disgrace for him personally and Albania too. Arriving in Tirana dressed in military gear with guns and grenades, surrounded by more people with guns and grenades, he brought even more violence to an already violent place. But he did a get a concession: as part of new elections to restore order, there was to be a referendum on the restoration of his father's ultimately artificial monarchy. He lost badly – two-thirds of voters rejected him. He rejected the vote as stolen and he tried his own violent response with attacks on government institutions. Like his father, he was forced to flee Albania again to avoid arrest for charges related to his quasi-coup attempt. In a fit of forgiving uncommon to Albania, he was later pardoned and allowed to return in 2002, got some of his property back, and remained an inconsequential political figure until he died in 2011.

Other Albanians also decided for the second time in less than a decade to destroy the state. The 1997 collapse, which some wrongly liken to a near civil war, destroyed Berisha's government, led to horrific violence, and required international intervention to set things right again. New elections in June 1997 put Berisha into opposition and brought the Socialists to power. They were far more willing to facilitate violence in Kosovo then the DP had been. In short, the KLA now had arms, an army, and thousands of Albanians from around the world started making their way to Albania to join training camps in northern Albania. The arms bazaar in Albania opened up all kinds of opportunities to the many groups that wanted to fight the Serbs. While the Tirana government was not involved at the start, they did help later as an uncoordinated free-for-all gradually became a coordinated program to get weapons to Kosovo.

But the international community was not quite ready to support Kosovo's independence or an insurrection. The policy was still to keep Yugoslavia intact – by then only Serbia, Montenegro, Kosovo, and Vojvodina – while pressuring Milosevic to give the Albanians their autonomy back, something that was hardly acceptable to the Albanians. In 1996 there was some hope as agreement normalized education for Albanian students. The agreement was never implemented, because there was no way Rugova, or any Albanian for that matter, would accept being part of Serbia again. Rugova's position was not so far from what had faced Izetbegovic in Bosnia in 1992. Stay in a Milosevic-ruled Yugoslavia or seek an exit. Life changed inside

Kosovo, as more and more youth, and not just from Kosovo, decided to head to the camps in northern Albania and prepare to fight for independence. And in spring 1998, war came to Kosovo. In February 1998 the KLA put out for the world to see the bodies of twenty men killed in the Drenica massacre. If you fly into Prishtina, you arrive at Adem Jashari International Airport. Jashari, very much a founder of the KLA and long considered a terrorist by the Yugoslav authorities, was killed along with fifty-seven family members in an attack on his family compound in March 1998. US secretary of state Madeline Albright warned other leaders that unless action was taken, the world was about to let another Bosnia happen.

In the early stages of the struggle, the KLA was in an extremely weak position and it would briefly be labelled a terrorist organization by soon-to-be allies. For the West, the situation was confusing. Was Milosevic just trying to quash an insurgency or was he making a bigger play – the creation of a Kosovo without Albanians? History shows it was the latter that motivated Milosevic's decisions. For the West to get involved took the usual rounds of diplomacy and a few massacres before anyone realized that Kosovo was another Bosnia in the making. Albanians were also routinely being forced to flee their homes: by the end of 1998 more than three hundred thousand people were displaced as Kosovo's harsh winter descended. Images of the thousands of displaced dominated the television screens in the West, and comparisons with the Second World War's deportations were front and center. Whatever Milosevic's plan was, he certainly failed when he moved to expel the Albanians.

Richard Holbrooke, the primary architect of the Dayton Accords, was again trying to get Milosevic to play ball, urging him to reduce force levels in Kosovo. But in January 1999 a major massacre in the village of Racak could not be ignored. Forty-five bodies were discovered, executed by Serb forces. Onsite was the Kosovo Verification Mission of the Organization for Security and Cooperation in Europe (OSCE), which was charged with monitoring the situation in Kosovo. William Walker, the mission's head, who remains a hero in Kosovo, declared the massacre a crime against humanity. The Serb side said the bodies were Albanian soldiers killed in fighting that the KLA had dressed up as peasants to look like a civilian massacre, for the benefit of the international community. But Walker asked, "How do you line up the bullet holes with the peasant clothing you put on the soldiers?" Belgrade moved to turf Walker out. The attack in Racak was in direct violation of two UN Security Council resolutions (1160 and 1199) that called for a cessation of hostilities in Kosovo. Racak, like the Markale massacre in Sarajevo in 1995, was the catalyst for international action. Both incidents, however, would be mired in conspiracy theories. The United States demanded action and backed it up with serious threats and the movement of serious military hardware to the region. The Contact Group, set up for the Bosnian war, which included France, Germany, Italy, Russia, the United Kingdom, and the United States, took over the file from the OSCE. Peace talks were set for February 1999 in Rambouillet, France. A deal would be given to both sides: take it or leave it. Whoever refused to sign would be punished: the Serbs would face NATO; the Albanians would be abandoned to their fate.

The Rambouillet talks and the ones that followed in Paris were complicated. Some even argued that the talks were designed to fail so as to enable NATO to use force and win back the raison d'être it had lost with the end of the Cold War. The most important thing to consider is that Milosevic did not go, but instead sent others. As would be the case when negotiations began over Kosovo's final status in 2007, the Serb side simply did not negotiate seriously, as they did not understand that Kosovo was, in effect, no longer theirs to play with. Kosovo was represented by President Rugova; Hashim Thaci of the KLA; Veton Surroi, the charismatic and eloquent spokesperson of civil society but also the publisher of Kosovo's leading daily, *Koha Ditore*; along with several other representatives. The agreement failed. The Albanians signed because they were told if they did not, they would be abandoned to face Milosevic and his forces alone. The Serbs did not sign but came back with a hopeless counterproposal. It was not a perfect deal for either side. The Albanians did not get a direct path to independence, as the agreement maintained the territorial integrity of what was still the Federal Republic of Yugoslavia. The final status of Kosovo was put off for three years, at which time an international meeting would be convened "to determine a mechanism for a final settlement for

Kosovo, on the basis of the will of the people," among other criteria. This was understood by Kosovo's negotiators to be a future
referendum. The Serbs has multiple issues and complained that it
amounted to a humiliating NATO occupation of Serbia and an international protectorate over Kosovo. The former was not true, but
the latter was. Many observers, including Henry Kissinger, said the
agreement was merely a pretext to start bombing. Holbrooke made
one last attempt to get Milosevic to back down. Milosevic did not,
preferring to take his chances that NATO would not bomb. I was in
Albania during the Rambouillet talks in February 1999 and again in
May/June 1999 during the NATO air war. During a February 1999
visit to Albania, I found it gloomy, with war in the air. Barely two
years out of the pyramid collapse, Albanians in Albanian felt that
events in Kosovo would bring another round of disasters. They too
wanted a deal in France.

Back in Kosovo the threat of expulsion always loomed, as forces
of the Yugoslav National Army, paramilitaries, and Interior Ministry
police were routinely terrorizing civilians. In Kosovo's hot spots,
houses were burned in a seemingly random way – burn two, leave
one. My friends remember those days well. Large numbers of people gathered in a single home, sleeping in their clothes, wearing
shoes inside the house, debating to leave or stay. When the NATO
bombing started on 24 March 1999, for many there was no choice
but to leave. Some left because they wanted to do so before someone
came to deport or murder them; others left because they were forced
to by Yugoslav forces or paramilitaries. They were driven by the
thousands to the borders. One of my friends recalled packed trucks
passing neatly lined-up bodies of dead KLA soldiers along the way
as a stark warning. Human Rights Watch estimated that nearly nine
hundred thousand people were expelled to Albania and Macedonia
and that several hundred thousand were internally displaced. The
Serb expulsion of the Albanians rendered the return of Serb control
over Kosovo impossible when the war ended.

The arrival of the refugees from Kosovo was incredibly difficult
for Albania. Just two years out of the collapse of the economy, the
Albanians did the best they could and called for brotherly solidarity. There was lots of that, but just as many people took advantage

of the vulnerability of the refugees and gouged them for rented apartments and other goods. After all, the Albanians of Kosovo were considered the rich cousins who had grown up under the glories of Tito, not Hoxha. Finally, 1999 was primarily the first time the Albanians of Kosovo actually saw Albania. They were devastated. In 1999, Albania was a wreck. It also looked like a victim of NATO bombing. The journey from the border near the northern town of Kukes was a mere 150 kilometers but took ten hours and was nothing more than a tour of Albanian misery – abandoned factories, barely passable roads, and ruined collective farms. Inside Albania, the refugees were housed in massive tent camps, available or run-down Albtourist hotels, and abandoned factories. Those with money got private apartments at outrageous prices from the locals. The Kosovo refugees, coming from a much more civil society than Albania, brought something that had not been there for a while: flowers. In an attempt to normalize their status in Albania, the refugees planted flowers in front of their temporary homes.

On the international front, NATO's first-ever intervention was justified on purely humanitarian grounds but went ahead without UN Security Council consent due to Russian opposition. The start of bombing poisoned the relationship with Russia more or less permanently. Russia not only rejected the intervention but also saw its own future as a later victim of NATO. French president Jacques Chirac, UK prime minister Tony Blair, and US president Bill Clinton all suggested that a genocide was underway in Kosovo and invoked the Responsibility to Protect (R2P) doctrine. They also told the Serbian people that it was Milosevic under attack, not them although few believed that. Former dissident and then president of the Czech Republic Vaclav Havel, who had serious moral authority, said the NATO action in Kosovo was completely ethical and brought the Czechs on board. A then-liberal Viktor Orban said he wanted Hungary to be on the right side of history for the first time, and Hungary was on side. Poland was also on board comparing Kosovar suffering to their own under Hitler and then Stalin. Bulgaria, not a NATO member at that point, took an even bigger risk when it supported NATO by allowing the alliance to use its airspace, despite the fact popular opinion supported Serbia. The flamboyant and often hyperbolic spokesman for NATO, Jamie Shea, compared what was happening in Kosovo to events in the Second World War. Images of trains being loaded by Serb security forces in Prishtina in late March with Albanian refugees destined for Macedonia confirmed this.

During my May/June visit to Albania to interview refugees, the United States had piled all manner of equipment at Tirana's airport in the event a ground war was required, something NATO hoped to avoid. Tanks plied Albania's few miserable roads north while Albanians looked on with astonishment. No tanks entered Kosovo until after the armistice was signed. In what was an almost entirely US show that exposed the limited capabilities of Europe, mostly US planes conducted thousands of sorties and stayed above fifteen thousand feet in hopes of a zero-casualty war. NATO mistakenly bombed the Chinese Embassy, struck fleeing refugees, and hit Radio and Television Serbia, causing avoidable civilian deaths. The air war undoubtedly escalated the refugee crisis, as Serb forces ramped up their expulsion campaign and almost a million people fled Kosovo to neighboring Albania, Macedonia, and Montenegro. Milosevic quipped that even the birds fled NATO bombs.

The majority ended up in Albania, where, to me at least, it seemed they would never get home. They were stripped of all documents and made stateless as they crossed the border. Milosevic was determined to at least secure a Kosovo that had no Albanians. In sending thousands to Macedonia too, which already had its own Albanian problem, no doubt Milosevic hoped to destabilize things in an already weak state with a marginalized and restive Albanian minority numbering almost 25 per cent of the state. In May the ICTY indicted Milosevic (and loads of others) for actions in Bosnia, Croatia, and Kosovo. What happened at Racak was part of the indictment. No doubt the ICTY hoped that by indicting Milosevic during the war it would prevent him from negotiating an immunity deal if he sought peace à la Karadzic.

Not only was Serbia (plus Kosovo and Montenegro) being punished by air strikes, the lie of the land of what was left of Yugoslavia was changed fundamentally. The duo of Bulatovic and Djukanovic in Montenegro started to fall apart even before the crisis in Kosovo heated up. In 1997, Djukanovic more or less broke with Milosevic, called him obsolete, set Montenegro on an altogether different course, and also permanently marginalized Bulatovic. This was an extremely bold and even dangerous move that deserves credit, as Milosevic was never magnanimous with his opponents. The Kosovo crisis was impacting Montenegro in ways that it could not afford, especially since refugees from there were headed to Montenegro too throughout 1998 and 1999. At all costs, Montenegro wanted no part of a war with either Kosovo or NATO and called for dialogue. As a place with fairly substantial military hardware, especially aircraft hidden away in cave bunkers, Montenegro was bombed too. But the always wily Djukanovic used the war to advance the case for Montenegrin independence, although he would have to wait until 2006 because the international community would block the creation of any additional post-Yugoslav states.

The NATO bombing campaign ended on 9 June, when Milosevic backed down and ordered his generals to sign an armistice after seventy-eight days of heavy bombing that did surprisingly little damage to the military infrastructure. NATO flew 33,000 sorties and used 14,000 bombs and missiles. NATO won the war entirely from the air and lost only three soldiers in accidents. The thousands of refugees went back home as quickly as they left it. Sadly, the refugees headed home before what would eventually become a 50,000-strong NATO force – known as KFOR, for Kosovo Force – occupied Kosovo. Interestingly, the Russians arrived first from their base in Bosnia and almost caused a conflict with NATO when NATO's supreme commander in Europe, Wesley Clark, told his men on the ground to evict the Russians by force. In any case, the Russians did not get an occupation zone and they proved harmless as they controlled only the entry to Prishtina's airport, where they opened a mini market of sorts to make some much-needed extra cash. The Bulgarians won even more friends when they denied the Russians the use of Bulgarian airspace to resupply their forces there. The returning Albanians wreaked revenge on the Serbs and Roma too, along with those of their own who had been branded as collaborators. The multiple murders that took place between January 1998 and December 2000 were destined to resurface in Kosovo when the EU established a special court to try people. The Albanians also attacked the historic Orthodox Church infrastructure. Although most Albanians were bilingual Albanian/Serbian speakers, speaking Serbian after June 1999 was a potential death sentence. Those Serbs who could, especially those who lived in towns and cities, fled north of the Ibar River, establishing a flashpoint in the city of Mitrovica, where the Serbs left the south and the Albanians left the north. North of the Ibar would largely become an extension of Serbia, and with the help of Belgrade, the Serbs there would ensure that they would never become a minority in Kosovo. Sadly none of Kosovo's leaders – either military or political – called on the Albanians to leave the Serbs alone and merely allow them to remain unharmed. The Albanians lost the moral high ground, and for the Serbs, the world was turned upside down as they had to retreat to a parallel society in a new Kosovo. Prizren, by far the nicest city in Kosovo and the birthplace of the Albanian national renaissance in the nineteenth century, stood out for the destruction of Serb property. NATO's substantial army there was also incapable of preventing so many savage reprisals. After all, as it said, it was not a police force. This was not the first time NATO would let down the Serbs of Kosovo.

Although the UN was bypassed by NATO, it gave an after-the-fact approval to the whole thing by essentially making Kosovo a UN protectorate. Kosovo was to become the UN's biggest mission ever, and for the thousands of do-gooders who came with the mission, the experience was to be very enriching. For the Albanians, however, it would often bring extraordinary misery. In what became known as the United Nations Mission in Kosovo (UNMIK), the UN would establish an almost colonial presence in Kosovo that was, at least in theory, designed to train the Albanians in self-government. UNMIK was headed by the Special Representative of the Secretary General (SRSG), who, like the High Representative in Bosnia, held ultimate authority – which ran counter to the demand for more democracy.

Albanians look fondly on the first SRSG, Sergio Vieira de Mello, who died tragically in a truck-bomb attack on UN headquarters in Iraq in 2003, and the second, Bernard Kouchner. On arrival in

Kosovo, the UN faced a place with no state whatsoever and it proved capable at providing emergency aid. NATO may have had thirty thousand troops there at the start, but there were no regular police. Kouchner adeptly kept the Albanians from heading to a civil war, given the various groups vying for power, by reminding them that bad behavior was not the road to statehood. Later events would prove that he was wrong. The KLA feared, with good reason, that the political process would marginalize them, and Kouchner kept the peace. Most of the warriors went on to form political parties that mostly represented fairly narrow business interests that were linked with the criminality that had solidified during the war. On the down side, the ineptness of UNMIK was revealed when the Serbs in North Mitrovica drove eleven thousand Albanians south to the other side of the Ibar River (south Mitrovica). The divided city of Mitrovica, with its heavily armed "Bridge Watchers" guarding access to the Serb side, would prove to be a major flashpoint in the years ahead.

Given the amount of security, tanks, and sand bags they were hiding behind in their downtown Prishtina HQ, it seemed the UN was more afraid of the Albanians than the Serbs had been. In any case, UNMIK proved to be incredibly expensive, given the small size of Kosovo. Salaries were high, and the location was great: you could grab a UN car and, in just a few hours, be on the beaches near Thessaloniki, or you could hop a flight to Vienna. It was development in the European context. Same pay as a really dangerous place, but without the danger. What could be better for the young ideologues eager to civilize the Albanians and try out all manner of governance experiments?

Inside Kosovo, it looked as though Rugova was a man of the past, kidnapped and humiliated by Milosevic during the war; it also looked like the KLA was set to be in control. The KLA established a rather nasty provisional government that hoped to settle some scores with Serbs and Albanians. However, the warriors would have to wait as Rugova was far from finished: he remained Kosovo's most popular politician and was the central figure there until his death in 2006. Milosevic would later argue during his trial at the ICTY that by kidnapping Rugova he actually saved him from being murdered by his Albanian opponents inside Kosovo. That was one of the few times that Milosevic was telling the truth. Hardly the altruist, Milosevic no doubt hoped too that in the end he would be back negotiating with a moderate like Rugova and not the KLA.

The UN presence was made legitimate by UN Security Council Resolution (UNSCR) 1244, which was never seen by any of the key players in Kosovo. Riddled with contradictory language, this agreement would in the end to do enormous harm to Kosovo as it placed the legitimate claim to independence on hold. The UN presence was one thing, but the agreement maintained the fiction that Yugoslavia's territory was unaltered. It was classic diplomacy in that it simply kicked the Kosovo status issue down the road. Not a single person then could have ever dreamed that Kosovo would wait nine more years for what was, even then, a compromised independence, filled with restrictions. Although an imperfect option in 1999 when the war ended, the best solution for Kosovo would have been to make it independent then. Milosevic was indicted; he had started a war that he lost; and the Russians, with the almost dead Boris Yeltsin in power (who hated Milosevic anyway), were too weak to care. But independence was not to be. The West worried about the fate of Montenegro but worried more that Kosovo independence would undo the settlement in Bosnia and invite another war. Kosovo had to wait with Montenegro. Things were made even more complicated when Milosevic was ousted in October 2000 and was later transferred to The Hague, where he died in his cell in March 2006. Serbia thus began an on-again/off-again transition to democracy that complicated Kosovo's quest for independence.

Even though Kosovo eventually became independent, UNSCR 1244 still haunts it. The agreement set forth the role of the UN, NATO, and the nascent Kosovo institutions. It reaffirmed that territorial integrity of Yugoslavia but also called for meaningful self-administration and autonomy for Kosovo. But 1244 did take into account to agreement signed at Rambouillet, where the Albanians were given a three-year time frame for a political solution to final status. UNSCR 1244 also suggested that while the UN began the process of helping Kosovo develop the institutions of self-government, the question of just what the end was remained open. UNSCR 1244, in essence, said one thing to Belgrade and another to Prishtina.

In terms of concrete, immediate effects, the UN quickly replaced the KLA's provisional government with its own people and oversaw local elections in October 2000 and "national" elections in 2001, as a step towards the self-government promised to the Albanians. The KLA transitioned to the Kosovo Protection Corps, which was a not an army but a civil agency designed for dealing with local issues such as floods. While UNMIK certainly outlived its usefulness, stayed far too long, and cost far too much, its nine years of administration did see some gains: it created the basis for a state; free and fair elections were held, which was not true in Albania; quasi-passports were issued, although few countries recognized them; a decent and multiethnic police service emerged; and the Albanians had a government that represented them, even though UNMIK was ultimately in the driver's seat. Nonetheless, UNMIK failed miserably with the judiciary and was unable to stop the explosive growth of corruption, which on some occasions even benefitted UNMIK staff. More important, the system it imposed was a hodgepodge of American and European examples. Finally, it was astonishing how little accountability and democracy existed in the system. The Albanian politicians blamed UNMIK, and UNMIK blamed the locals, with no apparent accountability on either side. What the ordinary citizen took away from all this was that only independence could solve every problem. The international community had something different in mind: it decided that stability was more important than democracy.

But the biggest failure was laid bare by the obvious disconnect with citizens on the part of both internationals and politicians. With UNSCR 1244 the Albanians were thrown into a deep existential crisis. The open-endedness of the UNMIK presence essentially denied them a future, and the situation became increasingly tense, although few recognized just how close to fracturing Kosovo was. In the absence of a meaningful discussion about Kosovo's future, there was a palpable sense of isolation and despair. This was true for the Serbs too. Those who had not fled north of the Ibar River, who were mostly rural, lived in NATO-protected enclaves. Those in the north of Kosovo set up a para-state that looked to Belgrade, not Prishtina, for support.

On 10 September 2001, on what was to be the day before the world changed, President Ibrahim Rugova arrived in Toronto for a week-long visit to Toronto and Ottawa. At that point in history, Canada was playing an outsized role in the Balkans, having already been a key player in UN peacekeeping missions in Bosnia. During the war in Kosovo, Canada had taken in five thousand refugees and kept offices open in Prishtina, Skopje, and Tirana. (These, along with the embassy in Sarajevo, have long since closed.) Rugova valued Canada's contribution to the Balkans. However, with the terrorist attacks in the United States on 11 September, Rugova went from being the man of peace to the Muslim from the Balkans being challenged for his thoughts on terrorism. Moreover, though just two years out of the war, it was astonishing how much pressure Rugova was under to placate the Serbs in Kosovo. Recalling then US ambassador Zimmerman's suggestion to Croatian president Tudjman that he offer the Serbs autonomy, one Canadian official suggested that Rugova govern in a coalition with one of the Serb political parties as a gesture of goodwill. Though in theory this was a great suggestion, it was naïve, as 2001 was not the time for that. Rugova dismissed the idea out of hand. He wanted to stay in power.

While Kosovo's new leaders and UNMIK sparred over competencies, its citizens drifted, as it seemed that Kosovo was in stasis. The place was teeming with celebratory visits from Westerners wanting to bask in the recognition of their role in 1999. Multiple big fish in little ponds descended to tell tales of their glory days, and the Albanians were happy to oblige because nobody puts on hospitality like the Albanians of Kosovo. The domestic Kosovo elite sought business-class travel more than a discussion with their constituents. When they were not traveling, they got used to feting international visitors. But outside the corridors of power it became clear that Kosovo was at the fork in the road: either solve the status question or face a catastrophe. To placate the Albanians to a degree and put off any discussion of Kosovo's final status, UNMIK instituted the "Standards before Status" policy in December 2003. It meant that Kosovo had to reach certain benchmark European standards of governance before any talk of status could start. The standards – democratic institutions, rule of law, freedom of movement, returns and reintegration, economy, property rights, dialogue with Belgrade, and the Kosovo Protection Corps – were actually impossible to reach. But Standards before Status would soon morph into standards and status, then finally, in 2008, status and no standards.

The events of March 2004 remain subject to numerous conspiracy theories, but some facts are clear. First of all, few experts inside or outside Kosovo knew just how fragile Kosovo was. Failure to move outside the capital meant that nobody saw just how easy it was to descend back into ethnic conflict. In what was exposed as sensational, inaccurate news coverage and the blatant inability of Kosovo's leaders to defuse tensions, news of the drowning of three Albanian children being chased by Serbs and their dogs spread like crazy throughout Kosovo. The story was not true, but the Kosovo Albanian media, despite being asked by UNMIK and the OSCE to defer broadcasting the story, went ahead with it. All major media outlets, despite almost five years of investment in developing a free and objective media, moved to a war footing and accepted the drowning story completely, with almost no regard for other opinion. Radio Television Kosovo started to broadcast old war footage from 1999 and photos of Adem Jashari with somber music in the background. The message was a simple one: get ready for battle. Fifty thousand people took part in two days of rampaging that left nineteen people dead (eleven Albanians and eight Serbs) and nine hundred injured. Thousands more Serbs fled Kosovo, and multiple Serb churches and monasteries were torched. YouTube has countless videos available of the tragic destruction. The international presence was exposed as weak, inward looking, incompetent, and despised by both Albanians and Serbs. NATO's KFOR mission was especially hopeless, given the amount of hard power it possessed and yet still failed to stop the violence against the minority population. It chose to avoid any risk to its troops. The Albanian leadership fared little better as it too did little to stop the violence. However, if the Bosnian Serbs had proven that you could establish a quasi-state through war and genocide, then by turning to violence against the Serbs and other minorities in March 2004, the Albanians also hastened the arrival of statehood in some unexpected ways.

As a direct result of the debacle in March, then UN Secretary General Kofi Annan asked the Norwegian diplomat Kai Eide to write a report and suggest the way ahead. Eide wrote that "little has been achieved to create a foundation for a multi-ethnic society." Hardly surprising, given it had been only five years since the war. Eide also caught the mood of Kosovo – the Albanians felt the international community was keeping them locked in the status quo. Eide said the time had come to start thinking about Kosovo's final status. Eide also noted that more power needed to be given to the Albanians and that Belgrade needed to be better included. Eide stressed Kosovo's weak economy – 60 to 70 per cent unemployment – and suggested that things were bound to get worse. By far his most important conclusion was that while he stated there never would be a good time to talk future status, now was the time to start talks. For Albanians, their perspective in particular was that the international community had stolen their future. However, Albanian behavior in March did serious harm to the type of state that they would eventually get in 2008, which would be a far cry from a normal state. Clearly, the Albanians would need to make incredible guarantees to the Serbs. For Serbs, March proved that the Albanians simply wanted them out. With Eide's report in hand, the UN did move to the next step, and in November 2005 appointed the former Finnish president Martti Ahtisaari to start talks on Kosovo's future status. Ahtisaari was joined by the former head of Austrian Foreign Ministry, Albert Rohan. The choice of an Austrian was good news for the Albanians as Austrian foreign policy was decidedly pro-Albanian, especially given the legacy of 1914. The talks were, from the start, a total waste of time as there was no basis for any kind of compromise. Anyone with any experience in the region knew that independence for Kosovo was the only option.

By 2006, a major obstacle in the path of Kosovo's independence had been removed: Montenegro was independent. As noted earlier, the international community allowed fragile and failing Bosnia to dictate, to a degree, the fate of Kosovo and Montenegro. After Milosevic's fall in 2000 and Serbia's tentative democratization, Yugoslavia ceased to exist, and the new State Union of Serbia and Montenegro appeared in 2002, which was a very loose confederation of two semi-independent states. It was joking called "Solania" or "Solanaland" because its creation was very much owed to the EU foreign policy chief, Javier Solana. The state union was a sham – its website was always under construction, and Montenegro aggressively pursued complete independence anyway with its own foreign ministry, different customs rules, and abandonment of the Yugoslav currency. In addition, the state union itself was subject to an exit clause: after three years, either unit could have a referendum. Montenegro took that option in May 2006, with a nasty catch imposed by the international community: it had to get 55 per cent support, not 50 per cent plus one like everywhere else in the former Yugoslavia. The 55 per cent threshold was mean spirited but doable, in so far as the Montenegrins, combined with the Albanians and other minorities, could get 55 per cent. What the international community did not plan for was a result in the grey zone – say, 53 per cent. In the end, the pro-independence forces got 55.5 per cent, and the sky did not fall. Serbia did not invade, civil war was averted, and life went on. Montenegro was independent, the third and final Yugoslavia disappeared, and Kosovo was next on the list.

In the talks between Kosovo and Serbia, a happy ending was impossible. The Albanians really negotiated seriously while the Serb side did not. But in their quest for independence, the Albanians gave away far too much and set all kinds of traps for themselves that appeared only later. Serbia was wedded to the notion of giving the Albanians an unheard-of level of autonomy but nothing more. Kosovo had had autonomy in the past, which had been crudely eradicated, so it was naïve to think that autonomy was on the table again. This position underscored the general attitude of Belgrade politicians since the founding of the first Yugoslavia in 1918: they wanted the territory, just not the Albanians. As an example, Belgrade never offered the Albanians a role in a new Yugoslavia, one that foresaw the Albanians as partners, rather than a national minority, in Kosovo. Could the Serbs ever imagine living in a state with the Albanians in which an Albanian could be the prime minister or president? Under the savvy leadership of president Boris Tadic, a real democrat who had always opposed Milosevic and was liked in the West, and the stridently nationalist foreign minister Vuk Jeremic, the Serbs scoured the world for support. Jeremic's main message to the world was that there were dozens of would-be Kosovos in waiting. Kosovo's independence, he argued, would end an international order based on international law. In any case, the Albanians moved further and further towards the goals of Ahtissari and Rohan, and the Serbs were left behind. They never had a chance, anyway, since independence was the end game because there was no other option. By no means does this mean that the Kosovo negotiating team was good – it was not – only that it was prepared to give away far more than the Serbs were and it had to undo the damage of 2004.

What this meant in principle was that Ahtisaari had to come up with a proposal that could protect the Serb minority. The Albanians had to offer up unprecedented decentralization and hand over extraordinary power to the Serbs. Unlike Dayton, Ahtisaari's plan was short and simple. He created an asymmetric state that was also, on paper, a multiethnic state. In many ways it was a perfect plan for a perfect world. Gone were minorities; in place was a community that included everyone. Ahtisaari's plan was not only shorter than Dayton, it was also in many ways far better in that it would allow the minority Serbs to possess autonomy and, through loads of qualified majority voting, a fundamental role in governing the new Kosovo. Kosovo remained, on paper, a unitary and sovereign state but it could not have an army. The Serbs would have reserved seats in parliament. Although not clear at the time, the Serb strategy was to avoid becoming a minority in Kosovo, and the Ahtissari plan laid the foundations for a Serb entity that looked a little like the RS in Bosnia, as it would territorialize Serb rights in the years ahead. As Veton Surroi correctly assessed, while the Albanians saw a period at the end of the Ahtisaari proposal, the Serbs saw a comma. EU mediation between Serbia and Kosovo in the years ahead would end up diluting Kosovo's sovereignty while providing more and more incentives to the Serbs.

The package, which was a real liberal and post-modern fantasy, was extraordinary for the incentives it gave to the Kosovo Serbs to play a role in the new state, and the Albanians made countless concessions. Although Serbia was losing territory, it was set to maintain decisive influence, especially in the Serb-dominated municipalities in Kosovo's north. The Serbian Ministry of Education was even allowed to supply textbooks to Serb schools. Given that this had already been implemented in Bosnia, with Croatia supplying books to Croats there and Serbia to Serbs there, and given that the results simply reinforced the wartime divisions, to do the same in Kosovo was pure folly. The Albanians got the demeaning supervised independence, which was really unfair and even absurd since that is more or less what they had under UNMIK since 1999. Ahtisaari's plan foresaw the departure of UNMIK after a Security Council resolution and a 120-day transition period before the arrival of an EU mission, the European Union Rule of Law Mission or EULEX, which would replace UNMIK. Kosovo, like Bosnia, would get an international office to oversee the implementation of the plan. EULEX was the biggest and most expensive mission of its type under the Common Security and Defense Policy. Indeed, the people got more aid per capita than anywhere else in the Balkans, on par with Palestine. (EULEX has an open-ended mandate that continues to be renewed but is expected to shut down in 2022.) EULEX's principal focus was to provide assistance to Kosovo in the judiciary, police, and customs authorities. In typical EU-style, nobody bothered to explain to ordinary citizens just what the Albanians had pledged to do, and very little public outreach was done by the Albanian leaders, either, to outline what the future looked like.

When Ahtisaari tabled his plan, known as the Comprehensive Proposal for the Kosovo Status Settlement, to the UN in March 2007, the hope was that the plan would be accepted by the Security Council and life would go on. This did not happen, because Russia opposed the plan and refused to endorse it. No vote ever took place in the Security Council. It was incredibly naïve to expect the Russians to get on side, especially since it amounted to a fait accompli for Serbia. In the year that followed prior to Kosovo's declaration of independence in February 2008 the EU tried to develop a coherent strategy among member states for Kosovo's imminent independence. It failed. Luckily for Kosovo, it could always count on the United States to speak with a single voice and cut through EU waffling. In June 2007, then US President George W. Bush paid a visit to the one place where he had almost 100 per cent support: the Republic of Albania. Bush's visit was beyond a milestone for the Albanian government, even though Bush allegedly had his watch stolen when he waded into an exuberant crowd. As to Kosovo, Bush was clear when he told a press conference that, "at some point in time, sooner rather than later, you've got to say 'Enough is enough. Kosovo is independent' and that's the position we've taken." That was that. It was up to the Europeans to get their policies in order as the United States would only wait so long.

In the end, the EU could not entirely get its act together. Five states, viewing Kosovo independence issues through the paradigm of domestic-minority issues, could not be convinced that Kosovo should be independent. These states were Cyprus, Greece, Spain, Slovakia, and Romania – all concerned about the precedent that Kosovo's independence would invoke in terms of their own minority issues. Given what transpired in Catalonia in 2017, Spain's intransigence on Kosovo independence seems almost visionary. The Americans, who were parroted by the EU too, kept repeating the same mantra, "Kosovo is *sui generis*," especially since with UNSCR 1244, Kosovo had been placed under UN administration. This was a case in which if you say something often enough, it becomes true, as Kosovo was not all that different from other conflict situations in the world, particularly if one looks at the fate of the Kurds, for example. The Russians had made their position clear too: Kosovo was part of Serbia, and Albanians were a minority in Serbia. Having spent almost a decade in limbo and then having embraced the Ahtisaari Plan as the basis for their future, few Kosovo Albanians understood just how much they gave away to a minority that made up only 5 per cent of Kosovo. Moreover, nobody thought that subsequent negotiations with Serbia would, in the long run, chip away at their sovereignty, often with the support of the EU. The asymmetry of the new state would always be there, and the Serb minority would keep pushing for more and more decentralization, and the battle over recognition would last longer than anyone expected.

Kosovo made what was called a Unilateral Declaration of Independence on 17 February 2008. Obviously, someone somewhere told it to go ahead, then wait for recognitions to flow in. The day before independence was beautiful, sunny, and warm. Independence Day was clear but bitterly cold. In the morning, the owner of Hotel Ora, Agim Caushi, dropped off a copy of the day's issue of the local paper, *Gazeta Express*, for me. It had a picture of pre- and post-World War One leader Nikola Pasic, communist leader Josip Broz Tito, and Slobodan Milosevic. The words simply said, "FUCK YU." It was over. The Kosovo Assembly gathered in the afternoon, and Prime Minister Thaci and President Fatmir Sejdiu collectively proclaimed Kosovo's independence and their willingness to adhere to the Ahtisaari Plan, which essentially was set to become Kosovo's constitution. The speeches were not impressive – somehow, it was obvious the people in power were not up to the task – almost as though they feared that independence might not be good for business. More could have been said to embrace the minorities, especially the Serbs, but at least they did not antagonize them. Given they had been preparing for this moment for so long, the absence of vision was depressing. Ordinary people, fed on the diet that independence solved all problems, hoped it would. When they awakened on 18 February, there was still no regular electricity or water.

The street party started. The VIPs had a private concert at which Beethoven's *Ode to Joy* was played. Despite the potential for violence, the whole thing came off beautifully in the Albanian areas. Serb areas were different. Violence occurred in northern Kosovo and in Belgrade, too, where looters went on a rampage and also attacked Western embassies and shops. On the day after, Kosovo still had the same problems: limited water and electricity, no industry, dependent on imports and remittances of roughly 15 per cent of GDP, and governed by a fairly mediocre and often criminal elite. A new international mission of the EU was getting ready to deploy. Supervised independence began. The Serbs stuck with the slogan that "Kosovo is Serbia." Kosovo did get a new and generic flag that nobody liked and a wordless national anthem. The flag and the anthem avoided any Albanian or Serb symbols. The flag included a map of Kosovo in yellow with six stars in white, denoting the different communities living there, against a blue background. One friend noted the map on the flag was a bad omen. Among European states, only divided Cyprus had a map on its flag. EULEX arrived, but UNMIK stayed – and so did UNSCR 1244.

## Conclusion

Kosovo's path to independence was not the bloodiest in the Balkans – Bosnia's was. Events between 1998 and 1999 in Kosovo cost almost 11,000 lives, with almost 1,700 people still missing. Moreover, Kosovo's path to independence was certainly the longest, as it had declared independence in 1991. Rugova's relentless pursuit of passive resistance and the solidarity of the parallel society should be lauded. But passive resistance yielded nothing, and the KLA took over. In the end, Kosovo did get lucky – for the first time in the twentieth century, just as the century ended – when NATO decided to intervene in 1999 to prevent a humanitarian catastrophe. NATO effectively became the KLA's air force. While Kosovo certainly should have been granted a kind of independence then, the international situation did not warrant such a bold and even visionary step. Albania's breakdown in 1997 helped to arm the KLA but did serious harm to the Albanian cause, in that nobody trusted Albanians to build a democracy. As the Republic of Albania was hardly a success story, why create another Albanian state? Milosevic's ouster in the fall of 2000 and the arrival of the darling of the West, Zoran Djindjic, as Serbia's new leader, did not help the Kosovo independence cause, as we shall see in the epilogue.

The legacy of UNMIK is mixed. Given the amount of money spent and the numbers of experts sent, it must be judged a failure. Just like the politicians in the region, UNMIK staff stayed too long, got paid too much, and got too cozy. UNMIK did serve as a bridge between the chaos of the late 1990s and the basis for self-government. Less talked about is the legacy of a sort of cosmopolitanism, given how international the staff of the mission was. Kosovo is quite tolerant, and had the refugees streaming through the Balkans in 2015 gone through Kosovo, it is doubtful they would have been harassed or chased away, as they were in Bulgaria and Macedonia. UNMIK taught the locals some bad habits, especially in terms of accountability, as UNMIK was extremely opaque. The near-total absence of accountability still permeates Kosovo life today. Unquestionably, UNMIK was less intrusive than the OHR in Bosnia, but that meant that it ignored things that should have not been ignored. The events of March 2004 hastened status talks but also, like 1997, cast a shadow on Kosovo's image, which came back to haunt the Kosovo Albanians during the negotiations for the Ahtisaari Plan. Coupled with the events of 1997 in Albania, it was clear that the Albanians could not entirely be trusted. As we shall see in a subsequent chapter, supervised independence morphed into compromised independence, as

Kosovo's sovereignty became more and more diminished and the elite really proved they were not up to the job.

The Ahtisaari Plan, which focused on the Serb issue, was flawed, but there was not much else on the table. Even before the plan was tabled, the Albanians had more or less already offered the same thing for the minorities, anyway, because they understood that they had to convince outsiders that they could provide an inclusive environment. It was not certain, though, that the plan was capable of fulfilling its main goal: a viable and stable Kosovo. Ahtisaari also hoped that the plan would bring a degree of prosperity. However, the level of decentralization and ongoing difficulties with Serbs in Kosovo and Serbia proper weakened Kosovo's ability to function as a normal state. The EU negotiators were filled with hubris in 2007 and believed the myth that post-nationalism was on the horizon and a new era of post-modern states was upon us. Thus they forced on Kosovo a post-modern state, when Kosovo had never been either a pre-modern or modern state.

Serbia was hardly post-modern or post-national either and obviously rejected both the plan and Kosovo's independence. It took the independence declaration to the International Court of Justice (ICJ) in October 2008 and more or less lost with the ICJ decision of 2010. But that did not change much. The majority of world states recognized Kosovo's independence, although in October 2017 Suriname rescinded its recognition. The Serb foreign minister, Ivica Dacic, declared a victory. The Kosovo Foreign Ministry said international law prevented Suriname from changing its mind. Global recognitions aside, supervised independence morphed into compromised independence. As we shall see in the epilogue, Kosovo remained a flawed and almost failed state. This impacted the ongoing talks with Serbia, especially as the EU continued to prioritize the Serb community's interests in Kosovo. The normalization of relations between Kosovo and Serbia, a priority if either was to join the EU, witnessed even more concessions from the Kosovo side in terms of the Serb community for the sake of European integration.

# 5

## Contested Heroes: Alexander the Great, Mother Teresa, and the Republic of Macedonia

Macedonia, at one point in its transition, was the regional success story. However, events in the past five years suggest that Macedonia is potentially the weakest state in the region, ripe for meddling from Russia and Turkey. As noted in chapter 2, Macedonia and Bosnia have some common features. Both republics would have been better served within a new and reformed Yugoslavia. As in Bosnia, the move in Macedonia towards a multiparty system witnessed the usual change from communists to socialists, the emergence of nationalists embodied primarily in the Internal Macedonian Revolutionary Organization– Democratic Party of Macedonian National Unity (VMRO-DPMNE), and the politicization of the ethnic Albanians there. Claiming the mantle of the 1903 Ilinden Uprising and the brief Krushevo Republic, VMRO-DPMNE was an early proponent of an independent Macedonia. The new president, Kiro Gligorov, a stalwart member of the old communist elite, would not fall for the often vulgar nationalism of the VMRO-DPMNE and would do his best to moderate things during his eight years in the presidency.

Faced with few alternatives, Macedonia held an independence referendum in September 1991, which was overwhelmingly supported by the ethnic Macedonians (95 per cent voted "yes") but boycotted by the Albanians, who expected more rights and an outright acknowledgment of their numbers. They hoped that given the legacy of oppression that had been aimed largely at them during the communist years, they could emerge somehow as equal partners in the new state, instead of being merely an ignored minority. Indeed, the fate of the Albanians in Macedonia is an under-reported story, as they suffered far more systematic denial of their basic rights than did Albanians in Kosovo, which had been transformed in the late 1960s and early 1970s, as already noted. No such dramatic advancement of rights ever came to the Albanians of Macedonia. Not surprisingly, the Albanian elite of Macedonia largely received the only "Albanian" education they could at the University of Prishtina during the heady days of activism there in the 1980s. Macedonia declared its independence in November 1991. The Macedonians, not surprisingly, feared the Albanians to a degree, given the overall problems with all their neighbors. Macedonia's official history, both before and after independence, hardly even mentioned the Albanians, and when it did, they were most characterized as inherently a threat to Macedonia and Macedonians. Plus, while the Albanians were 25 per cent of Macedonia's population, given their additional numbers in Albania, Kosovo, and Montenegro, their total numbers far outstripped the Macedonians. Fortunately, war was avoided for the decade that followed independence, but the regional conundrum would challenge Macedonia's survival in other ways.

The Macedonian story needs to be understood with attention to two interrelated factors. The first is the very name *Macedonia*, which is a seemingly endless source of struggle with neighboring Greece. The other is the Albanian factor, which eventually brought the country to a brief civil war in 2001. I say interrelated, because the Macedonian struggle for identity pushed the Albanians to violence, since Macedonia was a nationalizing state – although not quite at the same level as what went on in Tudjman's Croatia or Serbia under Milosevic. Rather, it is a state that prioritizes Macedonian interests and marginalizes the Albanians. Given the chronology, it makes the most sense to begin with the name issue, keeping in mind that the struggle for a solution to the problem is now more than twenty-five years old.

Given the permanently contested nature of Macedonian identity and the – to a degree – less-than-friendly attitudes of Greece, Bulgaria, and Serbia, the very name of the state created controversy from the start. The Bulgarians were happy to recognize the state of Macedonia; indeed, they were the first country to recognize it, but did not recognize a separate Macedonian nation or language. In 1993 even the *New York Times* wrote that two-thirds of Macedonians are of Bulgarian origin. The Macedonians, claiming the right to call their state whatever they wanted, became the Republic of Macedonia. The government chose the sixteen-pointed Vergina Sun as the new flag, which until then was not a symbol known to Macedonians at all. For Athens (and according to Greek popular opinion in general), the new state crossed a number of red lines. Macedonia, it argued, was a geographic, not an ethnic, description, and usurping the name *Macedonia* was explicitly a claim on Greek territory. In 1992, a million people demonstrated in Thessaloniki, the capital of Greek Macedonia, demanding the government take a hard line.

The Vergina Sun, for Greeks, was simply cultural appropriation, as while it was a symbol of Macedonia, it was a symbol for Greek Macedonia, not for a Slavic-speaking population that arrived in the area between the sixth and seventh century CE according to Greek historians. Even President Gligorov noted too that the flag was never used and he warned about linking contemporary Macedonians to Alexander the Great and other arguably Greek figures. Greek archeologists had discovered the star in the town of Vergina in northern Greek Macedonia in 1977, and it subsequently became a powerful symbol of Greek continuity with the ancient Macedonians. The Macedonians loved the new flag, but it was certainly a provocation that could have been avoided. Albanian parliamentarians boycotted the session when the flag was adopted. They found nothing in the flag to connect to and considered it a nationalist symbol associated with the VMRO-DPMNE. Besides, they had their own flag, the same one as in Albania – Skanderbeg's black two-headed eagle on a red background. In any case, Albanians were not permitted to fly the flag on public buildings, even in towns or cities where they were the overwhelming majority. While the flag controversy emphasizes the impact on relations with Greece, given that the Albanians were nearly 25 per cent of the population, the fact that the brand-new state chose to provoke the Albanians is telling. Taking advantage of the then weakness of the Albanians was one of countless blunders made by Macedonia's new leaders.

The Greek position was unwavering and could have been construed as bullying but must be seen in a wider regional context. Greek foreign policy in the 1990s did serious harm to Balkan regional cooperation and the general spirit of the neighborhood. For reasons that are still not entirely clear, Greece was the only EU country in the region that opted for a policy that ultimately supported Milosevic. In addition to beating up on new, weak, and poor Macedonia, the policy towards Albania was just as mean spirited, beating the nationalist drum of Greek territorial claims on southern Albania. Despite the UN admitting Macedonia in 1993 as the Former Yugoslav Republic of Macedonia (FYROM), Greece maintained unrelenting pressure on Macedonia. Multiple mediation efforts also failed to find a compromise name that included *Republic of Macedonia – Skopje*, *New Macedonia*, and *Nova Makedonija* in Slavic. They also tried *Slavomacedonia*, but the Albanians, since they were not Slavs, said no to that. Greece even refused a compound name and ultimately imposed an illegal embargo in February 1994 that blocked Macedonian access to the port of Thessaloniki. The Greek embargo was added to the already existing embargo on Yugoslavia, which had already taken a huge toll on a fragile economy. Macedonia was thus blocked in every direction. The much-heralded talk of reviving the Via Egnatia through Macedonia and out to the Albanian port of Durres was just empty talk. Nobody was building any roads in Albania, and in the five years of Democratic Party rule in Albania (1992–7), the party had added barely twenty kilometers to a nonexistent highway infrastructure. With the two embargoes, black market activity took over, unemployment went through the roof, and the Macedonians entered a prolonged existential crisis. Greek diplomatic and economic pressure was unrelenting.

The embargo ended in 1995 when Greece and Macedonia came to an agreement called the Interim Accord. The fine points of the accord are important. Greece agreed to recognize FYROM, and Macedonia got a new flag: out with the Vergina Sun, and in came what looked like a ceiling fan to some. There was still a sun in the middle, with seven yellow beams of light this time. On the technical side, Macedonia agreed to respect existing borders, made changes to the constitution, and both sides committed to avoiding hostile propaganda against each other. Finally, Greece agreed not to block

Macedonia from joining regional, multilateral, or international institutions. In essence, Greece was not permitted to block Macedonia's membership in either the EU or NATO as long as it did not use the name *Republic of Macedonia*.

In the years between the accord and 2001, relations with Greece improved greatly. Greece became a major investor in Macedonia, but it was always clear that the future of Macedonia depended entirely on the resolution of the name dispute. However, the name issue became secondary when the Albanians, taking a page (and the weapons) from Kosovo, formed the National Liberation Army (NLA), led largely by Ali Ahmeti, who had been part of the command structure of the KLA. The NLA sought to get results by force. In February 2001, so began another war in the Balkans. Ahmeti maintained that the types of constitutional changes the Albanians sought could be achieved only by war. Mercifully, owing to quick international intervention from both the EU and the United States, casualties were limited to two hundred, but thousands were displaced in what were by then routine ethnic-cleansing campaigns. Macedonia narrowly avoided a major civil war that would have split the country permanently and possibly caused a wider Balkan war. The war witnessed some surprising early victories by the Albanians and a miserable performance by the security forces. At one point, the rebels took a village that put them in a position to attack the capital, Skopje. For Macedonians, proud that they had avoided conflict until then, the Albanians' decision to take up arms was to many a total betrayal. Added to the name issue, it merely intensified their existential crisis. The best gateway to understanding the conflict between the Albanians and Macedonians is to watch Milcho Manchevski's *Before the Rain* (1994). Released seven years before war started, Manchevski depicts a spiral into violence among people trapped in an imagined past where revenge is in the air. Purposely overemphasizing the primitive and separate Macedonian and Albanian village life, with their tattered flags, traditional clothes, and battered homes, the two peoples are clichés. Brilliantly structured in three interconnected tales (two set in Macedonia and one in London) that amount to a circle, Manchevski's film captures how easy it is for two peoples to start killing.

The origins in the conflict to a degree relied on the availability of leadership, logistics, weapons, and uniforms from Kosovo. However, this is not to say there were not real grievances on the Albanian side. Although they had participated in a series of coalition governments since independence in 1991, the Macedonians prioritized their own problems, and change was coming far too slowly to the Albanians. They were particularly put off by their low representation in the public service and higher education. They wanted their own university, teaching in Albanian. The one they opened in 1994, in the quasi-capital of Albanians in Tetovo in western Macedonia, was declared illegal. They also wanted to fly their flag, but the Albanian flag, for reasons that should be obvious, inspired fear and dread in the Macedonians. But many Albanians were not disappointed only with Macedonian leaders. Some had anger towards their own leaders, too, who were simply bought off by the Macedonians. In any event, Albanians remained an underrepresented minority lacking some of the most basic of rights. For many Macedonians, the Albanian fight was not about more rights but rather merely a pretext for eventual secession from Macedonia and then unification with Albania.

The EU and the United States reacted with alacrity this time and showed none of the ineptitude that had characterized the early reactions to events in Bosnia or Kosovo. Negotiations were led by former French minister Francois Leotard and former US ambassador James Pardew. Meeting in the picturesque lakeside town of Ohrid, with its 365 churches and rare trout from the lake with Albania on the other side, the EU and the United States forced a deal on the Macedonian leadership that gave the Albanians almost everything they wanted. This led to the widespread belief that in the talks the EU and the United States favored the Albanians. The Ohrid Framework Agreement (OFA), like Dayton, was a top-down peace process made by EU and US negotiators – there was very little input from local actors. While the rebel NLA was not represented in the talks, the two mainstream Albanian parties (the Democratic Party of the Albanians and the Party for Democratic Prosperity) along with the two largest ethnic Macedonian parties (VMRO-DPMNE and the Social Democrats) were present. The OFA is often proclaimed as the

best of all Balkan peace plans for promoting interethnic reconciliation and laying a path for stability. That is true, but the bar is very
low. For ordinary Macedonians, it simply rewarded violence. The
main provisions of the agreement included a 3,500-troop NATO
peacekeeping force to disarm rebels and an entirely new stage of
constitutional and legislative developments. The NLA was declared
dissolved in September 2001. Its leader, Ali Ahmeti, would go on to
form a political party (the Democratic Union for Integration) and
become a mainstream Albanian politician, even though most Macedonians would have liked to have seen him in jail. The amnesty for
him and other rebels never sat well with the majority Macedonians.

Unlike Bosnia, Macedonia was maintained as a unitary state.
Even though the Albanians lived in compact communities in the
country's west and in a largely separate part of Skopje on the other
side of the Vardar River, the federal option was ruled out, despite
Albanians pushing hard for it. What the Macedonians got was mul-
tilayered sovereignty and massive decentralization. As in Dayton
(and later Ahtisaari), the goal was to get government as close to the
people as possible and put the same ethnic groups together, but the
OFA did not go so far as to offer autonomy, thus ruling out territorial solutions to ethnic problems, which had become the preferred
mantra of international mediators. What the slogan meant is that
you can get massive decentralization and enclaves but no border
changes. Much to the chagrin of the Macedonians, there was a redrawing of some local boundaries to better meet the Albanian minority's needs. Macedonia shifted from a highly centralized state to
the exact opposite. Ethnic Macedonians feared this soft federaliza-
tion as a stepping stone to partition, and some compared it to the
treaty after the Second Balkan War in 1913 that partitioned Macedonia among Bulgaria, Greece, and Serbia. A cornerstone was a reduc-
tion in the number of municipalities, the redrawing of municipal
boundaries, and de-centralization along the lines of what later happened in Kosovo. The difference was that the Serbs there received
autonomy, and the government in Belgrade was allowed to retain
decisive influence on the Serbs of Kosovo.

But there were other, more fundamental changes. The preamble
of the constitution was changed to reflect a far more civic identity so

that the Albanians, and others, were better recognized. In the first constitution of 1991, the Albanians had appeared at the end of the preamble, after a list of key Macedonian identity markers. In the 2001 amendment, the Albanians were moved to the first sentence of the preamble, which referred more generally to the citizens of the Republic of Macedonia. There were some of the Macedonian identity markers but these were moved further down in the text. Another amendment permitted the use of national symbols on public buildings and other forms of cultural promotion.

The Albanians took advantage of this, but so did the Macedonians. While the black double-headed eagle from the Skanderbeg family (also the flag of all Albanians) was everywhere, the Macedonians, foreshadowing an even greater nation-building campaign that would come later, started building huge crosses everywhere as part of a government campaign to strengthen the Orthodox Christian identity. This included a sixty-six-meter cross built in 2002 on Mount Vodno that is visible from everywhere in the city (it is illuminated at night), overlooking multiethnic Skopje. Built by the nationalist VMRO-DPMNE, it was officially designated as the millennium cross and meant to celebrate two thousand years of Christianity, but its political implication was just as clear to the Muslims. Reminiscent of the Saudi-built mosques in Albania, crosses appeared out of nowhere, often at the entrance to Albanian villages, as a reminder to anyone who cared to look.

A key feature of the OFA is that it never mentions the Albanians by name but instead speaks exclusively to a community that has at least 20 per cent of the population calculated at municipal levels. Only the Albanians have those numbers. What this means is that the vast provisions provided by the OFA at the state and municipal levels come into force only at 20 per cent. If the Albanians drop below 20 per cent at the municipal level, they do not receive the provisions of the OFA. Should another community, say the Roma for example, reach the 20 per cent threshold, they get the same deal. Macedonian remained the only language that enjoyed official status throughout the entire country and was the language of Macedonia in its foreign relations However, in the amended constitution, the language of the 20 per cent or more also became official and could be used at the municipal and national level. Plus, the OFA gave the Albanians veto rights over legislation that might impact language rights, culture, or education, among other things. As we shall see in the epilogue, the language issue was far from closed, as the Albanians would start pushing for full linguistic equality in 2016 and 2017, equality in symbols, and consideration as state-founding peoples in a new constitution.

The big difference between the OFA and the later Ahtisaari Plan was that the Albanians would get power based on their numbers. There was no asymmetry between the Macedonians and the Albanians. In what amounted to a kind of affirmative action, the Albanians would get the representation their numbers warranted in the public sector, especially in the police, where the Albanians were horribly under represented. A cornerstone of the OFA was a reduced number of municipalities, the subsequent redrawing of these municipalities, and substantial decentralization. By November, all the amendments were passed in the assembly, and Macedonia started a new life as a civic state on paper but with the nagging name issue still on the front burner. The OFA did fix some things: Albanians (and Macedonians too) got more power at the local level, the Albanians got jobs in the public sector, and they could speak their language and use their symbols. Finally, there was a requirement to provide university education in Albanian, and the Tetovo University, long a flashpoint in relations, achieved official recognition.

Among ethnic Macedonians, there was huge disappointment with the deal, which to them was nothing more than caving in to terrorists. Moreover, they considered it another blow to their already fragile identity. Greece denied them their name, and now the Albanians had taken a swipe at their identity too. Moreover, the OFA did not, in the long run, create the conditions for better relations, as both communities limited their interaction. Skopje in particular, was deeply divided. On the bright side, Macedonia survived, and the OFA was visionary in terms of providing the basis for peace and sustainable multiethnicity, as long as both sides embraced it. The Albanians have consistently evaluated the OFA in favorable terms. They could point to all kinds of improvements, especially the increase in jobs in the public sector, and their political parties took part in various coalitions with Macedonian parties. Like Bosnia, parties and politics remained ethnic, and few were able to capture the votes of both communities. The name issue lingered, but ahead in 2004 was a controversial referendum on the OFA-imposed municipal boundary changes, which some argued would have created the basis for future partition. If successful, the referendum could derail the peace entirely. However, the day after George W. Bush won a second term in the United States, the United States recognized Macedonia as the Republic of Macedonia. Greece was furious, but the Macedonians could feel just a little less pressure now that the United States acknowledged the constitutional name. (Canada would do the same in 2007.) Given the jubilation in Macedonia, the referendum failed for a simple reason: US recognition meant that the perceived potential fluidity of borders was over, for now. The existential crisis had abated. Plus, given the euphoria and partying, few people bothered to go out to vote the next day. Another reward came in 2005, when the EU declared that Macedonia was a candidate for membership – the first Western Balkan state to receive that distinction. Greece, however, continued to block the beginning of accession talks. But NATO membership was the real prize. It was vital for securing borders that were seen by many as potentially changeable and it was where the Macedonian leadership focused their efforts. They had a green light from Washington too.

Between 2006 and 2017, events inside and out of Macedonia shifted the country towards authoritarianism, which also worsened relations with the Albanians. The period is mostly associated with three interrelated things. First, was the rise of Nikola Gruevski, the leader of VMRO-DPMNE and prime minister between 2006 and 2016. Second, NATO membership failed to materialize; and third, Gruevski implemented a massive and exclusive nation-building campaign that was designed to offset problems with Greece, and the Albanians too, while empowering the Macedonians.

Only thirty-six years old when he became prime minister, Gruevski was originally heralded by outside observers as just the type of young reformer the country and the region needed. As a former finance minister, he had already earned a reputation as a capable technocrat. Either he was a born autocrat or events just got the better of him, because he took Macedonia down a dangerous road. (He would later resign in disgrace in January 2016.)

The NATO enlargement process in Central Europe and the Balkans had been largely a success story. NATO's relatively low standards for democratization made the process relatively easy. In the Balkans, only Serbia, given the legacy of NATO bombing in 1999, wanted to stay out. Bosnia could not join either, given local disagreements among Bosniaks, Croats, and Serbs. For the rest, NATO's success was that it was perceived by prospective members as providing security for them by guaranteeing borders. For NATO's founding members, by embedding potentially hostile neighbors in a multilateral organization, it could prevent a regional war. It eliminated the chance of a repeat of the interwar scenario, in which disputed borders and regional antagonisms prevailed and led to war and fragmentation. For Macedonia, NATO was essential to its foreign policy goals, and it was prepared to enter the organization, along with Albania and Croatia, at the April 2008 Bucharest Summit as FYROM.

However, certain unexpected things happened that kept Macedonia out of the alliance. The name issue was there still. In 2005 some other resolutions were tried, including a dual-use formula whereby Macedonia would use one name internally and another externally. That failed. In 2006 as well, Macedonia certainly provoked Greece when it named the tiny and dilapidated airport in Skopje Alexander the Great International Airport. Greece, considering Alexander the Great as an essential part of its cultural heritage, was more than annoyed by the Macedonian attempt to link Macedonians directly to Alexander the Great. Plus, Macedonia named the highway leading to the airport Alexander the Great Motorway. Any objective observer would agree that the airport naming was a provocation. This was a relatively new identity formulation for the Macedonians, and it signaled that the VMRO-DPMNE government was charting a new and destabilizing path. Skopje, Athens claimed, was violating the 1995 Interim Accord, which prohibited hostile activities or propaganda and the use of Greece's historic patrimony.

At the same time, the Greek position shifted a bit, and in 2007 Athens seemed open to accepting a compound name. For the first time, Greece was willing to allow the term *Macedonia* to be used.

The options included Constitutional Republic of Macedonia, Democratic Republic of Macedonia, Independent Republic of Macedonia, New Republic of Macedonia, and Republic of Upper Macedonia. Later, the Republic of Macedonia-Skopje was floated. Skopje said yes; Athens said no. The name was one thing, but what would the language be called? Everyone knew the term *Macedonian* would inevitably prevail. Greece did not really see a way out. Besides any deal signed, even if it included constitutional changes, could just as easily be reversed down the road.

In Bucharest, things did not go according to plan. Even though President Bush stated explicitly that three countries would enter NATO, only two, Albania and Croatia, did. The United States could not overcome Greek opposition and never really tried that hard, which is surprising. Unanimity among NATO was required, and Greece had some allies too. Yes, an effort to persuade the Greeks was made but it was a timid and half-hearted one. Given the primary role of the United States in NATO, the failure to win over Greece was totally preposterous. But clearly the United States did not care that much. Macedonia later took Greece to the International Court of Justice (ICJ). It ruled that Greece, by blocking Macedonia's entry into NATO, had violated the 1995 Interim Accord. The ICJ decision gave a moral victory to Macedonia but the ruling was hardly enforceable. Greece never bothered to take Macedonia to the ICJ when it started naming things after Alexander the Great.

Macedonia, thrown back into a deep existential crisis, was devastated and went almost into national mourning. The whiff of partition was back in the air, as maybe borders were not as inviolable as people thought. After all, the Albanian national identity was not contested, and Macedonia was being held back in terms of NATO and EU membership based on an issue that was wholly peripheral to them. Sensing new opportunities, Gruevski called for fresh elections, two years ahead of schedule. Gruevski's VMRO-DPMNE and its partners won easily, and the country embarked on a controversial national reawakening campaign and an inexorable drift towards authoritarianism and absurdity.

The final part of the story speaks to the period of "antiquization" and the "Skopje 2014" building project. Rejected by NATO, unable to begin accession talks with the EU and economically weak, VMRO-DPMNE turned the state bureaucracy into a growing preserve for political supporters by hiring like mad against the wishes of international creditors. There was already a long tradition in the Balkans that when a party lost power, the entire public sector, top to bottom, was purged. The only way to stay in power was to make everyone a state employee. Moreover, as Macedonia became increasingly statist, the state emerged as the country's biggest customer, which strengthened VMRO's control over media and civil society.

In some ways as an antidote to 2008, in 2009, Gruevski announced a major building project called "Skopje 2014." It amounted to a massive and extremely costly (and, some say, ghastly) transformation of the shabby and provincial capital. It foresaw a totally different city, with new statues, cultural institutions, and other buildings. Officially, at least, it was a rebranding exercise to show a different Macedonia to the outside world and give it a better international image entirely. Tons of cash was thrown as well at strange tourism- and investment-promotion ads on CNN that had a Monty Python feel and included some less-than-subtle jabs at Greece. For the locals, all this was supposed to improve their otherwise sour mood. It was, for sure, a completely mono-ethnic vision that said little to the Albanians or the other twenty-plus communities living in Macedonia.

Even Mother Teresa's legacy was disputed. She was born an ethnic Albanian in Skopje in 1908, in what was then the Ottoman Empire. Albanians and Macedonians, always looking for usable history and a real hero, claimed her as their own. Recall that the Catholic cathedral in downtown Prishtina is named after her, as is Tirana's international airport. Mother Teresa's relationship to Albania is worth explaining. She moved with her family to Albania after Macedonia became part of the post–World War One Kingdom of Serbs, Croats, and Slovenes. She left Albania in 1928, leaving most of her family there. Living in a country that waged war on religion, particularly Catholics, after the communists took over in 1944, Mother Teresa's family lived in obscurity and silence. In 2009, in what was simply a ludicrous move, then Albanian leader Sali Berisha asked India for the return of Mother Teresa's remains so she could be buried in Albania. The Indian government declined. In downtown Skopje, she has a statue and a memorial house devoted to her life and work. Only in 2017 would the Albanians develop a square in Skopje devoted to other, less contested national heroes.

The main features of Skopje 2014 are worth noting. Called kitschy, ugly, militaristic, and even totalitarian, it certainly had an unplanned nature. The centerpiece of the newly designed square was, not surprisingly, a giant twenty-two-meter statue of Alexander the Great and a smaller one of his father, Philip II of Macedon. Added to this were 130 additional statues, a triumphal arch, a new constitutional court, a national museum, and philharmonic. The statues facing the Albanian-dominated side of Skopje seemed to suggest the need to behave – or else. Only the Hungarians could out-statue the Macedonians. The costs, not surprisingly, were out of control, with most contracts going to friends and family of the governing party. Very little public consultation took place. The Albanians could only look on amazed, probably feeling things were eerily similar to pre-Ohrid days. Despite the obvious anti-Albanian undertones of the project, the Albanians were surprisingly quiet.

Skopje 2014 was inextricably linked to the VMRO-DPMNE-inspired "antiquization" campaign that also intensified in 2008. This was an entirely new national narrative. In essence, the campaign drew a direct link to the legacy of Alexander the Great or the ancient past. Some scholars at the Macedonian Academy of Sciences even claimed that the ancient Macedonian language was the same as contemporary Macedonian. Like the Albanian link to Illyrians, which is also tenuous, if you are ancient, you are there first. Lots of people bought into that but just as many still believed in the Slavic narrative which meant that not only were the Albanians excluded, many Macedonians were too.

## Conclusion

Gruevski and the VMRO-DPMNE governed until 2016. It was, by all accounts, a real party state, with serious shortcomings in what was a democracy only in name. Accused of corruption, wiretapping of opponents, and a crackdown on perceived enemies in civil society,

Gruevski and his crew refused to cede power, fearing their next stop was prison. The EU brokered a deal for new elections in 2016, which were highly contested, as VMRO-DPMNE won the most seats but the Social Democrats formed a coalition with the ethnic Albanian Union for Democratic Integration, which gave them a plurality of seats in the parliament. VMRO-DPMNE did everything possible to prevent the new government from taking office. Macedonians were scandalized when, in April 2017, they were treated to photos of incoming prime minister and Social Democratic Party leader Zoran Zaev bloodied by nationalist demonstrators, some of whom were masked, who stormed the parliament to prevent the approval of an ethnic Albanian as the new speaker.

As we shall see in the epilogue, the triumph of authoritarianism was not limited to Macedonia. As the prospect of EU membership diminished, which was the main driver of reform, local despots were empowered. They spoke the language of reform, which enamored them to Brussels and made opposing them difficult. But they governed as autocrats, and EU norms and values were applied by Balkan standards. Preferring stability over democracy, the once influential EU, along with an uninterested United States, watched the entire region fail. Already a generation has been lost to a never-ending transition.

Lauded as a success story in the Balkans in the 1990s, Macedonia ended up failing on a number of levels. First, in the years prior to 2001, the Albanian question was not dealt with effectively. The early nation-building efforts, despite Gligorov's moderating stance, did not provide the kind of solutions the Albanians deserved, and they ended up marginalized and bitter, which was made worse by Macedonia's poor economic performance. From the flag to the name controversy, the Albanians were perceived only as an afterthought. This is not to say that the Macedonians did nothing, only that they could have done more and faster. Macedonia was not Kosovo under Milosevic. Gligorov's successor as president, Boris Trajkovski, who died tragically in a plane crash in Bosnia in 2004, offered more concessions to the Albanians. However, the events in Kosovo in 1999 had changed things dramatically, and the Albanians were no longer weak, but Macedonian policy depended on keeping the Albanians weak or at least bought off. Unlike the Serbs, the Albanians did not have a powerful motherland that could defend their interests. The OFA proved to be visionary when compared with Dayton (1995) and the subsequent Ahtisaari Plan (2007). But the later nation-building campaigns, while somewhat justified given the fragility of Macedonian identity, did little to build trust in what was an increasingly divided and suspicious country.

# 6

## To Europe, for Some: Slovenia, Bulgaria, Romania, and Croatia

Between 1989 and 2018, four Balkan states entered the EU. Slovenia was the true post-Yugoslav success story, joining in 2004 along with nine other, mostly post-communist states (Cyprus, Czech Republic, Estonia, Hungary, Latvia, Lithuania, Malta, Poland, and Slovakia). As already noted, Slovenia, which unlike Croatia or Serbia, had no history of independence, simply left the Balkans and joined Central Europe. As we shall see, Slovenia's relative success, when compared with other former Yugoslav republics, was based on a number of built-in advantages, plus the absence of a war. Bulgaria and Romania also expected to join in 2004 but were held back until 2007 for reasons related to serious rule-of-law issues, largely linked to the judiciary and corruption. When they did enter, they were subject to a kind of second-tier membership. Goodwill from the EU – and pressure from the United States too – allowed them to enter with lots of problems still unsolved. Croatia, essentially a nationalistic authoritarian state until 1999, joined in 2013 and also left the Balkans. A plaque outside the University of Zagreb once said, "The first university in the Balkans." The plaque says something different now, along the lines of "The first university in these parts." Like Serbia, the Croats lost an entire decade in a nationalist frenzy before a new government gave people what they wanted: a European future.

With no previous experience with independent statehood and no dangerous national myths, Slovenia was better prepared for the future than any other Yugoslav republic, and a certain pragmatism prevailed. It was eager to reorganize the federation to lessen the financial burden imposed on it. In 1989, even before the breakup of Yugoslavia, the government already had a program in place called "Europe 1992." As we saw, Slovenia had a brief war that ended with the quick withdrawal of the Yugoslav National Army, a more or less peaceful path to an independence declaration in 1991, and quick integration into the wider international community. There was no Tito nostalgia either, as he quickly vanished from street signs and towns. In addition, the Slovenes were not burdened by the past, unlike the Croats or the Serbs. They could adapt better to the new circumstances and situated their past as having been part of the "cultivated" Roman world – when Ljubljana was known as Emona – and, later, the Habsburg Empire. Their national museums are decidedly detached and sanitized, as though they have no baggage, and even the material devoted to independence is decidedly staid. As the most west European of the former Yugoslavia and the most economically advanced of all accession countries, Slovenia simply attached itself to the central European states and quickly reoriented its exports west once the Yugoslav market collapsed with the start of the wars. Indeed, given its small and homogenous population, Slovenia had already carved out a nice niche as an exporting country, sending out more goods per capita than Greece, Portugal, or Spain. GDP per capita was about 70 per cent of the EU average. Unlike other countries, it opted for a gradualist economic transformation and eschewed the shock therapy/neoliberalism of Poland. The state remained a key player in the economy. Neoliberalism would come, but only after the 2008 financial crisis.

Already in 1993, Slovenia's leaders were setting out a defined economic and political agenda that would create a modern and democratic country that would, unlike its neighbors to the south, be firmly based on a sophisticated understanding of what a rule-of-law state was. In 1996, Slovenia signed a Europe agreement that came into force in 1999. As early as 1997, the European Commission noted that Slovenia had become a stable democracy, and Slovenia was invited to start negotiations. There was also huge internal consensus, indicated by enthusiasm for EU membership: all the major political parties were committed to Europe, and a referendum was held on EU membership in 2003, with 86 per cent voting in favor. For Slovenians, there was simply no policy alternative to EU membership for reasons of security and economic necessity. With membership in 2004, Slovenia joined the Schengen border-free zone in 2007, thus eliminating the formal border with Austria, Hungary, and Italy, leaving only an external border with Croatia. In 2007, Slovenia was the first country in the 2004 round of enlargement to enter the Eurozone.

In addition to these attributes, Slovenia's political-party system was the opposite of what had happened elsewhere in the Balkans. Alongside a general consensus on the country's future direction and a compelling anti-model found in the events that took place in all other former Yugoslav republics, Slovene nationalism was muted to a degree. As well, there were no extreme left or right parties at the outset, with the exception of the nationalist-minded Slovenian National Party. The biggest challenge to the otherwise ideal picture of Slovenia was the fate of the so-called "erased" people, the impact of government-imposed austerity after a near collapse of the economy, and the usual high-level corruption scandal. All of this proved that Slovenia was not such a model after all.

As to the "erased" people, Slovenia took a relatively hard line against people who had lived in Slovenia as part of the old Yugoslavia but who were not Slovenes. These included Albanians, Bosniaks, Croats, Montenegrins, Macedonians, Roma, and Serbs. However, Slovenia practiced a very liberal policy towards the Hungarian and Italian minorities. The initial legislation on citizenship looked liberal, but the criteria made it very hard for people to qualify. The former Yugoslav groups were essentially declared noncitizens, and their names were "erased" from the national registry, leaving them essentially stateless. People found out what had happened the hard way, as the entire process lacked transparency: they would show up to a doctor only to find they had no health insurance anymore and would find themselves with no ability to renew their driver's licenses. According to official sources, some eighteen thousand people lost all their rights in Slovenia. Other observers suggest a much higher figure. In a 2004 nonbinding referendum, 96 per cent voted against restoring rights to these people. For most Slovenes, these people had been on the wrong side of the fence when independence came. More likely, though, the notoriously frugal nation did not want to pay compensation. Slovenia's Constitutional Court more or less overturned the erasure, but nothing systematic was done to right what was a form of ethnic cleansing undertaken by the Slovene government. The European Court of Human Rights ruled in favor of the "erased" too. There were also admonishments from the EU and the Council of Europe, which did little to change things. Compensation, ordered by the courts, was hard to get.

The period between 2012 and 2013 proved to be contentious in Slovenia and elsewhere, as the bite of austerity after the 2008 financial crisis angered citizens and threw traditionally stable Slovenia into a series of crises. The government of Prime Minister Janez Jansa, of the center-right Slovenian Democratic Party, was forced to cope with the near collapse of Slovenia's banking sector, a possible international bailout, and widespread public protests demanding the country's ruling elite step aside for allegedly plundering the country like they did everywhere else in the Balkans. In addition, four members of parliament were deemed to have falsified their educational credentials. The protests really started in Maribor, Slovenia's second largest city, near the border with Austria. Citizens there accused their mayor of blatant corruption, mostly over €5 million of public money spent on radar cameras, with the proceeds of fines going to a private company. More than ten thousand people hit the streets, and the mayor eventually resigned.

What started in less-affluent Maribor spread to the capital, Ljubljana, where thousands were also out demanding the government step down. Under the banner of the "All Slovenian Popular Uprising" and with the slogan "They are finished," Slovenia got its own version of populism. The police used water cannon to disperse protestors. Jansa and the leader of the main opposition party were both charged with corruption in early 2013. Jansa's government collapsed in February 2013, and in June 2013 he was sentenced to two years in prison for accepting a €2 million bribe in return for a lucrative military supply contract. (He was later freed from prison owing to flaws in the prosecution's case.) In addition, Slovenia was headed down the same path as Cyprus with the imminent collapse of its largely state-owned banking sector due to a multitude of bad loans totaling almost a fifth of the country's GDP. Outside observers called on Slovenia to sell the state banks and allow smaller private banks to fail. Others noted that Slovenia was paying the price for the gradualist approach it had taken to economic restructuring since 1991. Ordinary citizens simply said enough was enough, and Slovenia no longer seemed to be the Balkan exception. It was clear that alpine, homogenous, and calm Slovenia had a political class that made immense illegal financial gains with no accountability.

But Slovenia was squeaky clean when compared to Bulgaria and Romania. These two states, although coming from somewhat different communist systems, followed similar and uneven paths towards Europe. Zhivkov's Bulgaria, the most devoted of Soviet satellites, was broke. The Romania of Ceausescu was solvent due to harsh austerity but otherwise humiliated and destroyed at every level imaginable. Both countries were environmental disasters too. Bulgarians and Romanians thought EU and NATO membership was a quick fix for everything, including bad geography, in that they could become part of the West, leave the East behind, and dwell in an altogether better neighborhood without actually moving. As we saw in chapter 2, the 1989 moment in the Balkans was compromised by the tenacity of the former ruling parties, supported by the security services. More important, as former communists controlled much of the state, they prevented any kind of assessment of the past, which would, in the end, do enormous harm to the transition process by eroding confidence in institutions and essentially sanctioning criminality. The absence of a reckoning with the past kept the wrong people in power, made institutional legitimacy impossible, and denied justice to victims of the old regime.

From the very beginning, both failed to meet the EU's economic and political criteria embodied in the 1993 Copenhagen Criteria which, in a very ambiguous way, set out the minimum standards for EU membership. The conditions included 1) stability of institutions guaranteeing democracy, the rule of law, human rights, and respect for minorities; 2) the existence of a functioning market economy; 3) capacity to cope with competitive pressures and market forces within the union; and 4) the ability to take on the obligations of membership. Foreign investors mostly stayed away and put their money in Central Europe, especially Poland, where there was real rule of law. When Bulgaria and Romania did enter the EU in 2007, it was primarily because they were able to leverage some foreign policy aspects that rewarded them for keeping cool and supporting NATO during the war in Kosovo. Plus, in 2007, it made some sense to suggest to the rest of the Balkans, still far from modern states, that EU integration was possible and thus keep the European perspective alive in Belgrade, Podgorica, Prishtina, Sarajevo, Skopje, and Tirana.

As noted, in Bulgaria, the communists became Socialists, and second-tier party hacks proceeded to dominate the political scene on and off again until 1997. The main opposition, embodied in the center-right Union of Democratic Forces (UDF), confronted the former communists, who had resisted meaningful reform for seven years. Not only had they resisted economic reform, but they had also blocked every single attempt to engage in a fair and open assessment of the communist past, which meant that personal and personnel files held by the security services remained closed. The Socialists won the first elections in 1990 easily because they controlled the media and the opposition did not have enough time to organize. In the 1991 elections, the UDF won. Filip Dimitrov, far better suited to a life teaching philosophy in the safety of a university then to the rough and unforgiving world of Bulgarian politics, was prime minister. He lasted just over a year, and then the Socialists were back in power. The period of the 1990s for was Bulgaria one of incredible political instability – there were seven governments before 1997 – characterized by intense political polarization. The minority Turks, numbering around 9 per cent of the total population, set up their own political party, the Movement for Rights and Freedoms. Led by Ahmed Dogan, who like many Bulgarian politicians had had a previous life in the security services, led the party from 1990 until he resigned in 2013. He had a near monopoly on the Turkish vote, which he used to advance his own interests and sometimes the interests of the Turkish community. Early in the party's life, the mainstream parties tried to sabotage it, as the 1991 constitution established a unitary state that forbid any type of autonomy, prohibited "political parties on ethnic, racial or religious lines," and acknowledged no ethnic minorities. Despite multiple court challenges, the party has never been banned, because its membership is open to everyone – although everyone knows it is the Turkish party. The party sat comfortably in the transition period as near-perpetual kingmaker. As a political entrepreneur and an extraordinary survivor, Dogan later expanded his appeal to Bulgaria's Roma population, some 4 per cent of the population who were marginalized, demonized, and lacked the single political voice that the Turks had. Unlike the Bulgarians, the Turkish and Roma population grew quickly.

For Bulgaria, the period from 1990 to 1997 was almost a lost era. The GDP dropped by more than 20 per cent. A fiscal crisis in 1996 and 1997 almost bankrupted the country, depleted hard currency reserves, wiped out savings, and certainly ruined the banking system, as a third of banks went bankrupt and hyperinflation started. Plus, in October 1996, former Prime Minister Andrey Lukanov was assassinated in what looked like a gangland killing. In the fall of 1996, people feared a food and fuel crisis as winter approached. Inflation hit 2,000 per cent. Only a massive intervention with very strict conditions imposed by the IMF brought about a colossal restructuring, including a currency board that pegged Bulgaria's currency to the deutsche mark and later the Euro. It would be fair to say that Bulgarian socialism only really ended in 1997 and that the real transition started with the election of the UDF with an absolute majority. This marked the beginning of serious engagement with Euro-Atlantic integration, radical and much-needed economic reform, and a reassessment of Bulgaria's strong ties to Moscow. Accession talks with the EU opened in March 2000, but the Bulgarians were held back on visa-free travel until December 2000. Moreover, it was a painful move: to begin the talks, they were forced to close their main nuclear power plant for safety reasons. That plant had provided almost half of their electricity needs.

But after only four years of UDF government, Bulgaria's political landscape changed with the return of the former king, Simeon Saxe-Coburg-Gotha or Simeon II. Simeon made his first visit to Bulgaria in 1996 and he was generally well received. By 2001 both main parties – the Bulgarian Socialist Party (BSP) and the UDF – were discredited. The BSP had given Bulgarians the financial collapse of 1996–7, and the UDF had failed to jail the people who brought the crisis on or benefitted from it. Simeon, as Bulgaria's first populist, created the National Movement Simeon II just two months before the election. With a landslide victory in the June elections, Simeon was the only monarch to return to power in the Balkans. He promised a new type of politics, which was readily embraced by many Bulgarians. He promised a government that would bring in real experts, especially Bulgarians who had worked or been trained abroad. He ended the period of Bulgaria's two-party system, promised to raise living standards, and set a timetable to fix the country in eight hundred days with lower taxes, a higher standard of living, and reduced corruption. Pledging to uphold the constitution, he said he was not there to restore the monarchy. Unlike his royal counterpart in, say, Albania, Simeon was at least willing to work hard, and the legacy of the monarchy attracted some genuinely positive nostalgia. Simeon held power until 2005 – when his support dropped dramatically. In 2009 his party did not win a single seat. After the eight hundred days had passed, it was obvious that Bulgaria's problems could not be fixed by the "king" either. In the 2005 elections, the Socialists regained power in a coalition with Simeon's marginal party and the Movement for Rights and Freedoms. At the same time, the far-right (or far-left) ultra-nationalist party Attack appeared and won twenty-one seats, becoming the fourth largest party in parliament. Despite the weak coalition, the government's main gain was to preside over Bulgaria's accession to the EU, which the vast majority of citizens supported as the only guarantee of prosperity, further democratization, stability, and a European future.

Power in Romania may have forsaken the Ceausescu dynasty but it passed to mediocrities who had lived on the second tier of communist power. They turned their newfound power into tremendous economic advantage. Keep in mind that Romania had the highest level of communist-party membership in the region, and more than 10 per cent of the population had been informants for the security services. There were still hundreds of Ceausescu loyalists hanging about in government and in the dreaded security services who had never been touched. The National Salvation Front, which later became the Party of Social Democracy (PSD) led by Ion Iliescu, easily won the May 1990 elections, which left much of the old order intact. As we saw in chapter 2, Iliescu had the miners as his shock troops to keep the opposition in line and stave off reform. Romania, like Albania, had an extremely difficult road ahead due to the legacy of isolation and the near-total destruction of its economy. Moreover, Romania was unable to develop a consistent narrative around its revolution or deal with the communist past in a way that had meaning for a people who suffered so much. A systematic reckoning with the past, which was required if Romania was to establish a democracy, was simply put off.

Governments were not capable of understanding what they had to do for EU integration, at least not until 1996, yet Iliescu promised a return to Europe. In 1993, Romania signed a Europe agreement and declared its commitment to joining the EU. This was disingenuous on the regime's part, as the rules of the EU did not serve its interests. In 1995 it applied for membership, and by 1997 the EU was already making it clear that things were moving too slowly, especially in market reforms, for Romania to be taken seriously. Iliescu held off major market reforms under the guise of protecting ordinary people, which was largely a foil to allow the plunder of the state's assets. Iliescu also claimed that he avoided the Polish-style shock therapy by offering what he called a quiet solution. Romania also got the cold shoulder from NATO, which did not include it in the enlargement of 1999 when membership went to the Czech Republic, Hungary, and Poland. On the plus side, the EU, fearful of a repeat of the interwar chaos, facilitated some important bilateral agreements, particularly with Hungary, that put to rest fears of renewed trouble over the large Hungarian minorities living in Romania.

The year 1996 would prove decisive in some ways. The anticommunist Democratic Convention of Romania, a coalition of parties, won the election and put Emil Constantinescu, a former rector at the University of Bucharest, into the presidency. Unlike Iliescu, he sought "shock therapy" reforms, massive privatization, and a real war on corruption. But Constantinescu could not deliver, and it turned out that the Iliescu's defeat was only temporary. Down but not out, the miners who had defended Iliescu in 1990 and 1991 came back in 1999 to lay siege to Bucharest again in a protest against cuts to mining subsidies. This was a direct attack on Romania's fragile democracy. The coalition fragmented and collapsed, and Constantinescu did not even bother to seek a second term as president. But he did succeed to some degree on the foreign policy front. In 1999, at the Helsinki Summit, Romania was acknowledged as a potential full member of the EU. Along with Bulgaria, Constantinescu won plaudits for supporting the United States and the UK's hardline position on intervention in Kosovo, which ran counter to the otherwise good feelings the population had towards Serbs and Serbia. The result was more enthusiastic support for Romania's EU dreams, especially from the UK prime minister Tony Blair. It did not win any friends in Belgrade.

The survivor Iliescu was back for another term between 2000 and 2004, serving alongside Adrian Nastase of the PSD. It was Iliescu's third term as president, a remarkable achievement, but it is worth noting that he was genuinely popular in rural areas particularly. Romania's nonstop bad luck was on display in the 2000 presidential election, which provided the usual options: mafia or crazy people. Iliescu was there, but so was Corneliu Vadim Tudor, the leader of the Greater Romania Party. In the Ceausescu era Tudor was the court poet, writing some really shocking odes to the dictator and his wife, referring to the latter as a "scholar and political personage, and mother at the same time" and "*a role model of charm and wisdom.*" Immediately after the revolution, he offered his services to Iliescu. He morphed into the official spokesperson of hate: hate for Jews, Hungarians, and Roma. (It is remarkable that he lived in a society that allowed a person like him to have a second chance. He later died, in 2015.)

In 2002 the EU made it clear that Romania's (and Bulgaria's) accession would be delayed until 2007 or 2008. That was the bad news. The good news was that Romania joined NATO in 2004, further proof of NATO's absurdly low bar for membership. Nastase proved to be unimaginably corrupt and he really plundered the county. Losing a bid to become president in 2004, he lost to Traian Basescu. Nastase was later indicted in 2006 for bribery, corruption, and embezzlement, but the legal process dragged on and on. He was finally sentenced in 2012, but when the police went to arrest him, he shot himself in a likely fake suicide attempt to avoid jail. He failed in both the suicide and staying out of jail. The election of 2004 was yet another turning point in the on-again/off-again transition. Until 2003, the judiciary was firmly in the hands of an often interfering executive. According to the EU, that had to end. Just as important was that in the years preceding accession, Romania was told explicitly to get some big fish in jail, and some investigations started that included Nastase and others. The 2004 elections also saw renewed interest in confronting the legacy of the past. This reckoning has been a long time coming, but the delay was simply because the people in power had too much to lose from the truth. Out of power, the Socialists, who were allied with an ultra-nationalist party run by a former Ceausescu stooge, called the process a witch hunt. Despite this, the Institute for the Investigation of Communist Crimes in Romania was established to document past criminal acts and possibly pursue legal action.

In 2006, the Romanians began a much-needed and systematic look at the past by opening the secret police files of parliamentarians, which exposed many PSD members as collaborators with Romania's secret services. Worried for their futures, many parliamentarians tried to have President Basescu impeached. The impeachment issue went to a referendum in May 2007, with voters supporting Basescu. It is worth noting that this madness occurred after Romania joined the EU on 1 January 2007. Basescu also introduced the Presidential Commission for the Analysis of the Communist Dictatorship in Romania. Although largely an academic exercise in that commission members were expected to document what happened during the communist period, it was important, as it amounted to a real confrontation with the past in all its brutality. In short, the commission assumed that Romania could never become a real democracy if it continued to deny the past. The commission's final report, which had no legal authority, named names and documented a violent society that had simply failed. Its presentation in parliament was greeted by nothing short of hysteria by its opponents.

Bulgarians and Romanians were enthusiastic in their embrace of the EU. Given their low levels of trust in their own institutions and politicians, they obviously trusted the EU more and counted on it to drive reform. However, just as elsewhere in the Western Balkans, and unlike in Central Europe, reform was largely driven by the EU without a corresponding commitment from the local elite. Because of this, there were some concerns that membership would be delayed until 2008, but by September 2006, it was clear that 1 January 2007 was the date. After joining the EU, both Bulgaria and Romania were saddled with additional burdens that maintained the EU's influence in key areas. The EU was forced to accept two states that had certainly not been Europeanized.

As such, their membership was tempered by the Cooperation and Verification Mechanism (CVM), which was designed to encourage further reforms in key areas. The CVM was not part of the accession treaties and had no time limit – the states had to comply. It was the usual carrot-and-stick approach that the EU had used everywhere else with undeniable success, as the EU would eventually withhold cash. The difference then was that these conditions were being applied to member states. The conditions were put in place so as to allow both states to enter the EU as planned on 1 January 2007. The main issues were weaknesses generally in rule of law and, in particular, in the judiciary, and rampant corruption. As well, as it was clear that in the past, privatization has been done mostly to benefit the regime and its cronies, which explains why so few foreign investors bothered with either country.

The CVM would, hopefully, improve the investment climate once foreign investors understood that the courts could actually protect them, not ruin them. Finally, a fearful EU did not grant full access to the EU labor until 2014, and when it came, there was much complaining, especially from the UK. Things were already bad in 2007, but they got worse when thousands Roma headed west to seek a better life and ended up in France and elsewhere; most of them were deported under despicable conditions. The EU said they had the right to stay and that France was discriminating against them, but nothing ever happened. The problem with the CVM was that penalties for not meeting standards were not all that onerous, and in 2011 several member states blocked Bulgaria's and Romania's memberships in the Schengen zone. Membership in the Schengen zone – and this is what continues to worry the EU the most – would make them frontier states responsible for maintaining borders in a tough neighborhood.

The CVM, in an open acknowledgment that Bulgaria was worse off than Romania, gave six criteria to Bulgaria and Romania only four:

## Bulgaria

1. Adopt constitutional amendments removing any ambiguity regarding the independence and accountability of the judicial system.
2. Ensure a more transparent and efficient judicial process by adopting and implementing a new judicial system act and the new civil procedure code. Report on the impact of these new laws and of the penal and administrative procedure codes, notably on the pre-trial phase.
3. Continue the reform of the judiciary in order to enhance professionalism, accountability and efficiency. Evaluate the impact of this reform and publish the results annually.
4. Conduct and report on professional, non-partisan investigations into allegations of high-level corruption. Report on internal inspections of public institutions and on the publication of assets of high-level officials.
5. Take further measures to prevent and fight corruption, in particular at the borders and within local government.
6. Implement a strategy to fight organized crime, focusing on serious crime, money laundering as well as on the systematic confiscation of assets of criminals. Report on new and ongoing investigations, indictments and convictions in these areas.

## Romania

1. Ensure a more transparent and efficient judicial process notably by enhancing the capacity and accountability of the Superior Council of Magistracy. Report and monitor the impact of the new civil and penal procedures codes.
2. Establish, as foreseen, an integrity agency with responsibilities for verifying assets, incompatibilities and potential conflicts of interest, and for issuing mandatory decisions on the basis of which dissuasive sanctions can be taken.

3. Building on progress already made, continue to conduct professional, non-partisan investigations into allegations of high-level corruption.
4. Take further measures to prevent and fight against corruption, in particular within the local government.

The EU planned to compliance and issue twice-yearly reports. More than ten years later, the consensus is that the both countries move too slowly and the Schengen zone may still be a long way off.

It is also worth noting that Bulgaria took one extra step in 2007 by establishing the Dossier Commission. Such a step should have happened in 1989 or shortly thereafter but was impossible at that time. As noted, both Bulgaria and Romania never effectively dealt with the communist past and allowed a large number of communist officials, especially in the security services, to remain in positions of authority. The Socialists, and sometimes the constitutional court, blocked any dramatic moves to deal with the past. The main argument of the Socialists was that since the security services has destroyed so many files in the early 1990s (estimates say 40 per cent of files were lost), truth was therefore impossible. But the truth did come out. One statistic says it all: between 2010 and 2011 the Dossier Commission revealed that 60 per cent of Bulgaria's ambassadors had been state security officers or secret collaborators. The commission, in addition to checking the entire Bulgarian elite (including the Orthodox Church leadership, which was rife with collaborators), gave total and unrestricted file access to all citizens. Even the president at the time, Georgi Parvanov, had been a collaborator, though not a big one. The research also revealed a hopelessly incompetent security service, with low levels of education, poor foreign-language skills, and rampant nepotism but totally loyal and very well paid. Although a bit late, Bulgaria went further than any state in the region in providing this level of detail and access. Worth noting is that while the EU drove virtually every reform in Bulgaria, the Dossier Commission was entirely the result of a domestic initiative.

With the former king marginalized, another populist party emerged that proved to be far more resilient: the Citizens for the European Development of Bulgaria. It was created by Bulgaria's ultimate everyman and quasi-populist, the then mayor of Sofia,

Boyko Borissov, a low-level state security employee, former body-guard to Todor Zhivkov and Simeon Saxe-Coburg-Gotha, football star, and karate lover. Lots of less pleasant things were said too about his alleged links to organized crime. He won the 2009 elections with the usual empty slogans about the war on corruption, and he has since become the dominant figure in Bulgarian political life. While he shared the former king's populism, unlike other populists, such as Viktor Orban in Hungary, he was anti-elite, but he did not set out to destroy Bulgarian institutions. Making his term even more challenged, Borissov had to steer Bulgaria through the impact of the 2008 financial crisis. Known for straight talk and a short attention span, he also promised a new Bulgaria.

The year 2013, like 1997, turned out to be another watershed for both states. What happened would lay bare the weakness of the transition to real democracy and the depth of the societal malaise. In January 2013, a series of nationwide protests, the like of which Bulgaria had not seen since the 1997 protests against the Socialists, began. In addition to street protests, six years after Bulgaria had joined the EU, seven people committed acts of self-immolation – all men, all unemployed, all desperate. What started out as a protest against electricity monopolies and skyrocketing utility bills turned into a wider indictment of Bulgaria's failure to tackle economic hardship as a result of austerity policies, corruption, state capture, organized crime, and cronyism. In short, Bulgarians wanted a normal state, the one they had thought they would get by the accession process but which had been denied them. Instead, not only did the protest highlight Bulgaria's failure to build a modern state, which drove more than a million people out of the country, but also – equally worrying – the fact that the EU could not rein in the country post-accession. Indeed, the EU seemed perfectly content with the miserable status quo there. The protests forced the resignation of the government of Borissov. New elections in May, with the lowest voter turnout since 1990, gave Borissov's party the most seats, but he passed on the mandate. The Bulgarian Socialists made a barely survivable coalition with the Turkish Movement for Rights and Freedoms that required the support of the far-right, nationalist, anti-Semitic, anti-Roma, anti-Turkish, pro-Russian, and xenophobic Attack Party.

But people were on the streets again in June. This time, the issue was the appointment of Delyan Peevski, an allegedly "shady" businessman and without a doubt Bulgaria's key media mogul, to the post of chief of the State Agency for National Security. Peevski, for many Bulgarians, was the archetype of the kind of people who had worked behind the scenes to destroy Bulgaria. Peevski did resign after the second day of protest, but people also wanted the government to step down. The Socialist/Turkish coalition lasted only until July 2014, when it stepped down for new elections in October. The Socialists had been damaged by the Peevski scandal and the cancellation, under EU pressure, of a gas pipeline under the Black Sea. This was the second blow to the Socialists' friendly ties with Russia, as Borissov had earlier jettisoned plans for Russian-built nuclear reactors that the Socialists had supported. Moreover, nobody outside Bulgaria liked who was governing either, especially after the leader of the Attack Party, Volen Siderov, was given a government position, and the government was largely shunned. The elections witnessed another appalling turnout, only 35 per cent, and put Borissov back in the prime minister's position after difficult and prolonged coalition negotiations.

Bulgarians voted again in March 2017, and Borissov won again but had to form a strange coalition. This time he joined forces with the United Patriots group, which included three nationalist parties – the Bulgarian National Movement, the National Front for the Salvation of Bulgaria, and the Attack Party. The National Movement is a pan-Bulgarian party that stokes trouble with Macedonia, the National Front wants to clean up Bulgaria, and Attack, as mentioned, is ultra-nationalist and racist. National Front leader Valeri Simeonov was made deputy prime minister and was put in charge of demographic policy and integration, despite an established history of anti-Roma remarks. In 2015 he referred to Bulgaria's Roma as "brazen, feral, human-like creatures that demand pay without work, and collect sickness benefits without being sick." Another government minister had to resign when a photo emerged of him giving a Nazi salute to a wax figure in an SS uniform. Attack leader Siderov causes the most scandals. It is hardly surprising that Gallup polls consistently show that Bulgarians are among the top ten most depressed people in the world. Borissov is hardly an Orban or Putin but he is hardly a liberal democrat either.

As to the CVM, which is keeping Bulgaria (and Romania) out of the Schengen Area, in 2017 things did not look promising. In January 2017, in assessing ten years of the CVM, the European Commission noted that "overall progress has not been as fast as hoped for." Later in the year, there were some helpful signals that membership was just around the corner. That is at least what French president Emmanuel Macron said in Sofia in August 2017 and was later echoed by European Commission president Jean-Claude Juncker. But member states like Austria, Germany, and the Netherlands quickly noted that both Bulgaria and Romania still had a long way to go.

Rapid population decline is now a major problem for Bulgaria owing to out-migration and a declining birth rate. Plus, for multiple reasons, Bulgarians are certainly not immigrant or refugee friendly. As well, right-wing parties point to the steady growth of the Roma population and what both factors mean for Bulgaria fifty years from now by stoking the fear that Bulgarians will become a minority in their own country. While all Balkan states have negative population-growth rates, Bulgaria's is the lowest in the region. The UN says Bulgaria's population will decline by almost 30 per cent by 2050. Bulgaria had almost 9 million people. In 2017, the population was estimated at 7.1 million.

Romania is losing people too, almost two million since 1989. And the reasons to leave show no signs of disappearing. In 2017, people were back on the streets in yet another battle with pervasive corruption in what were the largest demonstrations since 1989. The reaction was a response to a new law on corruption that would have decriminalized bribe payments that were less than 200,000 Romania leu (US$50,000). For many, it was an act that legalized corruption. The PSD government claimed the new law was meant to reduce overcrowding in prisons. Others noted that PSD leader Liviu Dragnea was poised to benefit, as he was charged with voter fraud and faced a trial for abuse of power. The government withdrew the law, but the people were back in the streets in August to protest against more changes, part of a wider judicial overhaul, to legislation deemed to undermine the anti-corruption agency and even allow a person with a criminal conviction to be elected president. The EU expressed its usual concern. In 2018, as Romania celebrated one hundred years of union with Transylvania, it was clear, at least to the EU, that the elite were not just stalling but actually reversing reforms in the judiciary and failing to combat corruption. Despite a harsh evaluation from the EU, the government tried to protect its own by using legislation to essentially throw out dozens of court cases dealing with high-level corruption.

Croatia, one could say, fell somewhere between Slovenian success and the utter failures in Bulgaria and Romania. Hardly angels during the war, Tudjman's Croatian Democratic Union (CDU) stayed in power only until he died from stomach cancer in 1999, and the usual suspects around him made quick conversions to stalwarts of the EU. Many speculated that had he not died at the moment, he may well have found himself in The Hague along with Milosevic. Tudjman's power rested on the politics of division, and by 1999, it no longer made sense. Although the CDU government had purged the country of 65 per cent of the pre-war Serb community in the 1995 Operation Storm, they had failed in their territorial goals to annex part of Bosnia. The CDU was a decidedly authoritarian government that used ethnic mobilization to stay in power. Plus, it managed the media to great effect and manipulated the electoral law. And as the 1990s progressed, its clientelistic voting system collapsed because it did have that many state assets left to parcel out and just could not create any more conflicts. The anti-Western message, a pillar of Tudjman's party, was totally at odds with the pro-Western population, who had hoped the country's path would have looked more like Hungary and less like Serbia.

As in Serbia, media was tightly controlled, delivering only the nationalist message that served to demoralize the regime's many opponents. State assets were handed out to supporters. Elections were highly manipulated. In one example, Tudjman intervened in the 1995 local elections in Zagreb to replace the winner with someone he preferred. The leadership demonized the EU (and loved the United States), which demanded compliance with the ICTY for actions during what the Croatians call the "Homeland War" in 1995, when Croatia regained occupied territory. How could war heroes be war criminals? Tudjman totally resisted any criticism of the actions taken against the Serb community in 1995. As Tudjman got older and sicker, he became the subject of increasing disrespect, and his death would lead to a total sea change in Croatia.

In 2000, Croatia started fresh. Tudjman's CDU was badly defeated in presidential and parliamentary elections. Its message just no longer resonated. Taking a page from Albania, the CDU demonized its opponents as communists. The opposition talked about low wages, corruption, and unemployment. A coalition led by the Social Democratic Party (SDP) won, and Stipe Mesic – a one-time ally of Tudjman and former prime minister who had left the CDU in 1993 – became the new president, running as a member of the Croatian People's Party. The election led to some stunning and abrupt changes – as if someone had merely opened a window. Croatia embraced the EU, and the new government pledged to finally cooperate with the ICTY, largely for war crimes committed during Operation Storm. The Croatians were so excited about their love affair with the EU that some expected membership would be possible in 2007 at the same time as Bulgaria and Romania, which made some sense given that from an economic perspective, Croats were twice as wealthy as their Bulgarian or Romanian counterparts. Mesic also worked to end the hyper-presidential system of Tudjman and had a new and reduced role by November 2000. He called for a new era in regional relations, promising to end the destabilizing role Croatia had played until then in Bosnia; begin the meaningful return of Serbs to Croatia that Tudjman had never countenanced; and mend fences with Bosnia. Efforts to fully acknowledge the negative role Croatia had played in the Bosnian war continued with even more intensity after 2010 as Croatia's membership in the EU approached.

A big test for the government came in 2001 when the ICTY indicted Ante Gotovina and others for crimes committed during Operation Storm in 1995, when Croatia had retaken Serb-occupied Krajina. The Homeland War in Croatia is sacrosanct; and Gotovina, with his good looks, a stint in the French Foreign Legion, and a womanizing and checkered past, was the archetypal Balkan hero. He led the Croatian attack on the Serb pseudo-state in 1995 during the Homeland War and thus was credited with restoring Croatia's territorial unity. The ICTY indictment claimed that in the aftermath of the victory, vast crimes against humanity were committed by Croatian soldiers. Serb properties were destroyed, and the elderly who could not flee were killed. Gotovina, likely tipped off about his imminent arrest, went into hiding, and Croatia had to find him. As Saddam Hussein also learned the hard way, it is impossible to prove you do not have something, and Croatia could not prove that Gotovina was not in Croatia. Since the Serbs had hidden Karadzic and Mladic, the Croatians had to be doing the same. The quest for Gotovina did serious harm to what had hitherto been a love affair with the EU, and it dominated public opinion. Deemed by the EU to have a functioning market economy as stipulated by the Copenhagen Criteria, Croatia applied for EU membership in February 2003, and negotiations were expected to start in March 2005 but were postponed due to issues of noncompliance with the ICTY. But it was clear from the outset that Croatia's EU dreams would be shattered if it could not deliver indicted war criminals, and the ICTY had proven useful in getting states to take EU conditionality seriously. As it turned out, Gotovina was not in Croatia but in Spain, on the island of Tenerife, where he was arrested in December 2005 and transferred to The Hague. In 2011, he was sentenced to twenty-four years, but in an appeal in 2012, the sentence was overturned, and Gotovina (and others) were free to go. He received a hero's welcome on his return to Zagreb. Many Croats felt vindicated. The leadership in Belgrade was outraged, claiming a serious blow had been dealt to regional reconciliation. Not only was Gotovina acquitted, but Ramush Haradinaj, essentially the number two in the Kosovo Liberation Army, was acquitted for the second time by the ICTY, which only fed feeling of anti-Serb bias in the ICTY.

The post-Tudjman era was largely shaped by governments that came either from the CDU or SDP. Even when the CDU returned to power, it maintained the new foreign policy goals. In 2008, alongside Albania, Croatia also worked tirelessly on the other issues – minority rights, refugee returns, and corruption. Lots of Serb-friendly laws were passed after 2000 that provided real gains to the Serb community. This was part of the EU accession criteria, which mandated massive decentralization. Returns of refugees expelled improved, although that could hardly be called a success story, as only 125,000 Serbs returned to their homes. Prior to 2000, the government was interested only in the return of Croats who had been displaced. While the EU's obsession with the rights of the Serbs represented one of the many cases in which the EU practiced double standards, the plight of the Roma was consistently swept under the carpet. The much-heralded "Decade of Roma Inclusion," launched in 2005, which brought together twelve European countries that pledged to close the gap between Roma and the rest of society, failed to deliver any substantive changes. The failure to deliver on minority rights for Roma never amounted to an obstacle to EU membership.

Determined to avoid another Bulgaria- or Romania-like accession, with all the attendant problems, the EU took a harder line with Croatia on rooting out corruption than it had with Bulgaria and Romania. Brussels expected the Croats to deal with the big problems before entering the EU, as obviously the CVM was deemed a failure. Nothing is more emblematic of this position than the case of Prime Minister Ivo Sanader of the CDU. He had been prime minister between 2003 and 2009 and was a long-time figure in the party, but he abruptly resigned in 2009 and disappeared. In 2010 he was indicted on corruption charges. He decided to flee in his car to Austria, although he later said he was not actually fleeing but had planned to return. The Austrian police arrested him, and he was later extradited to Croatia in 2011. In November 2012 he was jailed for ten years (later reduced to eight and a half) for taking bribes, including €10 million from a Hungarian oil company in exchange for controlling rights in a state-owned Croatia oil company and US$750,000 from an Austrian bank to give them a preferred position. Sanader's indictment and later imprisonment was just the type of proof the EU sought from Croatia regarding its commitment to the rule of law.

## Conclusion

If the accession of Slovenia came off without a hitch, the same could not be said for Bulgaria and Romania. Slovenia did have some issues, but in the end its accession was decidedly easy. Free of the baggage of Yugoslavia, pragmatic and practical, Slovenia did its disappearing and reappearing act. Bulgaria and Romania were totally different stories. The EU's acceptance of both was good for them but it did enormous harm to the fate of the rest of the non-EU Balkans. However, important lessons were learned. Things went so badly in both countries, even after they joined, that it could not help but make the process much more difficult in subsequent rounds of enlargement. Political decisions were a thing of the past, and the bar for admission just got higher and higher as things got worse and worse. Big-picture rule-of-law questions took center stage along with the need for stronger institutions and meaningful regional cooperation. Plus, the Greek financial debacle in 2008 and after added to the general distrust of the Balkans – with good reason, given how much every country had in common with Greece. What destroyed the transition in Romania and Bulgaria was all the above, combined with a political elite that was uninterested in real reform and that totally corrupted the system. In both countries, the 1989 moment came only in 1997. Despite the criticism of the EU's decision, membership in the EU did not make things worse and even improved life overall, so the EU's haste was the right decision. Without EU membership Bulgaria and Romania would have ended up like Serbia, caught between Russia and the West. The admission of both could even be deemed visionary if one ponders what would have happened without membership.

Croatia sits somewhere between the Slovenian experience and the Bulgarian/Romanian one. It lost ten years to war and vulgar nationalism. But its abrupt turn in 2000 was genuine and Croatia met even more demanding criteria for admission to the EU. Croatia took action against corruption, temporarily vanquished its nationalist demons, and even cooperated with ICTY fully, despite the fact that the Homeland War was so central to the very idea of Croatian statehood. Croatia was also forced to acknowledge and atone for actions in Bosnia too, where under the leadership of Tudjman, the state had willfully sought to dismember Bosnia. Not everyone accepts the new versions of the past. In November 2017, not long after Ratko Mladic got his lifetime sentence at the ICTY, six Croatians stood before the court to hear the results of their appeals for crimes committed in

Bosnia during the 1992–5 war. The sentences were upheld. One defendant, Slobodan Praljak, a former theater director turned general, denounced his sentence of twenty years for war crimes and crimes against humanity and drank a liquid from a vial, announcing that he had taken poison. He died later that day. Croatia's prime minister denounced the rulings, and the Croat member of Bosnia's presidency said Praljak's suicide had been "most honorable." The ICTY also upheld the idea that the Tudjman along with his defense minister and commander of the army had been part of a joint criminal enterprise to partition Bosnia and attach the Croatian part to Bosnia. This bothered most Croats more than the dramatic suicide. Could the Croats hold on to the myth that their behavior during the Yugoslav wars was merely defensive? The ICTY trial against the six Croats was expected to be the last trial before its shutdown. Reconciliation had to become local.

# Epilogue:
# Greater This or Greater That,
# Alone or in Europe

In October 2014, at Belgrade's Partizan Stadium, Albania and Serbia were playing soccer in a Euro 2016 qualifier. During the match a drone hovered over the stadium dragging a flag of Greater Albania (an Albania that included Kosovo, parts of Greece, Macedonia, and Montenegro). The flag also included pictures of the founders of the first Albanian state in 1912, Ismail Qemali and Isa Boletini, who had fought against Serb control of Kosovo after the First World War. The Serbian crowd went crazy. A Serb player grabbed the flag as the drone descended to the field, and a brawl ensued. Fans rushed the field to beat up the Albanian team, many attacking them with chairs. The crowd chanted, "Kill them." There were no Albanian fans in attendance because they had been banned from the match for fear of violence – otherwise things could have gotten even worse. The game was called off – no winners, but lots of people certainly looked like losers, and 2014 looked a lot like 1994. Back in Kosovo, where many of the players on the Albanian team came from, things went crazy too. Prishtina's streets, already filled with fans watching the game on an outdoor screen set up downtown, danced through the night in a bizarre "victory" celebration. When the Albanian team returned home to Mother Teresa International Airport in Tirana, despite the fact there had been no winner, thousands waited to hail their heroes in a nationalist frenzy reminiscent of the Milosevic era in Serbia. The streets of Tirana later thronged with thousands of fans partying. But celebrating what? A drone with a map? A political victory in a sports stadium? The events of October 2014 revealed a serious societal malaise in which inferiority complexes and routine failures could make even a drone with a flag a great victory. Worse still, 2014 was the dream year for the Western Balkans to join the EU.

The EU hoped that the lure of membership would be enough to drive reform when membership was promised at the Thessaloniki Summit in 2003. But membership was conditioned on ensuring that the Balkan states and their peoples could see some light at the end of the tunnel by maintaining what was called a European perspective. However, the economic crisis in 2007 and 2008 revealed serious shortcomings in the overall EU project. Bulgaria and Romania, not really members in full, were largely deemed to have been admitted too early. The fate of those two countries, plus what happened in Greece after 2008, confirmed beliefs that the Balkans share not only geography but also abnormal and predatory political parties, corruption, state capture, and clientelism. No country was able to create or sustain a political party that could break the power of the corrupt elites. Corruption, people could say with confidence, was the only the only transparent thing about their countries, as the elite openly flashed vast amounts of wealth. The Balkans, for the EU, looked more and more like the same cultural, political, and economic space. Plus, a Europe of regions as opposed to nations did not prevail. The nation-state proved to be more resilient, and not just in the Western Balkans. In Hungary, Poland, and Slovakia, the nation-state came back with a vengeance, and populist governments challenged the core values of the EU. The populist insurgency, to a degree led by Hungary's Viktor Orban, found loads of imitators in the Balkans after the migration crisis of 2015. Hungary's Orban-friendly media expanded to the Balkans, especially in Macedonia and Slovenia, with the same message: nationalist, anti-liberal, and the usual scapegoats found in left-leaning NGOs – multiculturalism, and the go-to bogey man for all aspiring autocrats, billionaire financier George Soros.

But there was some light in the tunnel. There was loads of money for infrastructure projects, and every state but Kosovo got visa-free travel to the Schengen Area of the EU. Macedonians, Montenegrins, and Serbians got visa-free travel for ninety day stays in December 2009. One year later, the same deal was offered to Albanians and

Bosnians. Successive governments in Kosovo promised the same but failed, mostly because the EU tied visa-free travel to certain unrelated issues, such as border demarcation with Montenegro. In any case, visa-free travel was a master stroke, encouraged largely by Austria, and it served to lessen tensions in the region and gave people something to celebrate, even if they could not afford to travel. Until then, getting a visa, especially for young people, was time-consuming, expensive, and often humiliating. It did not mean everyone traveled, but it was enough to know that you *could* travel. The EU was quick to remind everyone that if people did not play by the rules, the visa-free regime could just as easily disappear.

The foundations of the EU's intervention in the Western Balkans was based on the Stabilization and Association Process (SAP), which was a vast package to "Europeanize" the region in all aspects, based on contractual relationships between an aspirant state and the EU and embodied in the Stabilization and Association Agreements (SAAs), which replaced the Europe agreements of the 1990s. The reinvigorated process was launched in 1999, when the war in Kosovo laid bare all the failures that had occurred up to that point. The SAP was a much more ambitious agenda for preparing the region for membership. In essence, it was only then that even the prospect of membership in the EU was put on the table. Now, almost twenty years later, one can take stock of the successes and failures of the SAP and the role of individual states in making EU membership a reality. Before examining the state of the game in the non-EU Balkans, it is worth noting that the hopes of Thessaloniki 2003 are far from fulfilled. Although there have been undeniable gains, there have been huge setbacks, the biggest being the failure of the domestic elite to take reform seriously and build real democracies. The EU's attention, and that of the United States too, was diverted elsewhere, and the notion of stability first, democracy later became even more entrenched in policy. The main outcome of this was massive brain drain throughout the region as the young and educated left. The SAP was unevenly embraced by the region, and elites tended to blame external factors for their failures. As more than one analyst noted, EU norms and values were applied by Balkan standards. Some countries, like Kosovo, did little more than copy and paste laws from EU member states, which explains why landlocked Kosovo has such a nice law on the sea and advanced animal-rights legislation. But the authorities still shoot stray dogs at night.

In preceding chapters we saw how the world looked for Albania until 1997, Bosnia until 1995, Macedonia until 2016, Montenegro until independence in 2006, and Serbia until 1999. If we examine what happened in Albania first between 1997 and the present, we will see various common features for the whole region. In the wake of the pyramid collapse and the arming of Kosovo, Albania was stabilized by the international community but it was not made democratic. Highly contested elections were held in 1997 under strict international supervision, which put the Socialists in power. Given what happened to virtually every Albanian in 1997, there was no way Berisha's Democratic Party could win, as it was rightly blamed by most Albanians for the loss of their savings and the violence that ensued. Amazingly, and emblematic of a wider and very problematic feature of the Balkan elite, Berisha did not resign as party head but stayed on, hoping for another moment. Until only very recently, Albanian leaders recognized only the results of elections they won.

Freed after nearly four years in prison by the mobs who took over Albania in the state collapse of 1997, Fatos Nano was prime minister again and determined to get the most of out of life. He embraced hedonism as there was no way being prime minister could stand in the way of his second chance at a *dolce vita*. As an economist, at least a Marxist one, Nano needed first to restore political and economic stability. Plus, he needed to find the money from the pyramids, and the international accountants arrived in droves. Not much was found, and the international accountants left with their own sacks of cash. The new government brought wrongly named "crimes against humanity" charges against some key figures in the previous government for their roles in the 1997 collapse. Nano's main legacy was to allow his ministers to enrich themselves as he reveled in post-prison decadence. As a friend remarked, Albania under Hoxha was a real dictatorship with a real dictator; under Ramiz Alia it was a real dictatorship without a real dictator; under Sali Berisha it was a dictator without a dictatorship; and under Nano, just chaos.

As an indication of just how fraught the situation was, the controversial DP member and former student leader Azem Hajdari was murdered in downtown Tirana in September 1998. DP militants took to the streets, blaming the government for Hajdari's assassination. Berisha demanded the government step down in twenty-four hours. Fearing a coup was imminent and that he would end up dead, as it is doubtful his opponents would settle for jail a second time, Nano fled Tirana to Pogradec in southern Albania, close enough to Macedonia in the event he needed to flee the country altogether. The militants also took over state television. Protestors in the streets called for Nano's execution. He decided to resign instead, and the new prime minister was the thirty-year-old, well-meaning but seemingly not terribly bright Pandeli Majko.

Nevertheless, despite ongoing street protests and provocations from Berisha's party, the Socialists managed to stay in power for eight years, a period that witnessed dramatic changes to Albania. In some ways, Albanian elections offered bad choices. The Socialists proved better at building things; the Democrats excelled at destroying things. If the DP brought kiosks, the SP built a few mediocre roads, and Tirana added skyscrapers taller than the Hotel Tirana. Life outside the capital was still miserable, though, and thousands of people, especially from the impoverished north, made their way to Tirana to find work, putting extraordinary strain on an already dilapidated infrastructure. The Socialists also brought in a new constitution in 1998, approved narrowly in a referendum that derailed any attempts to establish the strong presidential republic Berisha had envisioned – Albania was a parliamentary republic. Berisha had done everything himself, as he rarely delegated. Outside his office, people just hung around waiting to catch sight of him, hoping he could get them a job, and often he did. It was highly personal rule, and things changed a lot. As noted, the country managed as successfully as possible the massive flow of refugees from Kosovo in 1999. Politics remained extremely polarized between the ruling Socialists and Berisha's Democratic Party. Boycotts and accusations were the norm. Without a doubt though, the Socialists were deeply corrupt, and with their coalition partners they captured and plundered the state. Everybody got something: a port, an airport, a border-crossing point, you name it – a bizarre form of privatization. But ordinary Albanians tried to get on with their lives, leaving the political struggle largely to both party's militants.

On the plus side, Albania saw the emergence of Edi Rama, an artist and former basketball player who became mayor of Tirana in 2000, when he was only thirty-six years old. Rama, who would go on to become leader of the Socialist Party and then prime minister, transformed Tirana, winning a Mayor of Year Award in 2004 and, in a real first for an Albanian politician, achieved positive fame abroad. Even the *New Yorker* in 2005 devoted a piece to his urban renewal projects, which gave residents a degree of self-respect that had long been missing. More important, kids could ride on Ferris wheels or simply play with their parents in a park. Much of what Rama did was simple: he brought a kind of civil society to Tirana and gave citizens possibilities that were commonplace in other European capitals. Rama had been minister of culture in Nano's government, and the first nice thing he did for the capital was to open a cinema. Prior to Rama, the DP mayor had allowed Tirana to become a real cesspool in what could only be deemed the era of "kioskism."

Tirana was simply awash in illegal buildings built in exchange for political support – kiosks selling cigarettes and snacks, shabby cafés, restaurants, and even hotels without permits or standards. The main park in the center of the city did not have a patch of green left. The tiny river that runs through Tirana, the Lana, became a rat-infested reeking toilet. When draft beer finally arrived in Albania in 1993 (the same year bananas appeared too, in what was the original pyramid scheme), it was great, but the pub near the Lana did not have a toilet. In power, Rama brought out the bulldozers and, in what was a politically risky and even dangerous move, laid waste to everything that was illegal. Before Rama, Tirana was gloomy and foreboding, even a bit sinister, especially at night. Rama restored Tirana's green space, added places for children to go, such as an amusement park, and restored the banks of the Lana River. Tirana's central park was back to its original grandeur. He brought some much-needed color by painting building facades, including apart-ments, in various bright colors. After a year the pollution ruined things, but his attempt to convince Albanians that civil society could exist outside your house or apartment was laudable. A complicated person, and very much a loner, Rama took risks that few were able or willing to take, and he had a vision that had hitherto been lacking in Albania's leaders. Rama brought back some of Tirana's pre-Second World War charm. In so doing, he earned the permanent hostility of Berisha, who never let up in his attacks on Rama. Given Berisha's legacy between 1992 and 1997, Rama called Berisha "Dr Rumpalla." (*Rumpalla* is a colloquial Albanian word meaning "disarray.") Berisha called Rama far worse things.

But despite Rama's achievements in Tirana and another Socialist victory in 2001, the opposition Democratic Party waged an unrelenting struggle against them with arguments that were predominantly locked in the past in an effort to maintain the link between the Socialists and their communist predecessors. In 2005, in what may be the greatest comeback of all, Berisha was back in power as prime minister. Given the legacy of Socialist kleptocracy and vulgarity, Berisha's campaign was based on a war on corruption with the slogan "With Clean Hands." And so began a forever war on the old regime's corruption, which meant there was lots of room for new corruption. Of course the elections were contested, and international observers noted countless irregularities, including intimidation and vote buying. It was the country's seventh national election, and the country still could not get it right according to observers. I once asked Berisha if he would respect the results of the elections. With a wry smile he said, "If we win, yes." He was only half-joking. Fatos Nano, in and out as Socialist Party leader since his release from prison in 1997, stepped down and stepped out too, but only briefly. Edi Rama, became the new leader but would need to wait eight years to become prime minister.

Berisha would see some gains for Albania in terms of its EU and NATO accession processes. In 2006, Albania and the EU signed an SAA, which came into force in 2009. In 2008, as noted earlier, Albania was invited to join NATO and formally did so in 2009. Also in 2009, Albania formally applied to join the EU. As already noted, in 2010, Albanians received visa-free travel for up to ninety days to the EU. In 2012, the European Commission, the executive arm of the EU, recommended that Albania be granted EU candidate status, contingent on further reforms in the judiciary, the public sector, and a meaningful fight against organized crime and corruption.

But the other side of the Albanian story was the disaster at Gerdec, a small village near Tirana. As part of its NATO membership bid, Albania was forced to dismantle and destroy the literally millions of weapons and ammunition it had, principally from China, to bolster its defenses in the 1970s. On 15 March 2008 a massive explosion shook the entire country as workers dismantled shells. Twenty-six people were killed, and hundreds were injured. To protect his allies, Berisha intervened in the process to bring those responsible to trial. It was also later uncovered that two youthful Americans were buying old and embargoed Chinese weapons from Albania and repackaging them for resale to the US Army in Afghanistan. The Albanian source for the entire story was murdered in southern Albania in September 2008. The whole strange episode is told in the Hollywood film *War Dogs* (2016).

Berisha's DP won another highly contested election in 2009, but Berisha was forced to form a coalition with Ilir Meta, who broke from the Socialists to form his own party, the Socialist Movement for Integration. Nobody can even guess what Meta's price for joining with Berisha was, but he fast gained the reputation as Albania's most corrupted politician, who turned any ministry he ran into a family business. The Socialists refused to accept the ballot. Rama even had parliamentarians go on a hunger strike, which was halted only when it became clear that people would actually die. In 2011, after videos showed Berisha's Meta appearing to ask for bribes related to a hydroelectric project, the Socialists took to the streets and attacked Berisha's office. Arguing that government institutions were under attack and that a coup was being planned, the Republican Guard shot and killed four demonstrators. Albania had been a NATO member for barely two years before Albanian authorities shot demonstrators in downtown Tirana. These few stories made a couple of things clear. One was just how low the standards are for NATO entry. Second, it was just as clear that rule of law was a long way off in Albania, as the courts made decisions that were clearly political, especially in the corruption case against Meta. The result was even greater distrust in institutions, leading to the slow and steady departure of thousands of Albanians for a better future elsewhere.

Berisha as prime minister was different than Berisha as president. He still micromanaged and he waged his nonstop war on the Socialists – the "blockmen" (a reference to the cloistered place where the communist elite lived in the communist period) or "Red Pashas," as he called them – and on Rama in particular, whom he accused of all kinds of depravity, but Albania by then had some of the trappings of a democracy, which held him in check. Civil society had gained some clout, and a few institutions could be deemed partially independent. To outsiders, Berisha's authoritarian streak was noted. There was increasing international pressure on Albania to get its act together and reduce political polarization. In 2012, when the country celebrated its centenary, hardly any foreign dignitaries showed up at all. The Greeks came but pulled out after Berisha spoke of some territory in Greece as being Albanian land. But Hungarian prime minister Viktor Orban, destined to become the EU's bad boy, was there to possibly offer advice to Berisha on the making of an "illiberal" democracy. In any case, the celebration was dire. Copying a giant cake in Kosovo in 2008 to celebrate its independence, the government produced an even bigger cake in front of the Palace of Culture, which ran the length of the whole building. A heaving mass lined up in front – hundreds deep – and seemed in a frenzy. The barricades went down, the pastry chefs on hand panicked, and people of all ages rushed to get their piece in what was, in the end, nothing more than a savage food fight. Angry youth in tight jeans and leather jackets climbed on the cake table and waded in. Old women in cheap shoes and nylon socks were there filling plastic bags too. It was a multigenerational disaster broadcast live on TV. The few VIPs in Tirana never got to see it as they were tucked away in a private lunch. It was horrific, and most Albanians looked on with shame. Europe, and not just the EU, seemed a long way off, literally and figuratively.

The EU and the United States stepped up their interventions in Albania to calm the political atmosphere by encouraging dialogue between the two main parties. Most citizens found it hard to identify real gains, and some politicians started playing the national-unification card. Berisha did too, although his credibility on that issue was weak. Early in his career, he did say that the division of Albanians could not be considered eternal, but in power, as president and prime minister, he rarely spoke of national unification. Besides, it was the Socialists – who as communists prior to 1991 had all but abandoned Kosovo – who did the most to help the Kosovo cause after 1997. Weak and dependent, whenever the Albanians spoke publicly of unification with Kosovo, they were quickly admonished by the EU and the United States. Besides, Albanians in Albania were largely indifferent to unification. They had enough headaches, and the stage of romantic nationalism was behind them. A nationalist party advocating a single Albanian state, the Red-Black Alliance (based on the colors of the Albanian flag), was formed in 2012 but never won any seats in parliament and more or less died. National unification had no value as a tool to mobilize voters. At that moment, attitudes were similar in Kosovo, but things would change somewhat as few could know then that the unification movement might find its home in Prishtina, not Tirana. Government failure in Kosovo went far deeper than in Albania, which bolstered the support for a Greater Albania there and helped drive youngsters to ISIS as well.

Albania's 2013 and 2017 elections, the country's eighth and ninth national polls, were the closest they ever got to free and fair. In 2013, Ilir Meta, always on the fence, saw which way the wind was blowing, joined the Socialist coalition, and abandoned Berisha. Rama's coalition won easily, and Berisha was out, finally. The win could not be contested, and Berisha knew it. He resigned, in a surprisingly graceful way, and handed the party over to the much younger Lulzim Basha, a former transport minister and former mayor of Tirana. The whiff of corruption lingered over Basha too for kickbacks related to a massive highway project linking Albania and Kosovo. The ever-loyal Berisha defended his protégé. Berisha also continued to call the shots from behind the scenes, though. Though prone to hyperbole, Berisha's attacks on the government always had a grain of truth, and he retains a deep and committed following in Albania. Berisha was outwardly austere in power, but his opponents and others claimed he had amassed huge illegal wealth for himself and his family. In 2014, Albania finally became an official candidate for the EU (after three applications that had failed, owing mostly to shortcomings in its electoral processes and its failure to implement a strategy to reform its judiciary). In 2017, Rama won again, but this time he won really big – sweeping most of the country, save the DP strongholds in the north. Rama no longer needed a coalition partner, and Albania began a long-overdue period of political calm. Probably for the first time since 1990, Albania seemed at peace with itself.

Albania still had problems though. According to the EU and the United States, its biggest problems were high-level rule-of-law issues, particularly in the obvious "justice for sale" process in its courts. But the real push for change came from the United States, which led the charge for dramatic judicial reform and a serious war on corruption and organized crime. This was the only way ahead for Albania, and the US ambassador to Albania openly chastised judges for their expensive watches and cars, noting that Albanian courts were politicized and that known organized-crime figures and corrupt senior officials walked Tirana's streets. One analyst noted that some 20 per cent of Albanian parliamentarians had known ties to organized crime. For ordinary citizens, corruption at all levels was just a fact of life, as most knew that the payment of bribes was required to get anything done at any level.

Organized crime in Albania is deeply linked to the traffic of humans, weapons, and drugs. It became part of Albanian life in the 1990s, chiefly as a response to the sanctions imposed on Yugoslavia during the wars. Albania's location between east and west – along with its relatively porous borders, ill-trained, ill-paid, and ill-equipped border guards, and weak judiciary – made it an ideal transfer country, with Albanian criminal groups acting as facilitators as goods moved east to west. Albania has also long been associated with turning a blind eye to marijuana growing and exporting, and is now awash in drug money, having become Europe's largest producer of outdoor cannabis. Possibly, the most illustrative example of this is the village of Lazarat in southern Albania, which symbolizes the depth of the marijuana business in Albania and its links to official state structures. The tiny village played an outsized role in marijuana growing, which is illegal in Albania. Everyone knew what was going on there, but the government was never able to shut it down, for a variety of reasons – the villagers were heavily armed, for one thing. According to press reports, Lazarat produced nine hundred tons per year, with a value of almost US$5 billion – almost half of Albania's GDP. But owing to pressure from the EU and the United States, in June 2014, eight hundred armed police moved in and took over, burning everything. Still, the growing continued. In fact, in 2015 and 2016 cannabis production increased, and at the same time, no major drug traffickers were arrested or prosecuted.

The crackdown on the drug trade, which has been uneven at best and even theatrical, was part of Rama's wider strategy to get Albania closer to the EU. What the EU and United States want is to see big fish in jail, as Albania has the lowest rate of serious crime prosecution in Europe, even worse than Bulgaria. Rama as prime minister, unlike any of his predecessors, seemed willing to deliver serious judicial reform and strengthened anti-corruption forces in 2016 and 2017. A sweeping set of constitutional changes in 2016 went the furthest of any reform to date. Berisha always waged wars with various prosecutors who got too close to the truth and he always protected his allies. Rama would not do the same. But he did face strong resistance from opposition lawmakers, who were aligned with judges who feared the new vetting procedures and who used the courts to delay implementation. For some, the biggest fear is that Albania, like Kosovo, will end up with international prosecutors, and some think that means jail for sure. However, Albania is not Kosovo, where the EU and the United States can do whatever they want. To be fair, as we shall see later in Serbia, going after big fish can prove dangerous and far easier said than done. Ultimately, in 2018, it was often-violent student demonstrations against Rama's government's failures to tackle corruption and poverty that provoked at least some major cabinet changes by getting rid of a number of the more odious members of his administration.

If Albania presents the case of extreme polarization and delayed democratic consolidation, Montenegro is its exact opposite in some ways, although it is not a democracy either. The Montenegrin branch of the League of Communists morphed into the Democratic Party of Socialists (DPS), and ever since then it has been in power, making it the longest-ruling party in the region. There was nothing to distinguish the state from the party. Critics inside and out of Montenegro noted that Montenegrin democracy was deeply flawed, but its internal stability won it support from the EU and the United States. Its success is mostly owed to its leader, Milo Djukanovic, who ran the country with only two brief interruptions in 2006 and 2010, since 1991. He stepped down only in October 2016, but reappeared to win the presidential election in 2018. His mastery of the whole country made Montenegro a preferred destination for foreign investors, and not just Russians. Even as part of Yugoslavia or the subsequent State Union of Serbia and Montenegro, the Montenegrin economy was far more open than Serbia's; it had different and lower customs duties and it even abandoned the national currency of Yugoslavia (the dinar) in 1999 and adopted the German mark and later the euro as its official currency, even though it was not a member of the Eurozone.

As noted, while starting out as a Milosevic ally, Djukanovic he earned a reputation as active in international cigarette smuggling during the wars and the sanctions that accompanied them. Smuggling, to be fair, was required to survive Milosevic's wars. The Italian authorities built a huge case against him later that was subsequently shelved for reasons of geopolitical stability. He was pro-Russian at one time, welcoming suspicious Russian money into the country with open arms from the likes of aluminum magnate and oligarch Oleg Deripaska, who took over the failing aluminum mill outside of Podgorica because no one else was willing to buy it and got the Montenegrin taxpayer to pay the mill's electricity bills. Djukanovic would later become the darling of those wanting to counter Russian influence in the Balkans. He shifted to the West just before the Kosovo War, provided refuge for Albanians fleeing Serb aggression, and later led the charge for Montenegrin independence in 2006. He never lost an election. Nonetheless, in 2015 he was named Person of the Year by the Organized Crime and Corruption Reporting Project "for his work in creating an oppressive political atmosphere and an economy choked by corruption and money laundering." Analysts always said Djukanovic's Montenegro is a family business. In 2011 he authorized a bailout of a bank owned by his brothers. His sister, running a small law firm in Podgorica, was named in the 2017 Paradise Papers. The EU's love affair with Djukanovic is the most telling example of the triumph of stability over democracy in the region. If the EU (and the United States for that matter) had been really serious about democracy, it is highly unlikely Djukanovic would have lasted so long.

The source of his success is his ability to sense where things are going. For our purposes it makes sense to examine the evolution of the independence project in greater detail and the later path towards EU and NATO membership. As we saw earlier, suffering from what can only be called the "Chicken Little Syndrome," the EU and the United States forced Serbia and Montenegro to remain together, fearing that more independent states would undermine things in Bosnia and Kosovo. The so-called State Union of Serbia and Montenegro in 2002 was a sham from the start. Montenegro never even pretended that it was prepared to stay and devoted all its energy to getting a referendum on the calendar.

The EU emerged as the main broker of the Montenegrin referendum. But it had to tread carefully, as Montenegro was almost divided evenly between pro- and anti-independence forces conjuring up images of violence by the losing side. As noted, the EU forced the Montenegrins on both sides to accept a deal that meant that a successful referendum was based on a 50 per cent voter turnout and 55 per cent support threshold. Thanks largely to the Albanian community, which had enthusiastically endorsed both independence and Djukanovic, support for independence was 55.5 per cent. The much-feared grey zone, which might have brought violence – a vote of, say, 54 per cent in favor – was avoided. It was a free and fair vote that was largely rejected by the main opposition parties, who blamed the EU for creating independent Montenegro. Serbia's reaction was civil; there was no violence between Montenegrins and Serbs, and life went on. The whole thing was an undeniable success in a country that people forget was quite multiethnic. The pro-independence coalition included Montenegrins, who were roughly 43 per cent, plus the national minorities (Bosniaks, Albanians, Roma, Muslims, and Croats).

Given the almost frightening uniformity of opinion around Djukanovic supporters, the country's EU and NATO aspirations were destined to be realized quicker than any other state's in the Western Balkans. Shortly after adopting a new constitution, Montenegro signed an SAA in October 2007, well ahead of Serbia. In 2010,

Montenegro was declared a candidate for membership and, in 2012, it started accession negotiations, which are moving ahead, albeit extremely slowly. The process for NATO membership, which is far more contentious in Montenegro than is EU membership, also went well. Montenegro became the alliance's twenty-ninth member in June 2017. The NATO process was sped up, largely thanks to Russian meddling in the Balkans. Russia, always eager to delay the Euro-Atlantic integration process and sow discord, happily used the Serbs in Montenegro to foment instability, just as they do with their Serb proxies in Bosnia. In the wake of Montenegro's fall 2016 elections, which was the first one the DPS nearly lost, the government alleged that it had uncovered a plot to assassinate Djukanovic, bring the opposition to power, and derail the NATO plan. The whole thing seemed to resemble a Tintin escapade. The coup plotters, an odd collection of people, included one person who was asked to throw Molotov cocktails at a party headquarters but got the address wrong. In later court testimony, he said he had no idea what he was supposed to do. Russia said the claims were absurd but at the same time it had always made it clear that Montenegrin membership in NATO was a "provocation."

Montenegro, the frontrunner to join the EU, has a lot to do, especially when one considers that it has been governed by the same party and same person more or less since 1990. Some analysts describe it as a mafia state where the interests of the government and mafia are essentially the same. Owing to international pressure, Djukanovic did step down in October 2016. But that was hardly enough, as the very same rule-of-law and judicial issues that plague the rest of the region are just as bad in Montenegro – probably worse. Djukanovic's inner circle was made extremely wealthy, and everyone knew that. The scent of organized crime had always lingered, and no big fish ever went to jail but instead moved freely around the garish seaside resorts with an entourage of body guards. The October 2016 elections saw widespread and legitimate accusations of fraud, intimidation, and vote buying. The EU called for a thorough investigation but not much more. But to be fair to Djukanovic, he was uncannily lucky, and most of his decisions were the right ones. In the EU and the US quest to get the geopolitics right and work on the other things later, Djukanovic was the man who always delivered and, unlike many of his counterparts in the region, always kept his word. Montenegro stayed stable and decisively pro-West. Djukanovic and his family got extremely rich. As in the past, Djukanovic's retirement was temporary – he won the country's presidency in April 2018.

Serbia, like Albania, witnessed the same on-again/off-again transition and deep polarization that took hold in Albania. Serbia, at least everyone thought, had its 1989 moment in 2000. Although Milosevic was no longer considered a statesman abroad after his indictment by the ICTY in 1999, his true fall thankfully came due to domestic opponents. In September 2000, Milosevic called for early parliamentary elections, believing that this would secure him and the Socialist Party more power. However, the presidential candidate of the Democratic Opposition of Serbia (DOS) – a coalition of eighteen opposition parties with very different outlooks – was Vojislav Kostunica, a constitutional lawyer with deeply held principles and also a strong nationalist who at least believed in democracy. Kostunica won the presidency with more than 50 per cent of the votes representing the Democratic Party of Serbia in DOS. Almost 80 per cent of eligible voters turned out. Under Milosevic, Serbian living standards had plummeted, making the country one of the poorest in Europe. Kostunica promised long-overdue economic reform.

Unaccustomed to losing, as he had never lost an election before, Milosevic refused to give up power. Anti-Milosevic demonstrators, who had taken to Belgrade's streets before, took to them once again. On October 5, 2000, thousands of people protested in Belgrade demanding Milosevic's resignation. Milosevic responded with tear gas but a day later, he gave in. Kostunica became the country's new president, and the young reformist Zoran Djindjic of the Democratic Party, its new prime minister after parliamentary elections in December 2000 in which the DOS coalition won 176 out of 250 seats. The end of Milosevic's rule was perceived as a turning point, both ending Serbian isolation and beginning Europeanization. The going would be tough, as Milosevic's Serbia had been really a pirate ship, totally criminalized, top to bottom, and the military-security forces-mafia complex stood to lose with Djindjic's plans. Plus, ten years of Milosevic had poisoned Serbian society. Milosevic's allies in the security services, army, and criminal world expected to be left alone by Serbia's new leaders. Moreover, it would prove to be much harder to undo Milosevic's legacy, particularly the exclusive nationalism he had touted, than most people realized.

The West loved Djindjic, although that was probably the triumph of style over substance. He was educated, handsome, and totally transparent, or so it seemed at the time. In Kosovo, there was panic. Independence would get a lot harder with a democratic Serbia. The taciturn and gloomy Kostunica, who sounded the same as Milosevic in many ways, at least to the Albanians in Kosovo, was something different, but at least Milosevic was gone. Djindjic wanted to move very fast and promised a European Serbia. After all, there was huge urgency. Serbia had lost more than ten years because of Milosevic. Djindjic decided to tackle the big problems first that revolved around Kosovo and the ICTY. Kosovo, as he understood it, had to be solved quickly, and he was certainly willing to open talks with Kosovo on a partition deal that would have given Serbia control over key northern municipalities. A similar deal would resurface in 2018.

Controversially, and contrary to President Kostunica's wishes, Djindjic agreed to Milosevic's transfer to the ICTY in The Hague in June 2001. This was an immensely dangerous decision: most Serbs harbored ill feelings towards the ICTY as something perceived to be both foreign, which it was, and anti-Serb. For many, it was as though all Serbia was on trial, which was true to some extent, in that most of Serbian society stood behind the very nationalist policies that had driven all the wars. This fact is often forgotten when Serbia trots out its victim status. In hindsight, probably expectations in the West and in Serbia were too high. Just watch Djindjic in a September 2002 interview with Charlie Rose in which he acknowledges that all Serbs had a little bit of Milosevic in them.

Djindjic and Kostunica squabbled about more than Milosevic. The tension between the two essentially derailed the entire reform agenda. Many DOS members were caught up in the usual corruption scandals, and it became clear that this was no 1989 moment. Kostunica's anti-communist credentials were impeccable, and there was no stench of corruption around him. He wanted to build a state based on rule of law and strong institutions and a slower pace for economic reform that would do less damage to ordinary people. One could perceive that Djindjic was more action oriented and less legalistic, easily prepared to bend rules to move Serbia ahead. They both agreed that Serbia needed to be integrated into Europe. But they failed, and support for them steadily declined. Even Djindjic, who seemed so earnest, allowed himself to be taken in by the lures of wealth that came with his office. The war on corruption, that mainstay of the empty rhetoric of all Balkan political parties, was merely theatrics. Despite Djindjic's and Kostunica's internal failures, the West did its best to save them, fearing a return of Milosevic's Socialists or the radical nationalists.

The West lamented that Djindjic could not do more to arrest members of the powerful mafia clans that continued to dominate Serbia. But to get into power and to stay there, Djindjic had made too many deals with too many people, and that made him reluctant to make too many enemies. Instead of making the war on crime a real one, he ramped up the Kosovo issue in classic nationalist style, even suggesting that if Kosovo were made independent, Serbia would be looking for a new conference to redetermine all the borders in the Balkans. Worse still, Djindjic was subsequently assassinated on 12 March 2003 in front of his government offices. The arrest of Milosevic was a direct path to his murder. A state of emergency followed, with an aggressive roundup of thousands of real and perceived criminals. The fragmented government could not re-group, and the DOS coalition died. Ordinary Serbs had to accept that they still lived in a criminal state that was also stridently nationalistic. Several top military commanders in a special operations unit in the Serbian State Security Service (known as the Red Berets) who were active during the wars and who had gone from war crimes to organized crime were later given long prison sentences for the assassination. Their goals, according to the verdict, were to prevent any more people being sent to The Hague and to bring extremists to power.

New elections came in December 2003, and DOS was finished as a coalition. As a sign of things to come, the Serbian Radical Party did well. Its former leader, Vojislav Seselj, had been sent to The Hague on war crimes charges in March 2003 (where he made a mockery of the whole process and was later acquitted), and his deputy, Tomislav Nikolic, led the party to a very strong showing, securing the greatest number of votes. Kostunica became prime minister in another shaky coalition, and in June 2004, the reformist Boris Tadic of the Democratic Party only barely defeated Nikolic. No big changes came. The slow pace of reform, in Serbia and elsewhere, drove many to leave the country. In 2006, when Milosevic died in his cell at The Hague, he was brought home, and Kostunica gave him something close to a state funeral. By then, Kostunica had slipped into the same nationalist rhetoric that had prevailed in the Milosevic era, even bringing in a new constitution in 2006 that explicitly stated in its preamble that Kosovo was part of Serbia. In 2007, Tadic appointed the strident nationalist Vuk Jeremic to be foreign minister and lead the talks on Kosovo. As we saw, Jeremic's lack of vision on the future of Kosovo doomed the Serbian side completely.

In the decade since Milosevic's death, Serbia has engaged in an on-again/off-again dance with the EU. The reformists who gained power in 2000 proved to be complete disappointments. As noted, in 2006, Montenegro gained its independence, and in 2008, Kosovo did the same. Serbia, supported by Russia, took an unsurprisingly uncompromising stand on the legitimacy of Kosovo's independence, so successive governments had to navigate a fraught political landscape. The EU and the United States delivered the same message: if you want Europe, you need to forget about Kosovo – you cannot have both. The Serbs were not willing to forget about Kosovo, although most accepted that there was no way independence was reversible. As noted in the discussion about Kosovo, what Serbia did was to use Kosovo to its advantage to get as many concessions from the EU as possible.

The year 2008 saw also the emergence of a new and what would prove to be decisive force in Serbian politics, embodied in the Serbian Progressive Party of Aleksandar Vucic. The party was a breakaway group from the Radical Party, made up of those who had decided that maybe Europe was the way to go after all. Prior to that, Vucic had previously served as Milosevic's information minister and had presided over some really ugly behavior towards the media, and later was later the main spokesperson for all the nasty policies of the Radical Party, including lauding indicted war criminals such as Karadzic and Mladic. But he had been converted, shown the error of his ways, and emerged as down-to-earth populist with the common touch who simply loved power. But given his nationalist credentials, he also had the credibility to make some bold decisions.

Also in 2008, with the arrest of the Bosnian Serb leader Radovan Karadzic and along with some important EU-sponsored agreements with Kosovo, Serbia seemed finally to be taking seriously its EU integration agenda. Some important regional reconciliation projects took place between Serbia and Croatia and Serbia and Bosnia. There was no apology for Kosovo, though, and the thousands of people still missing from the war were still unaccounted for. Drones over football stadiums aside, relations between Albania and Serbia also improved, although Albanian prime minister Edi Rama often stuck his nose into the affairs of the Albanians in Kosovo, and Macedonia too, and could not resist the occasional nationalist outburst, if only to say, "Look at me." However, Serbia's EU integration dreams are far more complicated than anywhere else in the region. Serbia's population does not show the same level of enthusiasm for the EU as elsewhere in the Balkans. If Albanians are 80 per cent behind EU membership, the Serbs hover around 50 per cent and never went over 55 per cent. Many Serbs, like the Greeks, have an irrational affinity for Russia that means they love Russia but would rather live in Germany, and they are smart enough to know that the Russian development model is not viable. The love affair with Russia is often unexplainable, given that the EU (and the United States) makes serious contributions to the betterment of Serbia – roads, bridges, hospitals, scholarships – while Russia more or less focuses on buying strategic assets. Because of the legacy of NATO bombing in 1999, NATO membership is off the table, and there is no Djukanovic in power to simply make it happen whether people want it or not.

In 2014 Vucic's party won a decisive victory and could govern alone. In early elections in 2016 they won again, and in 2017 Vucic switched from being prime minister to being president, a largely ceremonial post that he transformed into the center of all power. He pledged to maintain Serbia's EU path along with its special relationship with Russia and military neutrality. The EU and the United States has encouraged Serbia's leaders to choose between the EU and Russia. Until they absolutely have to, when membership in the EU becomes obvious, it is likely they will keep the ties with Russia alive. Like everywhere else, Vucic began the usual war on corruption, which so far has yielded few tangible results. Serbia now looks somewhat like the Hungary of Viktor Orban – brazenly populist, nationalist, and anti-pluralist – as it heads down the path of "illiberal democracy," meaning that there are almost-free elections but not much else. There is one very strong party in power, the opposition is in disarray, and Vucic has gathered immense power in his office. Serb voters, who never again came out in the numbers they did to oust Milosevic in 2000, are apathetic and exhausted. The politics of nation and nationalism never left Serbia and remain front and center in Serbian political life. Moreover, Serbian society has never really confronted the past and come to grips with the crimes committed in the 1990s, preferring instead to play the victim, the memory-free state. The EU seemed willing to turn a blind eye to the shortcomings of Serbian democracy. In one of the weirder moments, Vucic, who had vilified Djindjic in the past, led the charge to get a monument to him in Belgrade. One could not blame Serbs for looking at those power in 2017 and thinking that they had seen this all before, as Serbia had a president who had been active not in conflict prevention but conflict promotion. When Ratko Mladic received a life sentence at the ICTY for genocide and other war crimes in November 2017, Vucic said the sentence was unjustified and encouraged Serbs to look to the future, not the past. Moreover, Belgrade's Humanitarian Law Center released two dossiers on Serbia's chief of defense staff, General Ljubisa Dikovic, alleging that as a brigade commander in Kosovo in 1999, he had been responsible for the murder of more than one thousand Albanians. The charges were dropped.

Bosnia since Dayton is not a success story. Although the war did not return, Bosnia has remained stuck at a point in time. Indeed, Bosnia, as a mini-Yugoslavia of sorts, is the biggest challenge. The main political parties fought the same narrowly defined ethnic issues – as in the war but without guns. A big change came when

Milorad Dodik became the prime minister for the Serb entity in 1998. Dodik did not come from the traditional governing party and was, like Nikola Gruevski in Macedonia, at first mistakenly hailed by the West as someone who was a moderate and not a nationalist. But he later found the power of nationalism, as events were to prove. Dodik was so emboldened by the Montenegrin referendum in 2006 (as he would be further emboldened by Kosovo's independence in 2008) that he suggested, contrary the very fundamentals of Bosnia's constitution, that the Republika Srbska (RS) could have a referendum on independence too. At that time, he said that the referendum was not meant to begin the process of secession but was needed instead to make sure that the RS's status as an entity would never be altered. To be fair to Dodik, he does stick to the letter of Dayton, and his rhetoric is often shaped by real attacks on the autonomy of the RS from the Bosniak side and the Office of the High Representative. He has since altered his plan, with subtle support from Russia, declaring in 2017 that the RS will eventually be independent. But the RS will never be independent. The West would never accept it, and even Serbia has no interest in either an independent RS or one attached to Serbia.

Dodik's rhetoric revealed that Bosnia's problems are structural in essence and that Dayton, put there to end the war, needs to be revised or replaced if Bosnia is to engage in a serious way with the Euro-Atlantic integration process. There have, however, been several failed attempts to change the constitution, which is required for EU integration. The most oft-cited issue is related to essential conformity with European Human Rights Law. The Council of Europe, Venice Commission, which advises on issues related to constitutional law, among other things, weighed in with several recommendations to solve the problems. As a result, and pushed by the United States especially, it laid out a series of dramatic changes that were ultimately rejected. It tried again in 2008 and in 2009 but without success. What laid bare one of the main problems with the constitutional structure was the strange case of Dervo Sejdic and Jakob Finci. Both are citizens of Bosnia, but Sejdic identifies as Roma and Finci as Jewish. Both tried to run for public office at the state level but were barred from doing so because the Dayton agreement allows only constituent peoples – Bosniaks, Croats, or Serbs – to hold office at the state level. They could hold office only at the entity level. Alternatively, Sejdic could declare himself to be a member of another ethnic group. For the constituent peoples, opening up state-level institutions to others would upset the balance. And the Croats, numerically the smallest group in Bosnia, feared losing their spot on the state presidency.

The case ended up in the European Court of Human Rights (ECHR) in 2006, which, in a ruling in 2009, declared that Sejdic's and Finci's ineligibility was discriminatory. The aforementioned constitutional changes would have ensured that no citizens would be excluded from public office. The ruling remains unimplemented. The ruling plays a key role in the entire EU integration process. In 2008, Bosnia signed an SAA, but it was not put into force because of the ECHR ruling. What the EU hoped was that this would drive not only implementation of the ruling but deeper structural changes for the sake of EU integration. That did not happen.

The best example of state incapacity would be the central government's failed response to disastrous flooding in May 2014. Prior to that, Bosnians had taken to the streets to protest the privatization process and the fate of previously state-owned enterprises. In Sarajevo, protestors set fire to government institutions. The 2014 floods and protests put Bosnia back on the map, but only briefly. Based on a call for an entirely new approach to Bosnia by Germany and the UK in the fall of 2014, the SAA was unlocked, and Bosnia was back in line, so to speak. While some complained that the initiative allowed Bosnia to evade some key responsibilities, it put the emphasis squarely on Bosnia's dire economic and social problems. Bosnia's leaders were asked to sign on to implement a series of reforms. That youth unemployment and brain drain (Bosnia's population has dropped 20 per cent in the past twenty-five years) were more important than constitutional reforms was a major subtext to the plan. Sejdic-Finci could wait, especially since youth unemployment was more than 60 per cent. The British-German initiative was an altogether welcome shift in policy but it did not carry the day. Not surprisingly, it fell apart due to political infighting. Besides, Milorad Dodik went on to become president of the RS in 2010, and even though he aligns the

RS's legislation with the EU, he has always feared that EU integration would undermine the system of state capture.

Given the permanent crisis in Bosnia, a renewed interest in partition appeared. Pro-partition articles appeared in the West – often written by analysts hoping to restart their careers and get back to the Balkans (where they could at least get some recognition and free drinks) – which were refuted by local actors, with good reason. The partition argument for Bosnia generally suggests that the EU process is too slow to act as a catalyst for reform, that European populations are too uninterested in further enlargement to the Balkans anyway, and that something new must be done to end the gridlock, which is blamed on the triumph of ethnic politics. Multiethnicity, some argue, has failed, and new borders are required. In September 2018 the United States made it clear that while it would accept agreed-on territorial swaps between Kosovo and Serbia, Bosnia's borders were sacrosanct. But new borders do not solve the problems. They could, in fact, revive the problem raised in 1990s that new borders for Bosnia would give rise to a weak Muslim republic in central Bosnia surrounded by hostile neighbors run by nationalists. As it stands now, regular Bosnians can easily believe that what goes on at the national level is mere theatrics and that the three ethnic leaders meet socially to agree on divvying up the pie and compare bank balances in Swiss accounts. It is undeniable that the elite maintains the tension purposely and ramps it up to win elections and get rich too. Elections in 2018 offered the same ethnic scaremongering, and RS leader Dodik made as much use as he could of his friendship with the Russian president. For Bosnia's three ethnic leaders, maintaining power simply means keeping the country on the brink of war.

Yet ethnic politics, and the nation-state for that matter, have proven to be extremely resilient, and not just in the Balkans. Kosovo, like Bosnia, is emblematic of this. When we left Kosovo in chapter 4, independence was a reality but it was compromised on three related levels. First, the Ahtisaari Plan opened the way for further incentives to the minority Serb community and the erosion of Kosovo's sovereignty. Second, the Kosovo elite is not up to the job and has always pursued narrow financial gains ahead of national interests. Bold and visionary leadership is hard to find. Third, a number of states in the EU did not recognize Kosovo, which hindered the EU and the EULEX mission, making it what was called "status neutral." Serbia of course refused to recognize Kosovo, despite the decision of the International Court of Justice (ICJ) in 2010, but it still held most of the cards in the negotiations with Kosovo and never missed an opportunity to needle the Kosovar leadership.

A good example of provocation was a new train between Belgrade to the city of Northern Mitrovica in part of northern Kosovo largely inhabited by Serbs. The area is one of the most contentious aspects of the negotiations on normalization of relations between Belgrade and Prishtina. In January 2017, as the inaugural train headed south from Belgrade, it was obvious that in addition to passengers and staff dressed in colorful Serbian national costumes and Serbian colors everywhere, the train has had a clear political message written on it in twenty languages: "Kosovo is Serbia." The train almost brought more conflict. The Albanians called it a provocation and a message of "occupation." Serbia's leaders suggested Kosovo wanted a war. The train never made it to the destination, because the Kosovo border authorities blocked its entry. The international community, which had invested so much time in fixing Kosovo-Serb relations, worried the whole process could come off the rails.

Small problems like that aside, in the decade that followed independence in 2008, Kosovo has been a failure. Its economy remained extremely fragile, and owing to its climate, it could not easily turn to cannabis, as Albania did. Imports were usually ten times exports. The economy was weak, consisting mostly of small-scale services like mini markets, tire repair, car washes, gas stations, and travel agencies. It lost a number of chances to build a modern education and health care system, failed to capitalize on the vast potential of the diaspora, and invested the state budget almost exclusively in building costly new highways. Remittances, which are vital for all of the Western Balkans, were most critical in Kosovo: there, they sometimes reached 20 per cent of GDP. Albanians clung to the myth of the resurrection of the once-viable mines in Trepca in the north, but that seemed unlikely. Their leaders also boasted about their vast reserves of lignite. Ranked as the most corrupt country in the region, foreign investors stayed away.

In terms of relations with Serbia, there were some important gains, but the victories went mostly to Serbia. In the decade of independence (2008–18) Kosovo gradually gained international recognition, to the point where most of the world recognized its independence. In addition to the five holdouts in the EU, Bosnia also refuses to recognize Kosovo's independence, fearing it as a precedent for RS independence. Russia sides with Serbia, even though it used the Kosovo precedent for recognition of breakaway territories in Georgia. The Islamic world was very slow to come around to recognition, seeing Kosovo as a US project and the Sunni Muslim majority as America's Muslims. Moreover, Serbia, with an international network based on more than one hundred years of statehood, successively resurrected Tito's nonaligned movement, with non-recognition policies triumphing in key countries in Africa, South America, and Southeast Asia.

The internal political milieu was similar in some ways to what occurred in neighboring Albania: intense polarization between the main political parties, obstructionism, massive corruption, and out-migration by the country's best and brightest. New parties came and went, but the scene was largely dominated by Democratic League of Kosovo, the Democratic Party of Kosovo, and the Alliance for the Future of Kosovo. The latter two parties were war parties and led by key figures in the Kosovo Liberation Army (KLA) – Hashim Thaci for the Democratic Party of Kosovo and Ramush Haradinaj for the Alliance. Both had opportunities to be prime minister, and Thaci became president in 2016. Haradinaj is exceptional in that he was sent to The Hague twice to face war-crimes charges and was acquitted twice. On both occasions prosecutors blamed witness intimidation and murder for the verdicts. Since the bar was so low for indicted war criminals, he won plaudits for turning himself in for his first indictment, when he was prime minister in the pre-independence period in 2005. He was retried by the ICTY due to accusations of witness intimidation and acquitted once more in 2012. He was again arrested in France on a Serbian-issued warrant in January 2017, but the French courts refused Serbia's extradition request and, after four months in France, he returned to Prishtina. In the fall of 2017, he became prime minister again. One of his first decisive acts was to double his salary, saying he needed to purchase better clothes. For Albanians who came of age in 1999 and after, the sight of the same people still running Kosovo is extremely depressing. Kosovo's elite is generally shunned internationally: no one wants them around. The only place they go with any fanfare is Tirana, but even there, they look out of place.

While parties came and went, only one group proved capable of shaking up Kosovo's moribund political landscape and challenging the state capture of the ruling elite and the willingness of the international community to tolerate the intolerable. The movement Vetevendosje (or Self-Determination, in English), emerged as an often-violent protest movement that captured the hearts and minds of thousands of marginalized youth. It was led by the charismatic Albin Kurti who had spent time in a Serbian prison. Kurti called for a new approach to everything, especially in negotiations with Serbia and the Serbs in Kosovo. Vetevendosje fought UNMIK and its quasi-successor, EULEX, and they fought the entry of Serb products into Kosovo. Kurti had no time for Rugova's notion of a separate identity for Albanians in Kosovo and called for unification with Albania and a place for Albanian symbols in Kosovo, which were mostly forbidden by the Ahtisaari Plan. For Vetevendosje's civic activists, UNMIK and EULEX represented governance that was "unaccountable" and "undemocratic." This was true. But EULEX did have some success, even though it was often accused of corruption within its ranks. It built on UNMIK's success in establishing professional police, by far the most trusted institution among Albanians, and customs services, but it failed to tackle organized crime and corruption and to establish an independent and multiethnic judiciary. Political interference in Kosovo's judiciary remained a major problem. Citizens generally hoped that EULEX would put corrupt people in jail. That never happened.

Vetevendosje transitioned into a quasi-political party in 2010 with a leftist and ethno-nationalist bent. Their candidate for mayor of Prishtina, Shpend Ahmeti, defeated the establishment parties in the 2013 local elections. Ahmeti is one of the few bright spots in Kosovo and has actually tried to represent the interests of Prishtina's citizens. His predecessor, like most Kosovo politicians, had hid behind the curtains in an Audi Q7, with loads of bodyguards hanging about, and had allowed his supporters to build willy-nilly in Prishtina without proper permits. Ahmeti was out in the streets and accessible. In the June 2017 national elections, owing to its ability to get out voters who never bothered to vote and to the disintegration of the clientelistic voting of the past (since the governing parties had little left to give people), Vetevendosje became the largest party in parliament. In the local elections in the autumn of 2017, Ahmeti won a very narrow victory in Prishtina, despite the fact that the traditional parties did their best to thwart him in the second round. Vetevendosje also did well in other municipalities. The internationals who still rule over Kosovo have marginalized it as much as possible. Fearing instability and the fake bogeymen of nationalism and unification with Albania, they do everything they can to keep Vetevendosje away from power, preferring to deal with the elite in the traditional ruling parties, whom they can cajole with threats of indictment by special courts. The international community lacks leverage over Vetevendosje, and its isolation has been a serious mistake since, in the case of Kosovo, it is the nationalists who are the good guys, for now. The establishment parties, with the support of the international community, blocks Vetevendosje at every turn. Sadly for Kosovo's youth, who saw in the party a chance for a better future, and reflecting an established trend elsewhere in which protest movements hoping to transform the political landscape die or are co-opted, Vetevendosje split in March 2018. Some members sought to pull it from its leftist nationalism to a more liberal orientation. Kosovo's traditional ruling parties did not hide their excitement. They had long ago agreed that they would alternate power and share the proceeds of state capture. Ahmeti, in some ways Kosovo's best hope, opted to lead the dormant Social Democratic Party.

Vetevendosje had some strong points related to the negotiations with Serbia. The EU, as noted, considered Serbia's stability as key to an overall transformation of the Western Balkans. The EU feared Serbia's potential for a Weimar syndrome, in that the democracy would collapse, and so resisted over-humiliating Serbia. As Serbia was the largest and wealthiest of the Balkan states, this tactic made a degree of sense. But what this meant for Kosovo, governed largely by an inexperienced and even uneducated elite, some of whom had criminal ties, was that Kosovo negotiators were always out of their league when compared to Serb negotiators. The asymmetry of the Ahtisaari Plan just would not go away. For the EU, the challenge was to normalize relations between two abnormal states. The result was a series of baby steps that whittled away at Kosovo's sovereignty.

Blocked by Serbia at the international level, which kept Kosovo out of the UN, and at the regional level too, the first step for the EU was to get Kosovo at least integrated at the regional level. As Serbia held to the legitimacy of UNSCR 1244, it meant that even after independence, in any regional meetings, Kosovo was still represented by UNMIK. Kosovo representatives could attend but could not have a seat at the table. The EU facilitated a deal that got Serbia closer to candidate status and got Kosovo to the tables. The downside was that Kosovo got a new name to be used in regional meetings in 2012. It was no longer the Republic of Kosovo but Kosovo*. The asterisk then referenced UNSCR 1244 and the ICJ opinion of 2010, which stated that the 2008 independence declaration did not violate international law – essentially saying that for some, Kosovo is part of Serbia, and for others, it's independent. Kosovo's negotiators had a hard time selling the deal but tried to convince people that Serbia, by accepting it, had almost recognized Kosovo. This was not true. Edita Tahiri, one of Kosovo's lead negotiators with Serbia, said the asterisk was a snowflake that would melt away. Nobody believed that either. Vetevendosje had further evidence that Kosovo leaders were too willing to bow to international pressure.

Kosovo could now sit at some tables but not others. For example, in the fall of 2018 Serbia worked to effectively block Kosovo's membership in Interpol. The Kosovo government responded by placing a 100 per cent tariff on Serbian goods in violation of regional trade agreements. The EU worked towards two key agreements that would later be judged as historic, but which were not. The two agreements were both made in Brussels in 2013 and 2015. In 2013, the EU, with Aleksandar Vucic, a seemingly pro-European leader in power in Serbia, began a normalization process designed to end or at least limit Belgrade's influence in northern Kosovo and set the two states on a new path. The EU thus oversaw further decentralization and empowerment of the Serb municipalities there. It allowed the municipalities extensive powers and the right to form an association. What it meant in practice was the territorialization of Serb rights, which had been a key demand from Belgrade. No longer did Belgrade seek to possess northern Kosovo but merely to control it, as the new agreements granted Serbia an immense role in the affairs of the Kosovo Serbs. For what happened in 2013, Serbia later got candidate status for the EU, and Kosovo signed an SAA. The August 2015 agreement, which has been challenged by Kosovo's constitutional court, formalized the Association of Serb Municipalities and added a new and unexpected layer of governance to Kosovo, one not foreseen by the Ahtisaari proposal. The new body, with a charter, a president, vice president, and assembly, and with essentially executive powers, was to oversee education, healthcare, economic development, and urban planning in Serb-dominated areas. It attacked with vigor by Vetevendosje as a sellout. The party subsequently tear-gassed the parliament in October 2015 and again in March 2016 when the issue came up for discussion. Vetevendosje leader Kurti and other party members were later dramatically arrested in front of the parliament in November 2017 to face charges for the attack on parliament. The jailing did not get much reaction from the international community. The group later received suspended sentences but were warned that next time they would find themselves in jail.

With the Brussels agreements, the Serbs seamlessly avoided being a minority in Kosovo. But it is worth noting that the Serbs living in the north were never consulted, and not all of them were prepared to cooperate with the government in Prishtina just because Belgrade and the EU said so. In January 2018, Oliver Ivanovic, the most important leader of the Serbs in the north, was assassinated outside his office in Mitrovica. Ivanovic's murder, given the sensitive state of talks between Belgrade and Prishtina and given that he had been a key proponent of engagement with the government in Kosovo, could spell problems. One thing is clear: the main beneficiaries of Ivanovic's death are criminals on both sides of the Ibar River who know that zones without rule of law, like the territory north of the Ibar, are far better for business.

Serbs in Kosovo and Serbia had a choice. Stick with the "Kosovo is Serbia" mantra, which is to deny reality, propose something new, or accept Kosovo as a state. Some argued that the agreements merely advanced the criminal interests of both sides, who had been cooperating since the war. For the historic agreement, Serbia started accession talks, and Kosovo got its own international dialing code – 383. Albania's prime minister, Edi Rama, lamenting the slow pace of Kosovo's integration and playing the nationalist card for domestic purposes, said in April 2017 that if the EU continued to close its doors to Kosovo, then the two countries would have to unite "in a classical way." Like the drone, this resonated in Kosovo, where support for unification is much higher than in Albania. Rama was quickly attacked, especially by Belgrade's leadership, and the EU said such provocations were unacceptable. The trend in developments in northern Kosovo suggested to some that a partition deal, along the lines of what Zoran Djindjic floated in 2000, was back on the table. Northern Kosovo would go to Serbia, and parts of Albanian-inhabited Presevo Valley in Serbia would go to Kosovo. Some states might would accept such a deal as long as both Belgrade and Prishtina agreed. In exchange, Serbia would recognize Kosovo, and Kosovo could begin in a serious way the EU accession process. Partition would be an extremely difficult sell for the Albanians, as it would amount to another decisive Serb victory and it is utterly opposed by the vast majority of Albanians living in Kosovo. As a serious idea, it seems to live only in the head of Kosovo president Hashim Thaci, who hopes that by maybe winning a Nobel peace prize he can stay out of jail. On the plus side, it would certainly nullify the Ahtisaari plan. One more thing is clear. Serb president Vucic wants to solve the Kosovo conundrum and he has the authority in Serbia to do it. He can make historic decisions that are not necessarily palatable for the majority of Serbs. Sadly, he has no real counterpart in Kosovo. Neither Haradinaj nor Thaci have the authority or legitimacy to negotiate territorial swaps, and any attempt to do so would invite civil conflict in Kosovo between Albanians. The people of Kosovo, whether veterans of the war or just ordinary people, did not sign on for partition.

If Kosovo's sovereignty was undermined by the deals with Serbia, there is one more element worth examining. In 2010, Dick Marty, a Swiss senator at the Council of Europe, published a damning and lurid report of human rights violations by KLA fighters during the war and after, He pointed the finger at then Kosovo prime minister and now president Hashim Thaci. The most gruesome accusation was the charge that the KLA had abducted Albanians and Serbs alike, transferred them to a "yellow house" near Burrel, in northern Albania, where their organs were removed and sold. Marty's report also established a strong and identifiable link between the KLA and organized crime. The EU took Marty's report seriously and followed up with its own special investigative task force, which documented human rights violations by senior KLA officials. In the end, knowing that the Kosovo courts were not up to the job of prosecuting these crimes, by a constitutional amendment Kosovo was given a special war crimes court in early 2017 that would try the cases that spanned from 1 January 1998 to 31 December 2000. Given the legacy of blotched trials and widespread witness intimidation in the past, many argue that the court is a required step if Kosovo is ever to obtain legitimacy. For others, since it was set up largely by outsiders with no parallel institution for Serbia, the court is just another restriction on Kosovo's sovereignty. Still others condemn it for maligning a just liberation war and for seeking only to indict the KLA, and state that it is therefore by definition anti-Albanian. The court insists that only individuals are to be judged, not the KLA. Regardless, across all aspects of Kosovo society, the court is perceived negatively. Given that more than ninety files are open, some of the leadership have tried to block it and received stern warnings from the EU and United States. Blocking the court would isolate Kosovo even more. If the court does adhere to its mandate, the so-called war parties – Hashim Thaci's Democratic Party of Kosovo and Ramush Haradinaj's Alliance for the Future of Kosovo – may be doomed. There lies the silver lining, possibly.

In February 2018, Kosovo celebrated ten years of independence. The independence party, as President Hashim Thaci promised, lasted ten days, but there were few real reasons to celebrate. Sure, problems with electricity and water had largely been solved, but providing Kosovo's people with better prospects has proven difficult. Saddled with a mountain of overlapping agreements, many ask why Kosovo has signed on to so many bad deals. First, the elite lacks the proper training to negotiate effectively. Second, governments are almost exclusively staffed at most levels with family members or party loyalists who are woefully underqualified. Third, and this is what most people on the ground believe, looming indictments mean that Kosovo's leaders do just what the international community tells them to do, even when these demands run counter to the most basic of Kosovo's national interests.

Macedonia also faced a series of crises in 2016 and 2017 that it actually survived, and maybe it will end up providing a potential alternative for other Balkan states caught in the same trap of pseudo-democracy. When we last examined Macedonia in chapter 5, the long-running control of Macedonia by the VMRO-DPMNE came to an end in a series of scandals. It became clear that the government was waging a clandestine war on its opponents and was engaged in the wholesale plundering of the state. Some twenty thousand people were allegedly under surveillance, and a wiretapping scandal caught government officials in all kinds of illegal acts. In the aftermath of the December 2016 elections, the country's president refused to allow the Social Democratic coalition with the Albanian Union for Democratic Integration to take office, claiming it was set to dismantle the country based on Albanian demands. The United States, not the EU, intervened decisively to get things back on track. VMRO-DPMNE leader Nikola Gruevski was sentenced to two years in jail in 2018 for his role in soliciting a €600,000 Mercedes from a cabinet minister, which he planned to use for personal purposes in 2012. He appears finished as a politician. Due to show up at a jail to begin his sentence in November 2018, Gruevski instead enlisted his allies in Hungary to help him flee there by car. Once there, his request for asylum was processed instantly with a favorable ruling. Considered by some as a man who represents the pinnacle of effective state capture, he probably has the cash to live comfortably in exile in Hungary. His party was decisively defeated again in the fall 2017 local elections. What stood out about the Macedonian case in 2016 was the level of engagement from the population, both Albanians and Macedonians. It was largely citizen activists, determined to end the emergence of a one-party nationalist authoritarian state like Hungary, who forced change. The coalition of Social Democrats and the Albanian Democratic Union for Integration did its best to revitalize the flagging EU and NATO integration projects and mend fences with Greece. The courts and the public prosecutor's office were purged of Gruevski's appointees.

In an extraordinary gesture of goodwill, in February 2018, Alexander the Great Airport became Skopje International Airport, and the Alexander the Great Highway became Friendship Highway. There was even talk of taking down some of the statues. Talks between Athens and Skopje intensified. The left-wing Syriza government in Athens had come to power hoping to reverse the austerity program imposed on Greece by the European Commission, the European Central Bank, and the International Monetary Fund and overthrow the neoliberal consensus. Having failed in that, it did make a historic decision to normalize relations with Macedonia when it accepted the name *Republic of North Macedonia* in June 2018 in a landmark agreement with Skopje that opened the door for Euro-Atlantic integration. North Macedonia was to be used internally and externally, and the Greeks agreed to accept the name of the language as Macedonian.

The Macedonian government put the new name to a consultative referendum in September 2018 with a somewhat biased question that asked, *"Are you in favor of European Union and NATO membership by accepting the agreement between the Republic of Macedonia and the Republic of Greece?"* US defense secretary Jim Mattis and even German chancellor Angela Merkel, among others, went to Skopje to urge people to support the deal. Nevertheless, by any measure, the referendum was a failure. Although roughly 90 per cent of voters supported the new name, turnout was a lackluster 36 per cent, well short of the numbers needed to make Prime Minister Zaev's pitch to parliament easier, as he needs the support of two-thirds to change the constitution. The nationalists will now do everything possible to derail the deal. Even Macedonian president Gjorge Ivanov called the deal with Greece a violation of Macedonian sovereignty. The low turnout has a number of explanations. One, huge numbers of people, exhausted by decades of nonsense and incompetence, simply would not vote. Moreover, there is credible evidence that Russia actively interfered so as to stall the Euro-Atlantic integration process by stoking the Macedonian fear of the Albanians with Facebook posts suggesting, among other things, that the name change was a sop to the Albanians. Russia has officially deemed the referendum illegitimate, designed to pull Macedonia and Macedonians into NATO and the EU against their will.

While Macedonians may be ready for a new name and the prospect of EU and NATO membership, most Greeks remained opposed to the use of the term *Macedonia* in any way, and *compromise* is not necessarily a good word in Greece. For many Greeks, having sold out – at least to some – their economic sovereignty for the sake of remaining in the Euro zone, selling out on the name issue was just too much. But Greeks have at least come to recognize that Macedonia is not a threat to Greece and that normalizing relations will undercut Turkey's growing influence there. Unlike everywhere else in the Balkans, the Greeks like the Russians and perceive Russia as an ally on the name issue. Moreover, Russian president Vladimir Putin is the most popular international politician in Greece. To move ahead, Greece will need substantial guarantees that this is a permanent change, as statues can be put back and constitutions can be changed. The name issue remains an emotional one. The legacy of expulsions still lingers, especially since many living in the Greek region of Macedonia are descendants of Greeks expelled from Turkey during the 1920s population exchanges. It is therefore not absurd for some people to imagine being uprooted. Regardless of which Macedonia you live in, both Greeks and Macedonians are easily mobilized and oppressed by the past. Both Greece and Macedonia put the issue to a parliamentary vote in January 2019 after Macedonia had already adopted major changes. In an extraordinary and hitherto absent spirit of a vision of a better future, both votes passed.

Part of the crisis in 2016 and 2017 related, not surprisingly, to the Albanians. VMRO-DMPNE had whipped up the usual nationalist fervor about expanding Albanian demands that if implemented, would, they said, destroy Macedonia. It is true that the Albanians were asking for more, and most of their demands clustered around the Albanian platform, which had mostly been formulated in Tirana, with some help from Edi Rama. Its main goal was to gain greater equality for the Albanian language in Macedonia, which would entail making Macedonia a bilingual state. Macedonia's leaders do need to take some bold steps to make things work better, as most Macedonians are a long way from seeing Albanians as equals. Education needs massive reform, especially since Albanians are still denigrated in textbooks and underrepresented in national history. Bilingualism could help too, as it would deprive the ethnic Albanian parties of their single issue. Plus, some point to the growth of political Islam and the potential for radicalization. In 2016, Besa, a new Albanian party emerged, with support from Turkish president Recep Tayyip Erdogan's Justice and Development Party. While the Albanians never got anything on the level of absurdity provided by the Skopje 2014 project, they did get a big square in a part of Skopje where they dominate to honor their national heroes. Whether trust between the Albanians and Macedonians can be restored is not clear.

The EU had hoped that the lure of membership would have been enough to drive reform. It was wrong – and not just about the Western Balkans. In Hungary, Poland, and Slovakia, the nation-state came back with a vengeance, and populist governments challenged the core values of the EU. In Bulgaria and Romania, things actually deteriorated after membership in 2007. But does that mean that everything is the EU's fault? The ethnic bloodletting of the 1990s is thankfully behind us, but the region is still tense. Governmental crisis and economic stagnation are the norm in many states, and much-needed regional cooperation has been suppressed by renewed nationalism. Youth face a choice between unemployment or exit. It no longer seems possible to change things locally. Wars on corruption have proved to be rhetorical or focused on really small fish. The international community no longer seems ready to step up to the plate, and the United States, by far the most influential player, has hardly mentioned the region since Trump came to power in 2017.

The local political elite are often hopeless, almost always corrupt, sometimes lazy, and decidedly predatory. They almost always eschew making historic choices but prefer short-term solutions that preserve their power and state capture. It appears that for most rulers since 1989, cash matters the most, as corruption is the most transparent part of the Balkans. The people in power have amassed enormous wealth. They have run roughshod over populations that have been in transition for more than twenty-five years, and destroyed or co-opted challengers to their rule. In addition, Russia is back in the Balkans, happy to sow trouble for NATO and the EU wherever there is corruption, instability, suspicion across ethnic lines, and state dysfunction. Having successfully helped to force the EU and the United States to turn inward to a degree by promoting all manner of anti-establishment forces, and after having been more or less excluded during the period of Yugoslavia's disintegration, Russia has influence. It offers cheap oil and gas, nuclear power plants (with loans to pay for them), fake news, and the promise of "traditional values" – a vision of the future based on an imagined past. To gain influence, Russia is willing to encourage ethnic rivalries too, as was evidenced in the Macedonian name referendum and its embrace of the RS in Bosnia.

Outside of these pressing short-term issues, there are some larger structural problems in the states that live under internationally designed and imposed peace treaties. Dreams of stable and integrated multiethnic countries have been replaced by fear, suspicion, and parallel societies. Bosnia, Kosovo, and Macedonia are post-communist and post-conflict. This has led some to suggest that the key to future stability is new territorial arrangements, given that the treaties that ended the conflicts have failed to deliver stability. However, the idea of a new map wrongly implies that the problem in the Balkans is primarily ethnic. It is not. It is primarily political. Does this political instability, which is often related to ethnic rivalries, mean that the region needs new territorial solutions? Or does it mean that the problem is political, in that brain drain and demographic decline have simply left these countries in the hands of opportunists, fools, or criminals unwilling and incapable of delivering a European future? It is primarily the latter: new borders leave the same people calling the shots and may bring other problems. The border issue is important, but borders need to be reaffirmed, not altered. Too many people in the region think the borders are malleable, and this lends itself to a kind of existential crisis. Speeding up NATO enlargement to Bosnia and Macedonia would relieve tremendous pressure and would do more to reduce regional tension than anything else. Knowing that borders are truly inviolable would amount to a paradigm shift.

Corruption, which is the main source of the general distrust of institutions that pervades the whole region, is front and center. The Balkans, still largely a crossroads of sorts, is one of the most fertile grounds for corruption and organized criminal activity. Every country now engages in a rhetorical war on both, but nothing changes. The 2016 report of Transparency International (TI) noted some improvements (excluding Macedonia), but across the region it painted a bleak picture of klepto-capitalism's powerful executives and political parties capturing the state. While former president of Georgia Mikheil Saakashvili would eventually go off the rails, his war on corruption was successful, proving that it is possible to win the war. Reduced corruption and crime in general is indeed one of Saakashvili's most enduring legacies. But in Georgia there was the political will to tackle the problem.

While country-specific opinion polls suggest people identify unemployment as the biggest issue, some analysts note that the elimination of corruption could be the key to solve a whole range of other problems. Those states such as Russia and local individuals who seek to weaken the EU's credibility in the region cannot thrive without corruption. TI's most recent report on the region tells a grim story, noting that most countries lack the institutions or laws to even be effective. Kosovo, for example, which is ranked the lowest in the region by TI, has done absolutely nothing to combat corruption. Political parties, which are an outgrowth of the chaos and wars of the 1990s, remain the West's main interlocutors and are by far the least-trusted institutions and the main conduits for corrupt practices. The few alternatives to the mainstream parties that emerge are usually destroyed, co-opted, or shunned by the West as dangerous disturbers of the peace. For ordinary people, success in the war on corruption means some big fish should be in jail. But the big fish are not in jail because the international community wrongly assumes that these big fish are the key to stability.

In 2016, Turkish president Recep Tayyip Erdogan hosted the wedding of his daughter. Foreign guests included Prime Minister Edi Rama of Albania and Bakir Izetbegovic, then Bosniak president (also the son of the late Alija Izetbegovic, Bosnia's first president). The allure of market authoritarianism as an alternative model, whether in

China, Hungary, or Turkey, has existed for a long time and is getting stronger. While analysts come up with a plethora of words to describe things – illiberal democracy, electoral democracy, stabilotocracy, aggressive majoritarian democracy – the Balkan states offer an array of low-quality democracies, which is the essence of the whole dilemma. The stability-over-democracy path – the very same path that was chosen after the First World War, when the bar for success was set so low – prevails. That is also the consensus of the few enlightened leaders left in the region.

But the Western Balkans do have an advantage over other regions facing similar challenges. The first advantage is size: populations are small, with only 17 million people in the Western Balkans, especially after so many people have left (although the small and declining populations in each state make all politics local, in that these states are run like corrupt small towns where everyone knows everyone). On the plus side, the end destination is clear: despite Brexit and the resurgence of the nation-state, the EU and the EU enlargement process is an undeniable success elsewhere in post-communist Europe. For the most part, there is a consensus among populations that the EU is the right destination because it alone can make their politicians behave while guaranteeing security and prosperity. That Albania, Bosnia, Kosovo, Macedonia, Montenegro, and Serbia will join has never been taken off the table, and there is no viable Plan B. One could hardly say the same for Turkey. Since the Thessaloniki Summit of 2003, one could conclude that the EU (rightly or wrongly) did prioritize stability and sought to fix the region's geopolitics first. That job is barely even half done. But there are some encouraging signs. Russia's malignant interference needed to be countered, and the refugee crisis of 2015 put the region front and center, as refugee flows could not have been managed to the EU's liking without the Balkan states at the table.

In 2014, the EU did finally breathe some new life into the enlargement process. Enlargement fatigue, it was feared in the region, was not just about Turkey but also the Western Balkans. Moreover, the stomach for new member states among European publics was no longer there. The Greek crisis, Balkan criminal groups (especially Albanian ones), plus an extraordinary influx of Roma from

Romania had pretty much turned public opinion against the Balkans. EU commission head Jean-Claude Juncker had already stated in July 2014 that there would be no new member states added for the next five years. He largely blamed the Balkan states for that, as he stated that none of them could come close to qualifying by 2019. But 2025, at least for Montenegro and Serbia, seemed a bit more likely, he said, but added that the Balkan states needed to work much harder. However, Juncker, not shy of clichés, added that the "tragic European region" needs a European perspective, otherwise "the demons of the past will reawaken." Instead of imminent membership, German chancellor Angela Merkel launched the Berlin Process in 2014. Hoping to replicate some of the early success of the beginnings of European integration in the 1950s, the Berlin Process envisions regular summits and support for locally driven and conceived regional cooperation projects. No longer would external forces drive the agenda. If coal and steel could help mend fences between French and Germans after the Second World War, then the same could be done in the Balkans with energy, transport, and people, particularly the youth. It was not naïve to think this would help, as the region is decidedly unintegrated on a number of levels. An important example of this type of project is the joint Kosovo-Serbia highway between Nis and Prishtina. While regional mobility has increased dramatically, new transport links can only improve relations among the western Balkan states and peoples, especially the youth, who to date have been the biggest victims of the transition.

# Guide to Further Readings

There are a number of really classic surveys of the Balkans. Interestingly, some of the earlier works are still the best, with a few exceptions. L.S. Stavrianos's *The Balkans since 1453*, originally published in 1958, is a treasure. No other book has yet to match its breadth and achievement. Robert Lee Wolff's *The Balkans in Our Time* is also superb. More recently, Charles and Barbara Jelavich have published seminal works on the region in the nineteenth and twentieth centuries. There is also a good introduction to the region by Andrew Wachtel entitled *The Balkans in World History*. Mark Biondich's *The Balkans: Revolution, War, and Political Violence since 1878* is largely academic but also accessible and extremely well researched. Mark Mazower's *The Balkans: A Short History* and Thanos Veremis's *A Modern History of the Balkans: Nationalism and Identity in Southeast Europe* are also useful surveys. A real standout for its readability and thorough research is Misha Glenny's *The Balkans: Nationalism, War, and the Great Powers, 1804–1999*. Although much maligned in academic circles, Robert Kaplan's *Balkan Ghosts: A Journey through History* is still a great read, as the author captures well a precise moment in time. Kaplan was nowhere near as wrong as many people thought. For a brilliant assessment of the interwar period, country by country, there remains nothing better than Joseph Rothschild's *East Central Europe between the Two World Wars*. For those interested in geography and shifting borders, Paul Robert Magocsi's *Historical Atlas of Central Europe* covers the region well.

Country-specific works are also plentiful. For Albania, Anton Logoreci's *The Albanians: Europe's Forgotten Survivors*, published in 1977, is still a classic. Later works by Elez Biberaj, Bernd Fischer, Nicholas Pano, and Miranda Vickers are essential for understanding Albania's communist and post-communist life. I recommend Biberaj's works on Albania's communist period, the country's bizarre relationship with China, and the transition from communism; Fischer's study of King Zog and Albania during the Second World War; Pano's seminal history of the People's Socialist Republic of Albania; and Vickers's general history of Albania. Elidor Mehilli's *From Stalin to Mao: Albania and the Socialist World* explains in a readable way just what was happening in Albania during the period of alignment with the USSR and later China.

Readers interested in Yugoslavia in all of its variants should look at the works of Ivo Banac and John Lampe, as well as those of Sabrina P. Ramet. On the wars, there are simply endless things to read. An extraordinary achievement is *Confronting the Yugoslav Controversies: A Scholars' Initiative*, edited by Charles Ingrao and Thomas A. Emmert. Florian Bieber, Armina Galijas, and Rory Archer's edited collection *Debating the End of Yugoslavia* is worthwhile as well. As I noted in the text, some of the journalists covering the wars did astounding work. In particular, I note the work of Misha Glenny, Tim Judah, Allan Little, Joe Sacco, and Mark Thompson, but there are countless other solid journalistic accounts. The BBC documentary *The Death of Yugoslavia*, which first aired in 1995, is a must-watch. It remains the best of any source on the wars. The International Crisis Group wrote dozens of reports on the conflicts, all of which are available on the web. They are great sources for context, but readers should avoid the lofty recommendation sections, which were always completely out of touch with the reality on the ground.

As noted in the book, Bosnia has generated an extraordinary amount of academic and non-academic literature. The best history remains Noel Malcolm's *Bosnia: A Short History*. Interested readers should also look at the available works of Florian Bieber, Dejan Guzina, and Soeren Keil. As well, the work of the European Stability

Initiative has always been excellent – it is just too bad that nobody listened to it. All of its reports are available on the web. For Croatia, the most read writers and analysts are Ivo Goldstein, Dejan Jovic, and Marcus Tanner. Kosovo's history is well covered by Noel Malcolm's *Kosovo: A Short History*. It is loved in Kosovo but largely loathed in Serbia. The aforementioned Tim Judah has two very readable books, *Kosovo: War and Revenge* and *Kosovo: What Everyone Needs to Know*. On the KLA, there is James Pettifer's *The Kosovo Liberation Army: Underground War to Balkan Insurgency, 1948–2001*, a book that heaps praise on the KLA and its leadership. Finally, on the role of UNMIK and later EULEX, see Iain King and Whit Mason's *Peace at Any Price: How the World Failed Kosovo* and Andrea Lorenzo Capussela's meticulous study of the EU in Kosovo, *State-Building in Kosovo: Democracy, Corruption and the EU in the Balkans*. For an understanding of Macedonia, start with the works of Keith Brown and Ulf Brunnbauer. Andrew Rossos has a good survey of Macedonia's history in *Macedonia and the Macedonians: A History*, and there is also Hugh Poulton's *Who Are the Macedonians?* The best histories of Montenegro are to be found in Kenneth Morrison's *Montenegro: A Modern History* and Elizabeth Roberts's *Realm of the Black Mountain: A History of Montenegro*. On the transition years, see the work of Srdjan Darmanovic. For Serbia, the aforementioned Tim Judah is one of the best analysts. Sabrina P. Ramet and Vjeran Pavlakovic's edited collection *Serbia Since 1989: Politics and Society under Milosevic and After* is both balanced and nuanced. Srdja Pavlovic is excellent on both Montenegro and Serbia.

For Bulgaria, the work of Richard Crampton is still the best available. His *A Concise History of Bulgaria* is excellent, as is his book *The Balkans since the Second World War*. Clive Leviev-Sawyer's *Bulgaria: Politics and Protests in the 21st Century* is a great journalistic read with lots of telling anecdotes. Equally interesting but more academic is the sad picture of Bulgaria's corrupt elite in Venelin Ganev's *Preying on the State: The Transformation of Bulgaria after 1989*.

A good start on Romania is provided by the works by Dennis Deletant, Stephen Fischer-Galati, Keith Hitchins, and Vladimir Tismaneanu. For more recent developments, Florin Abraham's

*Romania since the Second World: A Political, Social and Economic History*, Tom Gallagher's *Romania and the European Union: How the Weak Vanquished the Strong*, and Lavinia Stan and Diane Vancea's edited collection *Post-Communist Romania at Twenty-Five: Linking Past, Present, and Future* are essential for understanding the flawed transition and particularly the perseverance of the old elite.

# Index